Footsteps in the Forest of Vedanta

Footsteps in the Forest of Vedanta

A spiritual awakening

Derek Thorne

vedantarama.com

First published by Vedantarama, Fenny Castle, Somerset, UK. 2024.
Enquiries to vedantarama.com

ISBN 978-1-0687526-0-5

vedantarama.com

DEDICATION

For Sue, my wife who has supported and participated in this majestic spiritual evolution in all its elements from beginning to end, over all these dynamic years. We both know it is a perfect destiny.

CONTENTS

INTRODUCTION

Dear Reader,

The book before you is a rich tale of a spiritual awakening unfolding between Amelia the seeker and her teacher, Ram. Their dynamic encounter takes place in Bowslip, a mystical forest landscape where Ram lives, which holds many discoveries and challenges.

This treasure of experience arises in response to a most compelling desire in Amelia's mind. That same desire comes to many others in this life and perhaps one of those people is you. It is a power in humanity that has been present for as long as living beings have been able to feel and think. We call it the seeker. Seeking of course is a common thing, curiosity and exploration is part of human nature, apparent in every sphere of activity, scientific, artistic and cultural. In the case of the spiritual seeker however, this enquiring force is targeted in a particular profound direction, toward the meaning of life itself. Why am I here? What is all this? What is divinity? Who is God? These questions are the seeker's passion.

Out of this evolutionary restlessness has come the philosophical, spiritual and religious movements of the world. The result is a beautiful storm of hopes, ideas, dreams and propositions of what is real and what is not. The seeker is both intrigued and perplexed by this marketplace of possibilities and stands at a crossroads. What to do, where to turn? Well, inevitably destiny will take its course and that is exciting for us all. You are about to meet Amelia, perhaps you will recognise some of her characteristics in yourself or if not, I am sure you will be sympathetic to the drives that move in her and the sincerity of her responses. Amelia travelled around the stalls and alleys of the spiritual marketplace and came away unfulfilled. She came to realise that what she wanted was not stimulation and entertainment to pacify her restlessness, but something much more than that. Her heart was yearning for the authentic, the stable, the reliable, the deep and the true. She found an offering of these very qualities in Vedanta, the 5000-year-old world respected tradition of spiritual discovery, originating in the mystical Upanishads and thriving most dynamically ever since. At that point she meets her teacher, opens her heart, frees her mind and engages in the fire of Self-discovery.

The content of this book is a compilation of the annual journals distributed to members of our Vedanta organisation over a period of six years. Each chapter originated as a separate self-contained story but their nature is such that they connect together in a cohesive and progressive tale. This is evident in the way Amelia changes, she is different at the end when she encounters Shiva in the snowfield, to when she begins her sadhana camping out for three nights on Bowers Hill. In recognition of that persistence and accomplishment, Ram sometimes calls her his hero.

I hope you enjoy witnessing Amelia's most personal discoveries. This is part one of her story and not the end of her tale but it travels a long way, concluding at a most magnificent and satisfying point. She has told me that she is happy to share her story with you in this way and hopes that there are many things in the pages ahead that will bring you intrigue, insights, discovery and joy. Maybe a little part of you will fall in love either with Amelia, Ram, or with Vedanta itself, as the voice of reality revealed.

May your intelligence shine and your heart respond.

Derek Thorne
Fenny Castle
Summer 2024

vedantarama.com

Chapter One

New Beginnings
before the forest

Amelia was not like you and me. Her life was full of experiences but she had no insight into those movements and was restless and perplexed, not like you and me. There were questions, lots of questions but where were the real questions, the questions behind the questions, the ones that would transform and satisfy? She did not know her own questions. For that to be resolved she had to be exposed to the unexpected, there is no other way. The thing about the unexpected is you never know where or when it may arise, or who will be its catalyst.

The teacher Ram was with the atheists debating the nature of God. The thing about a debate is that it is based on propositions supported by reasoned argument, so if the intention is to win a debate, it is a good plan to have a developed strategy of tactics and responses. The moderator at the university debating house set out the scene and explained the rules to an expectant and enthusiastic audience. The atheist team were invited to begin with their opening argument as it was they who were putting the proposition that God doesn't exist. Their speaker, Dr Franklyn, had prepared well, laying out the case convincingly. The audience were appreciative, it was stimulating and engaging.

Ram's response was hopeless by comparison, ill-conceived and poorly explained; there was heckling. The atheist team, inflated like puffed-up cockerels, entered into their countering arguments, putting forward forceful positions about evolution and physics, Darwin and the inconsistencies of religion. They were cheered. Ram came back and spoke unconvincingly about how the politics of religion and the complexity of science obfuscated reality. Dr Franklyn was out of his seat in a second; propelled by the back slapping of his team, he took to the podium for the summary and conclusion of their case. It was riveting and powerful, accompanied by much nodding in the audience followed by whistles and applause.

The moderator invited Ram to the podium. He took his place and said nothing, it was awkward, then, he began to chant. The audience sniggered, shuffled, shouted out and then progressively settled. Silence descended. The atheist team looked perplexed and got into a conflab with the moderator to protest. But Ram had his ten minutes; he was entitled to his ten minutes. The chant was mesmerising, lilting in its cadence, complex in its tone and rhythm, repetitive and penetrating. After eight minutes with his green light still on, he stopped abruptly and stood powerfully and majestically commanding the podium. For two minutes the audience of five hundred people sat silent; coughs and shuffles, clearing of throats but silent. His red light came on and he stepped down from the podium. The atheist team raised an objection that there had been no proper rebuttal of their proposition and that this was a foul. Ram was invited to respond to the point of order. He stood; the audience fell silent.

"I have lost this debate, for it is impossible to win, not because the resolution isn't available but because the method is hopeless. Mankind will debate forever in the quest to understand themselves. I leave those clever and reasoned words to my opponents. These men and women," he said, pointing to his challengers, "can increase their knowledge, their position and their confidence, they can become accomplished and revered because of it but they will still be ignorant men and women. You cannot know the nature of God through the concepts of clever people, but you can feel it and be it, living as a reflection of that divine being and expressing as that. That is the difference between us. I have not been here to argue God, I have been here to live God and you have been here for that too. Some of you will believe that and some of you will not, some of you will know it and not declare it, some of you will protest it and deny it. Critics will say that belief has no place in a debating house and I say that debating has no place in the experience of God. Thank you for your time." He left the stage.

The atheist team demanded a vote on their proposition. They won convincingly on the numbers declared and went off to the after-debate dinner, buoyed up with satisfaction and pride, scoffing at the inadequacy of their opponent and his preposterous explanation of himself. The moderator remained neutral but later confided in his colleagues that for the first time in the history of the debating house, renowned for its rigour and decisiveness, more than thirty percent of people had abstained, declaring themselves undecided, an unheard-of percentage.

Outside the hall, Amelia bustled out urgently. She had a place at the dinner but had forgone it, she looked around purposefully as she wriggled into her coat, her heart beating strongly and her mouth becoming dry; she was anxious and motivated, she wanted something and she was doing something about it. Ram was at the head of the taxi queue; it was a busy evening with lots of movement and activity on the street. She felt nervous but determined, she moved. A taxi pulled up, Ram spoke to the driver and opened the rear door to get in.

"Sir, will you be my spiritual teacher?" she said, suddenly up close to him and feeling the tingles of embarrassment on her skin and in her eyes.

He looked at her for four seconds.

"You can share my ride if you like," he replied, "where are you going?"

Her address was out of his way but he negotiated with the driver on a mutual route.

"Get in."

She sat beside him. They sat in silence; the driver had pulled shut the dividing screen and she didn't know what to say or do. The moment was powerful. Was it desire? It made her feel reckless and also uneasy; there was something inexplicable, something important. The taxi moved through the traffic. The silence deepened into a great peace, she could lose herself in it but now was not the moment, it was too urgent; the ride would be over soon.

"Sir," she said, "I was very affected by what you said tonight; will you be my spiritual teacher?"

The look he gave her in response was heartbreaking, deep and compassionate; she felt the lump rising in her throat.

"I am not your teacher yet," he said, "this is your teacher."

"What is?" she enquired.

"Life and mind, all of it; challenge, confusion, opportunity, adventure, passion, achievement, disappointment, success, the search for God and taxi rides."

"But I want someone to guide the way through all that," she pleaded, "to make sense of it and find the meaning in it, to make it easier."

"You may want that but you shan't have it. If you realised the opportunities being brought to you in the simple, ordinary moment, you would be worshipping the teacher in that and would have no desire for a conventional teacher; if I was to deny you all that through becoming your agent of appeasement, it would be a great spiritual injustice. If you could see the big picture right now you would withdraw your request in an instant and defend to the death your pilgrimage through ignorance and these life events. The guidance you are asking for is commonly desired but its granting is for weaker minds. No one who approaches me as you have is in that category. These circumstances are your perfect sadhana but you do not know it. Life and mind, both inner and outer, is either your indulgence, your tyrant or your Guru. The defining factors that distinguish between the two are insight and faith, so which is it to be?"

It was no longer clear where she was. The sounds of the traffic, the vibration of the engine and hum of the heater at their feet were like a soundtrack to some fantastic journey. Memories spun through her head; an image of childhood, the smell of horses, a flash of a great expanse of desert, stars, a lover's affection, the rush in her body building as a tingle then a pulse, warm waves. She was unable to respond, his startling critique of the conventional teacher as an agent of appeasement rocking in her brain.

"Because you do not know these things," said Ram, his voice echoing in her stunned mind, "you need just one instruction from me."

"What is it?" she asked, snapping into alertness like the hawk spotting her prey.

"Engage, stay alert and engage."

The taxi was three minutes from her door and she suddenly felt very anxious, as if she was about to lose something of fateful importance.

"How will I know what to do?" she asked.

"No one knows what to do, it is impossible to know what to do, just be alert to what happens, watch it and act. In the absence of not knowing you have to respond and commit, otherwise you will perish. That's what I have been saying to you, that is your precious opportunity; to observe. Every moment is shaping your destiny and every moment is offering you freedom."

"But what is that destiny? If I don't know what to do can I get it wrong, can I waste opportunities, will I have regrets?" The taxi pulled up at her door. If asked to describe her feelings at that point she could only have babbled and even the babbling would have been inadequate.

For some, the path is linear and organised, progressing in common steps, trickling slowly, a constantly negotiated comfort as things are repeatedly put back to a more convenient time. For some, the path is stuck in recession. For others, the path is hard labour as the consequences of the past fix like mortar that will not yield, and for some, the path is passionate, characterised by wild encounter, intensity and exposure. Ram knew that he could only ever be the teacher for that.

"Can I call upon you again?" she asked tremulously, emotion

swelling in her; it felt like grief but she knew it could not be that. She remembered that same feeling at the end of a teenage holiday romance; tenderness and pain like some precious intimacy being cruelly deleted.

"For what?" said Ram, "what is it you want to know?"

"Who I am, and you, the meaning of all this."

He spoke to the taxi driver who nodded and turned off the engine. They sat there, poignant and alone in the street, the windows misting now the air circulation was off. Ram gave Amelia the tapas of Atma Vichara; it was an initiation. You know how things are like that, when you are either being shown or told something in a routine way, or information is transferred to you with power and meaning. After five minutes of silence only punctuated by the fidgeting of the driver behind the closed glass, it was apparent that they had come to an end.

"Can I call on you?" she said finally.

The answer surprised them both.

"Yes, when the twilight falls, come to me, after the daylight has blazed and when the twilight falls. Observe your mind."

And that was it. The door closed, the taxi pulled away and he was gone. She watched silently voicing the words 'I think you are my Guru'. Two minutes later she realised with a jolt of pain that he had left no details.

When the student is ready, the teacher appears, that's what she had read. What did it mean? She had been told that guru just means teacher but she had never liked the word believing it to be some kind of false projection. As time passed, she would come to understand guru to describe the potency of the teacher, not just any teacher but one that can reach in, touch your heart, inspire your mind and transform perspective. Many things can reflect this power; a picture, a text, an inspiration, an idea but sometimes all that is guru comes forward in a person that you can talk to and walk with and live out your days. 'Observe your mind.' Assimilating that mystical instruction, was to take her travelling through texts, temples, the architecture of ancient times and the wild forest of adventure. And all of that would begin on a Somerset hilltop in a Big Conversation.

Chapter Two

The Big Conversation

three years later

on the hill

"Come any time, Amelia," Ram had said, "any time between April and September. We will camp on the hill."

He was so casual about the details, claiming that planning and management had come to an end and was not something that should have much of a bearing on matters of the heart anymore.

"That is all we are concerned with now."

"Haven't we always been concerned with that?" I had asked. He had widened his eyes and shaken his head.

"Managing the superficial, that's what we have been concerned with, I'm tired of all the management, now is the time to be unmanaged. Come to me for the Big Conversation, sometime between April and September."

"So, what date exactly shall we meet?"

"Day One, I want a new Day One, a new Big Bang between us."

"What is the Big Conversation?" I implored.

"Leave it until we meet; come to me on the hill."

I had been with Ram now for three years. It sounded like a long time but then again it felt like just a moment. The number three seemed significant, a kind of milestone but then again it was just another day. I thought of the story in the Upanishads where the student goes to the teacher and gets various directions and is told to return after twelve years and then another twelve years, on and on. I had always found that poignant; there was something special about dedication and commitment; it moved me. Now we were going back to the same place, where six months after our taxi encounter I had found him again, or he had found me, at the oak tree grove on Bowers Hill. I had no idea why that location was suggested this time but it was intriguing if nothing else. I had been back to that particular hill since, it was a beautiful spot, a good place to tramp around, with a public footpath across it but I had never again discovered the oak grove itself, I couldn't seem to find it.

"Don't take the common route," Ram had said, "you will never get anywhere that way. The grove is not for the public, it's for the sadhaks; it's on the other side of the hill, a completely different direction. You have to find the Fern Road by the willow tree." He gave me some instructions but they were pretty vague. I tried to prepare, studying maps and at the end of March I took a drive over there just to get the lay of the land. After an hour of exploring I finally managed to find what he had called the Fern Road. It wasn't surprising I had missed it because it was completely neglected and wasn't even a path; just an alignment of tall ferns snaking up the hill. His path was not between the ferns at all but through them. From the 25th I began assessing the weather daily, watching the changes as the five-day forecast predicted first cloud, then sun, then a bit of both. My anticipation of our camping trip would be affected by all these things and the sunrise and sunset. I monitored those times too, imagining puja in the dawn and fires in the dusk. I imagined many things; many, many things. For when you are invited to a hilltop with your Guru it's important to have a plan and be prepared, isn't it?

'Don't drive' was the single statement on the back of the plain postcard that arrived at my home on the 26th. It was signed *'R'*, otherwise I would have had no idea what this random instruction was all about. The card itself, a simple woodland scene, depicting Tuttenham Clumps was marked as having been posted in Lochinvar. It was maddening to get sent such an ambiguous message, irresponsible when I couldn't seek clarification, what I wanted was some kind of itinerary, a programme. I ranted a little bit as my sense of injustice speculated on what this crude instruction could possibly mean, even though I knew very well. It meant don't drive to Bowers. "Why?" I muttered to myself. "Ridiculous, I should ignore it, I won't do it!"

I remembered a similar occasion when Ram had given me a particularly challenging direction. I had complained it was impossible and I couldn't do it. He never said anything about it, not a word and we just readjusted the arrangements. But that was the thing, readjustments never allowed you to experience what may have been on offer in the first place. When you are provoked into uncertainty by your Guru, what do you do? When do you say yes and when do you say no, and what is the criteria for deciding?

I recalled how he had once responded to a similar dilemma. I was sat in a class he was leading and the questioner had asked, "How do you know you can trust the teacher and that his words are authentic and that there isn't some hidden agenda?"
Ram had replied, "It depends if that teacher is speaking as a person or as the guru of your own reflection. If it is as a person, then it is routine, fallible and all social parameters apply in the common way. If it is the voice of your own reflection then you should see beyond the person speaking and pay deep respect to the current of the words, or the actions, depending on how the communication is conveyed. If the teacher before you is restricted by the person, that is routine relationship, if the person before you is absorbed by the guru, that is mystical relationship, outside of time."
"And how do you know which it is?" the questioner continued.
"The power conveys it," was the response, which I could tell was inadequate for the questioner who continued to try and elicit explanation from the man she saw speaking, whilst I was tingling in the corner from the half-second glance of those guru eyes that had accompanied the words.

In the absence of a start date I decided I would go to the hill on the 28th and stay two nights, maybe three. He had previously told me I only needed clothes for camping. "What about equipment?" I had asked.
"Just clothes and a sleeping bag, a blanket and three litres of water."
Even though there were car parking spaces at the bottom of the hill,

I had decided I would accept the 'Don't drive' challenge. The only practical way without a car was to take a bus which stopped a mile and a half away, or a taxi. So, at 2pm on Tuesday 28th with my rucksack by my side, I paid the taxi driver, walked away from the public path and around the western flank of the hill, along the wooded track and across open ground as the track petered out. An eroded gully came down the side of the hill and forked at the base into two dry stream beds. At the side of the fork was an immense, ancient willow tree. These two features were the only landmarks I had been given in my wholly inadequate meeting instructions. Fifty metres away the Fern Road ascended the lower slope of the hill and into a wooded area ahead.

It was nothing like I remembered it from three years ago when through a set of circumstances and a broken heart, I had been here before. It had been a very chaotic time for me. I was desperate for some way of feeling better about all things. A woman I had met at a meditation class said that she was going to visit her spiritual teacher and I should come along. Over the years I had often questioned that, it was a very strange offer as I hardly knew her and then lost touch with her very quickly afterwards; why would she do that? I remembered how I had walked up the hill proudly, feeling special that I was embarking on a magical quest. There would be techniques, practices, formulas, I would be distracted from my problems and initiated into a new state. I felt sure there was a proper track here then; I remembered a clearing at the top of the path, a lean-to hut and a veranda of sorts. We had ascended together out of the bushes and there he was, just like that, it was him, Ram! I couldn't believe it and felt instantly embarrassed. I know I had talked a lot, describing my thoughts and ideas, telling him what I had done since meeting him in the taxi. And then there was that painful moment, the sensation of it flashed again in my senses as I walked through the ferns. I had been explaining a recent retreat and how I was planning to explore this new enlightenment practice and did he know about it? I had paused, just to allow the politeness of a response, my mind still alive with the next thing I wanted to say. Then, I noticed it, the look of disgust on his face. Later my friend had said, of course it wasn't disgust, and I thought about that a lot. Eventually I concluded that she was right, it wasn't disgust, it was disinterest. What I was seeing was someone who I could not draw in, fascinate or impress, he was not intrigued at all in what I was saying, or in me. That non-effect felt so terribly insulting and it had made me mad. Eventually my companion broke the silence and suggested tea. He got up and went into the bushes. I was really upset; I didn't know why but I felt ghastly. My friend gave me a hug and said I should just listen to what might be said to me. We had tea in silence; it was excruciating, I sat there with my eyes closed and felt terrible, emotional, invaded and anxious; fighting to maintain an appearance of stillness, even though I was raging inside. After ten minutes of tea drinking a bell was rung.

He looked directly at me, an intense and penetrating scrutiny. "Do you have a question?"

And that was the most frustrating thing, I didn't. A million issues were pouring through me but I could not find the courage or the relevance to raise any of them, I was speechless.

"Turn within," he said, "encounter what is there, investigate what you find. And now you can leave."

I had never been so dismissed. Gathering up my things aggressively, I made a point of conveying my dissatisfaction, or at least I think I did. I spent the whole way down the track telling my friend how rude I thought the teacher was. She defended him by saying he was just clear and not playing to the common game but I didn't buy it, as far as I was concerned, I did not feel wanted and I had wanted to be wanted. I was upset for days, churning it over in my mind. There was no engagement, that was the thing, just absence of impact but I could not forget the instruction, or that look, or the bombardment of my sensibilities. It was that which opened up the great adventure.

It was about 3:00pm when I came up through the ferns and into the trees. Even though the hill was only two miles from the town, this section was completely secluded. The upper slope was thickly wooded, there was no path at all through the cluster of trees, "You just go up," Ram had said, "go up and just keep going, why do you always need a particular marked route?"
It was hard on the path, nettles and brambles to negotiate and the incline was tough. I stopped to take a breath leaning against a huge old oak tree. The drilling of the woodpecker echoed through the wood. "Just go up." Suddenly I found that truly hilarious, boundlessly funny, my chuckles grew into great laughs and sniggers, it was beautifully liberating, clearing any remnants of those old memories.

The final ten metres to the top were a scramble through the brush; I came over the lip of the hill on all fours. On the western edge of the small plateau were the remnants of a wooden structure, just the foundation now and dismantled joists lying abandoned to the side. Next to it a tarpaulin raised up and stretched out across a lattice of branches and in the front, a fire pit with a cooking frame positioned above it. Two cheap camping chairs stood positioned on the opposite edge facing out over the landscape. I put my pack down and explored the encampment. It was rough. Ash in the fire pit showed that it had been used. There was a sealed plastic box behind the ruined hut. Prising off its tight lid, I found a bag of lentils, a bag of rice, a bag of oats, a bag of tea and a big box of matches. A tied black plastic sack contained a sleeping bag and two pillows. A ten-litre water container was half empty. It was 3:30pm. The top was peaceful, the afternoon sun gently warming on my face as I lay back on the grass and stared at the sky observing the clouds move, reflecting on how things had changed in me since the last time I was here three years ago; all the sadhana, all the life experience and adventures. It was poignant and I felt ready for whatever the night might bring. I assembled the cooking rig and went ahead boiling up rice and dhal. There was nothing to flavour it with, I looked around for herbs or leaves but there was nothing obvious, so my meal was a bland mix of mush eaten out of the single pan with my fingers, I started to feel miserable. The darkness came in and just as old fears began to rise in me, a rustling and crashing in the bushes accompanied by the flickering and flashing of torchlight heralded the arrival of Ram. I checked my watch, it said 9:15pm. He strode in, bold and big and I immediately felt the joy in him and the echo of that as it rose up in me.

"Good night for camping," said Ram, as he took the pan of cold mush, scraped some out onto a flat stone and ate with his fingers. "Delicious, needs some salt, don't you think?"
"There isn't any salt."
"I know."
"How did you know I had come?"
"The fire. I have been looking out for it, well done for getting it going."
We built up the fire together, prepared the bedding and cooked up Tulsi tea. Sitting together in the dark, the lights of the town twinkling in the distance, I gave all my attention to engaging with my teacher. After a silent half hour, punctuated with the crackling of the fire and the sounds of owls, Ram stood up, clapped his hands and spoke.
"We are here to have a Big Conversation."
"What's it about?"
"The seer's knowledge and the seer's action."
"Is there an action?" I asked excitedly.
"Yes, there is an action and we are here to initiate it but first you

must absorb the knowledge. It's nothing you haven't heard before but tonight is different; tonight and tomorrow I am to transmit it to you, not just talk to you about it."

"What's the difference?"

"It's a guru thing, don't worry about it." He sat down again, silence prevailed between us and the minutes ticked by, it felt different up here tonight, different from how we usually squared up to each other. There was no paraphernalia, no incense, no special objects or positioning; we were just sitting on a rough hilltop with the sky above us in natural isolation. I felt relaxed, very relaxed, then a growing awkwardness, as if it was expectant on me to start something. He looked at me for a long lingering moment then nodded, just once.

"How do you start a Big Conversation, Ram?"

"By saying something big," he answered, looking at me mischievously.

"Well, the moon is big," I said pointing at it.

"And ancient," said Ram, smiling, "we like the old, I think."

"How old are you?"

"13.8 billion years, give or take a few million."

"But you know what I mean, how old are you really?"

"As I say, 13.8 billion. How old do you think you are?"

"It's my birthday this year."

"Congratulations. But who will be having the birthday?"

"Me of course, it's my birthday, another year older."

"Really? Who or what do you think you are then?"

"Me, this body, this mind, my life."

"Oh, that little thing, I wouldn't give that so much attention if I was you."

"Okay, I know what you mean but that is what I am here and now, this daily life, that's what's relevant."

"This is serious," he said, with an enforced comical graveness to his voice.

"Is it?"

"Certainly, I don't think you know what I mean at all."

"I do, I know about time, existence, identity, spirit. I have read the Upanishads; I can quote it to others."

"You mean you can speak it?"

"Yes, I can speak it, I know it."

"Speaking it is not knowing it; what do you think is necessary to know the reality of the Upanishads?"

"Information, study and understanding."

"No, for other skills in life that is true but for this that is not enough, we need realisation. Information and understanding is thinking."

"And is thinking wrong?"

"Of course not, by no means, it's natural, productive and essential to life, jnana is the beautiful pursuit but for realising this knowledge, thoughts alone are only the beginning."

"So thoughts aren't important then?"

"Thoughts are very important, real in the instant they arise and then unreal when they have gone but particular thoughts, ideas, attitudes, opinions and events are what in this conversation we must identify as content. Realisation of this knowledge is not content; it is the experiencing of the content. Do you see the difference?"

"No, I am not sure I do, surely the content as you put it is the important part."

"No it isn't, it really isn't, it's a preliminary component only. Tell me, are your dreams real?"

"No, they are dreams."

"There you are then; you are already making a distinction of content. An event on this hill is real to you and an event in your dream is unreal. That evaluation of content is your common perspective; it is not what we should be concerned with here, now, tonight."

"That's an extraordinary thing to suggest."

"What do you think I am suggesting?"

"That the content of things is not important."

"I haven't said that at all. Of course, the content of a thing has significance to it. Life is a theatre of content. There must be an interest in the content otherwise nothing would have any value. But I am saying something else to you. I am saying that the intrigue and fascination you attach to navigating the changing content, consumes your attention and captures your identity. That phenomenon is masking something deeper and more magnificent; something simple yet elusive, it is masking the experiencing power itself and I am here to show you that."

"Has our Big Conversation started now?"

"Yes, this is our Big Conversation, first comes the seer's knowledge and then the seer's action. So, tell me why is your dream not real?"

"I suppose it's like a hallucination."

"But it happened. It was experienced."

"Yes but it felt different, not solid. I am not connected with it in the same way; I don't understand my dreams like I understand these actions now, here talking to you."

"So what? Such understanding has no value in realising the experiencer."

It seemed a radical thing to say. "What? That can't be right, understanding is the objective surely, otherwise how do you make sense of anything?"

"By going beyond thoughts and ideas. A foundation of understanding is essential, in fact critical but you already have that in abundance. You can't keep pursuing that same direction endlessly. The quest for perfect understanding is a mirage, it's an addiction that will drag on and on constantly seeking confirmation. Such a pursuit is just more of that same mental activity driving you further and further away from experience. Once a core and sound understanding is in place it is experience that then holds maturity of vision, not thought. There is something about you that is thinking and evaluating the content and there is something else which is experiencing that thinking as it happens."

"You mean the ego and the Self."

"Aha! See, you can speak that knowledge from the Upanishads very well but it's still only ideas in you, however grand they may be. We are here to realise it not to think it, my question to you is simple, is your dream real?"

"No."

"Why not?"

"Because last night in my dream a tiger came inside me, right inside my skin."

"Did it? Gosh!"

"And that's not real."

"Why not?"

"Because obviously a tiger did not and cannot climb inside my skin."

"But it did in the dream and that was real when it happened."

I was feeling exasperated now and hesitated without responding.

"If I tell you to invite the tiger in and somehow you did, losing your identity in that tiger persona, then felt you must go out and tackle a nagging problem with uncompromising ferocious determination to conquer it and defeat it, what would you say?"

"That it was a dangerous hallucination."

"And you might be right but even so you would not deny that the event happened."

"No, I would say I imagined it and it is not the real me."

"Aha! That is the exact point! When you say that, you are basing your evaluation on common identity. Perfectly understandable in the everyday world and sensible, no one wants to negotiate with tigers but what I am conveying to you in this Big Conversation is not the particular activity of content but something else, a different power that knows the experience happened."

"Okay, the experience happened but it was a false experience."

"What is it in you that says that, what is working to make all these distinctions in the content of events?"

"Isn't it just intelligence?"

"Quite so, judgement, intelligence and memory are the tools, all perfectly normal but who is it in you that wants to categorise everything in this way, to shape it, feel it, live it and own it? Surely you know, tell me you know."

"I thinks it's the ego, or rather, the I thought. Is that a better way of pinning it down?"

"Yes, the I thought, not the intelligence itself but the I thought that seems to direct it, wield it and suffer from it. How many times have you heard the spiritual teaching of the I thought?"

"Well, quite a few."

"And to date, you have approached it as a philosophical thing, as something to meditate on and understand. All good but now there is something else more subtle to see, hence this encounter between us here on this hill. What is the I thought?"

"This imaginary person."

"Oh, imaginary is it? That may be what texts and teachers have said to you but how has that helped you? Has it changed the experience and made the I thought dissolve like the tiger in your dream? Tell me, is there still an individual there or not?"

"I don't know, I am not sure anymore," I sighed.

"I know," he responded with compassion in his voice, "in such conversations the sadhak is perplexed and doesn't know where to turn but this is a Big Conversation Amelia, note the word Big, we must be bold and we must be sure. All that urgency to understand it that has driven your seeking is an exquisite passion, you can't avoid it, you must pursue it but it also cooks your brains. We need to get beyond that now. Of course there is an individuality present, operating here and now, the natural flavour of Amelia and those who through some misplaced rigidity deny that, are mad. There is individuality but it doesn't define you or contain you, that's the point. Describe the I thought to me."

"It's the ego, as I said."

"Just a word, it's not descriptive enough, is it? It doesn't help and it doesn't transform. Just to say ego is unacceptable."

"Well, how do you describe it then?"

"The teacher describes it by perceiving it in himself and then speaking about what he sees. That is how you do it, not from books and concepts anymore but from direct description. The I thought is obvious when you have established the distance to view it. The I thought is the sense I am a person inside this mind and the feeling that is my identity and my reality. It is the belief that the functions of thinking, wanting, doing and feeling are what I am, the sense of a personal embodied 'me'. It's what the texts call the doer or Jiva. Do you see this distinction? It is this identity that we are exposing and not the movements themselves, not the content?"

"Yes and that identity doesn't exist, I don't exist."

"That's not good enough, that doesn't cut it; such statements do not do you or all the other sincere seekers justice. When poorly understood this bleak thinking just confuses and makes you frustrated and tense. You can say, "I don't exist" if you truly mean the I thought itself but if you mistake that for intimacy then you are making a terrible error. The I thought is the concept I am a separate me and that we are indeed rejecting but not the intimacy of existence itself. This is the distinction of the wise. There is a clear experience of existence and intimacy, that is real and that we are not rejecting but more of that tomorrow, I think. This is a Big Conversation Amelia; we are enhancing the Upanishads."

"Can you enhance the Upanishads?"

"Not the knowledge but the articulation, we are enhancing the articulation. Even then it's not enough. If I give you the most skilful articulation possible then my verbal duty to you is delivered but it might still cook your brains and feel unattainable. The guru's duty is partly words but is beyond words also; it is energetic. When the words drop, that energetic communication prevails in the silence without words. There must be silence Amelia, without silence the duty between us will wither and fail."

"Is there a duty then?"

"Better to call it a destiny, it draws us into association."

"Is it pre-destined then?"

"Everything is pre-destined; you, me, the meeting between us. But don't be confused, pre-destined only means generated by the prevailing helix of events. Nothing is stand alone; everything is generated by that which preceded it."

The impact of his words lingered in the air as a growing sense of thrill trickled through my senses. This was different, something new was operating between us, something potent that was shifting my sensibilities. "What is the guru?"

"That which breaks through in you. All these questions you ask and have ever asked can be answered theoretically; a clever person with a scholastic understanding of these things can defeat any argument about the nature of reality. But if you only understand the architecture you still don't know it in experience, you don't feel it and you cannot convey either its detail or its beauty. To know it in experience and paint its beauty you need more than philosophy; the energy of that and its art defines the guru but now we are off the point."

"There are so many points."

Ram laughed. "Yes," he said, "so many pointless points. What is here is the point, what is being experienced is the point, what is happening is the point and we are to talk about all of that before you leave this hill but not yet. First we must finish this I thought business. What must we do about the I thought do you think?"

"Destroy it!"

"That's a term used in some texts but not by me. I find it a brutal word, it also implies a direct action, some kind of practice as if there was a technique for it. Things are more subtle than that, more natural. A better way of describing destruction is deconstruction, a letting go, a giving up. Tell me how do you give something up?"

"By not doing it I suppose."

"Yes, but what if you really want to do it, what if it's a strong habit you can't break, even an addiction, if you want to stop that and give it up, then what do you do?"

"You get determined."

"Great! You get determined; I like that. What is it that makes you determined?"

"Well, you have to want to do it."

"Precisely, you have to want it, there has to be a vitality, an energy, a force, an affection for it. It's not an external thing, it doesn't come upon you from outside as if you were some passive agent, there is no point waiting for it like that, it comes up from inside and you know it as an enthusiasm, a commitment, a destiny. You have to want it, what makes you want it?"

"I don't know, evolution or something, previous lives maybe?"

"Perhaps but right now these are abstract causes. Truthfully that which makes you want it is distaste for the current situation. That is what is at the heart of the motivation within you that has brought you here, a non-fulfilment and an objection to the common values displayed in the world around. This inherent dissatisfaction leads to the preliminary spiritual search that eventually matures into Big Conversations like this… today's the day, Amelia."

"For what?"

"For the transference of the seer's knowledge. First the clarification of the I thought that we have just shared, then the description of the Self as you have come to know it and for that we need to be somewhere else. I will meet you in the morning at 7:30am in Percy's."

"What's Percy's?"

"It's a cafe in the town, go to the bottom of the hill and walk to the industrial estate. It will take you two hours but now there must be silence."

"But Ram, I have a thousand questions about the I thought and you

and everything."
"Silence is the only possible response to those questions now."
He went into the bushes and then arranged himself in the sleeping bag. I followed. It was uncomfortable, bleak under the tarpaulin on the rough ground but also magnificent to be there, in the dark on the hill, out in the air and the sky, next to my Guru. I listened to his breathing and the sway of the breeze in the trees, trying to avoid thinking about the dampness and creeping things. I dreamt of tigers padding, prowling, nestling, then curling and purring next to me. When I woke at dawn, aching and stiff, he was gone.

I entered the busy little café at 7:30am. It was noisy inside. The steam rising from the hot water boiler on the counter and the hissing coffee machine competed with the loud clatter of crockery being washed in a deep, white industrial sink alongside the spitting and crackling sounds of the cast iron frying pan pushed over the gas ring by a large sweaty cook, in between plunging trays of chips into a sizzling fryer. The fat fumes seemed to suck all the goodness out of the air; I found it hard to breathe screwing up my face watching the fug condense on the bay windows like a fog. The place was busy, full of lorry drivers and traders, men and women dressed mostly in overalls, heavy working clothes and boots. Two waitresses weaved about between the tables. Ram was squashed into the far corner on a small table for two, cradling a big white mug of tea. He waved and beckoned me over, calling to the waitress at the same time. I moved through the throng.
"Sit down," said Ram cheerily, kicking out the straight-backed wooden chair, "I've ordered us egg and chips."
"Chips? It's half past seven in the morning!"
"Chips are what you eat here."
I was horrified, feeling shocked, this was surely not the place to meet your Guru. "Ram, why on earth have we come here? It's awful!"
"Because God is here too," he said, looking straight into my eyes. He

was deadly serious, his words landing in me like a punch. The table was uncomfortable and very cramped; the large man behind me kept pressing his chair into my back. I shuffled into a better position.

"I don't feel right here, I feel out of place, people are looking at us. Can't we leave? Why couldn't we stay on the hill or meet in a temple? There is a 13th century church down the road; we could sit in the temple garden."

"This is much better than a temple, when you are up on the hill gazing out over the beautiful vista with nature all around, you feel a sense of clarity. When you meditate in the temple and all the movements of mind cease, you perceive a purity and openness and you feel content, close to God. Now, amidst this clamour and activity you feel uncomfortable, it is like you have lost something. There is a single reason for that."

"What is it?"

"You believe the Self is only the peace and nothing else. This is not so, the Self is the experience of all of it, including this egg and chips and your uncomfortable feelings. What a perfect place this is to have this conversation. It's the temple of the world."

The waitress noisily placed two bulging plates before us, a great mound of chips, three eggs and a huge hunk of bread and butter.

"More tea please," Ram ordered and she returned immediately with two enormous steaming white mugs, the cook was just lining them up on the counter for anybody who wanted them.

"What is the default property of a lake?"

"Water," I answered, pushing the chips around the edge of my plate.

"Yes, but I mean its observable properties, what is the default state of the water's surface?"

"I don't know, stillness maybe?" My eggs were so fatty; I tried to mop them up with the bread, scowling as I did so.

"Yes, stillness, that is the original state of the lake and the state to which the property of water inevitably returns but it is not always still. Now you can't say the water is lost, when it is agitated, it is obviously still water, still itself. It isn't wrong or harmed, neither is it something else, it is exactly the same with the power that we call the Self. It can be understood as the illumination within the experience and that does mean any experience."

"So is the Self everything then?"

"You can say so but it is best and most lucid to understand it as the experiencing of everything."

"So that means the I thought that we were discussing last night is also the Self."

"Ah, a conundrum of philosophy you are so quick to make, see how tempting it is for this working mind to propose complexities? From the ultimate position that is a true statement but it is not a helpful statement. The I thought is a position of ignorance, it is an event within the Self. From a viewpoint of ignorance you cannot perceive the reality. If the water surface is only ever turbulent it will never know the nature or beauty of its still and reflective essence. It will never know what it is, it will just know what it has become as a result of its agitation, crashing about, running off in all kinds of eddies and rivulets. If the I thought is accepted as yourself and life unknowingly lived from that position, it's a confused perspective, just like the agitated water. The point is, the permanence of the Self is the power of illumination; which you know as the power of experiencing. The activity within the Self is the impermanent manifestation of the content of experience, that is the major point. There is nothing wrong with the impermanence, it just cannot be said to be the enduring, formless Self or I. Let me put it another way. There is a mind; it is that power in which all these fluctuations arise and move including the I thought. What you are is that which is experiencing the mind, not the movements within the mind but that which is experiencing the mind; for ease it can be called consciousness. The seer's knowledge is to know this constantly, even during the changing experience. This is Self-realisation, to know the substance of the Self, even whilst movement plays and ripples flow.

Ignorance is to have no knowledge of this at all and to be possessed by the belief that I am the movements and fluctuations. The mistake the sadhak makes is believing that only peace is legitimate and that agitation is somehow wrong or bad. Now, it may be unwelcome but that's another matter, that's to do with preference and character. It is perfectly understandable that the sadhak wants to align herself with the inspiring and distance herself from the mundane or challenging. That is sensible and wise, it sweetens experience but even in those times when circumstance is mundane or challenging, the Self still prevails because the Self is the Being within the experience, or to use the traditional language, the witness. That's what the Upanishads have been calling the Self for thousands of years, the witness, or as we are enhancing the Upanishads today, I will call the witnessing power. Do you recognise that that is here now?"

"Yes, it must be."

"That's right, it must be here now for there to be any existence at all. It is here for you, for I and for everyone else who is alive, even here amidst noise and steam and crush and fatty chips, and listen, I want to emphasise to you the amazing thing, the thing that once you see it, changes everything. This presenting power that we are calling the Self with all its awesome majesty and incredible properties of manifestation and creativity, is here completely spontaneously and naturally. It is the effortless illumination of the moment; effortless I say in the sense that there is nothing whatsoever that you have to do to generate or sustain it, that is truly stunning. This effortless, spontaneous power is the ground of existence upon which everything else stands; it is Being itself. So magnificent is it, that we can understand it as the very substance of God, living as all this, as you."

"Some people don't like the word God."

"I don't care, they don't like the word God because they have a contrived and limited view of what God is, they think it's some external, fatherly being directing the universe and that seems medieval and absurd to them. Or they don't like the word God because they don't see why they should submit to some power other than their own intelligence. Well, let me tell you, no one knows the workings of this universe and no one knows the possibilities. Anyone who looks in an unprejudiced way into the heart of things will see power, creativity and beauty but that's not all, they will see love and more, they will see divinity and if they don't, they are only limited by their own ignorance. We should celebrate the word God, we should reclaim it, it's a liberating word, a majestic expression. I will not apologise or be hesitant at the use of the word God because God is what I see and God is what moves in me and God is what I am inspired to express. The point is, my ability to express at all is utterly dependent on the architecture of the Self, call it by any name but that fact remains the same. Are you an artist?"

It seemed a random question and it took me aback. I said I was.

"Fantastic," he replied, "I am glad you are admitting it at last, we must all be artists of one type or another. If, as an artist, you happen to paint a picture, you see the content, the detail; the picture may be sublime or horrible, inept or genius, there is infinite variety of possibility in the depiction of the picture but there is one constant that is vital and indisputable, the canvas on which it is painted. You never see the canvas which is steady, all-accepting, all-embracing, but the canvas is the key structure, without that there would be no possibility of picture at all, no base upon which that creativity could be expressed. Also, the canvas is timeless and versatile, only temporarily occupied by the picture. It can be changed, over-painted, erased, deleted. When it is gone, the object will be gone but not the substance upon which the object depended. The Self is like that; Amelia is a temporary experience. All the struggles and aspirations, objectives and accomplishments are Amelia's mind, it is part of nature, part of this tremendous project of creativity and evolution, it is a way of expressing cosmic art. And within that mind are all the conflicts and potential; ancient habits of the past versus pressing aspirations for the future, hungers for selfish gain and promotion versus generosity and kindness, and all shades in between. As such mental life runs the theatre, personal life plays out and there are consequences moment by moment, on and on. That which knows it, that which contains it, that which illuminates it, that which gives it life and in which your personal consciousness itself appears, is the Self. The individual is a mode of expression, the human being is a vehicle of perceiving and expression. Within that, the experience of a mind is part of this grand project."

Ram paused and mopped up his eggs with his bread. The man behind me banged his elbow into my back again as he raised his arm and shouted out for the brown sauce. The waitress threw it and he caught it like a baseball player. The table next to him broke out in applause and cheers. It was extraordinary that we were having this advanced and exquisite conversation amidst these everyday, crude circumstances. I thought of the Upanishads and the forest ashrams in which they had been delivered. Was this any different, did it matter at all? I suddenly felt profoundly moved and felt real affection for the man sitting behind me even as the back of his chair ground into mine.

"Ram, can I ask a stupid question?"

"Yes, definitely you can and you should."

"Am I alone?"

All that he had said, all that he had ever said inspired and thrilled me but I had always had this nagging sense of not wanting to be alone; it frightened me and I avoided it but now it was out. Ram didn't so much look at me in that moment, he seemed to encircle me, almost absorb me; I loved him more than life. The seconds ticked by in the noisy bustle around us.

"An individual mind may feel loneliness but that's only an experience. It's impossible to actually be lonely because there is no single, separate person to be alone in the way that has been imagined."

"But the Upanishads speak of the aloneness of Being and if that is the Self I think I am afraid of letting go into that, is that aloneness real?"

"Perhaps we can just spell it differently."

"What difference does that make?"

"A huge difference, stick an 'L' in it."

"Where?"

"Oh come on, come on!" Ram took his pencil and wrote on the napkin:

Aloneness = All-oneness

"It is all oneness," he continued, "Self-realisation is the expanded state of all oneness; a profound shift in perspective. It's simple and ordinary but majestic and full at the same time; it is freedom. Loneliness is impossible in that and if it appeared, it would only be a thought. But your question points to something. You do need courage because in surrender and sacrifice there is the fear of loss and the fear of death to overcome. It's a kind of grief you see."

"What is?"

"The realisation that you are not what you thought you were, a kind of grief like a divorce. You see, you don't want to let go of what it is you perceive of as your identity, in other words, this person. It's not that a potential release from that is unwelcome but it is, nonetheless, a threat of loss, or we might say, death. It changes quickly into immense, sustaining relief and ease but there may be a phase of uncertainty, even fear. Hence, your fear of aloneness and that's why the texts constantly talk of faith. This identity that you are afraid of losing is entirely mental; it is a set of ideas, or rather a concept. The affection and security at the heart of your Being is not in any way a product of that concept. Self-realisation is the loss of that concept, there is no loss of affection and security, only an enhancement of those things, not loneliness but fullness."

The waitress came and cleared our plates. I felt embarrassed that mine was hardly touched; Ram's was clean. I paid the bill and we left the café. Standing outside in the lorry park I felt like a giant outside of time and inside of something else, I was exhilarated, fizzing, unsure of where I really was but fully present and so capable.

"I need to do something but I don't know what."

"That's great, inspiration and motivation are the gifts, the what can come later. I will see you tonight on the hill; cook for 7:00pm."

"Where are you going?"

"Oh, here and there, how about you?"

"I think I will go and explore that church and then maybe I will find a shop and buy some salt."

Ram nodded his head and then wandered off.

I watched him pass the time of day with one of the drivers and then leave the car park and disappear down the road. It was amazing, so ordinary, so simple and yet so mystical. I headed off in the opposite direction towards the church tower in the distance.

Ram arrived at 7:20pm and sat down in the camping chair beside the fire. He turned up his nose comically at the paper plates, cups and wooden forks I had lined up on the stone.

"Smells tasty," he said, examining the salt and curry paste at the side of the pan.

"I bought chapatis, Ram, and tomatoes."

"Nice, better than egg and chips."

We ate as the twilight overcame the hilltop and the edges of the trees got increasingly lost in the darkening night. Two owls called to each other in the woods behind us. I felt we were in an ancient place, in Vedic lands prior to civilisation before things had become so complicated. Being on the hilltop around the fire was like a forest ashram and I liked it. Even though the café conversation had been exhilarating the reality was, I preferred it here. Childlike happiness soared and played in me and I lost myself in that gentle reverie. Ram cleared up and brought the blankets to the fire. We sat in the chairs with the blankets around our shoulders and chanted the mantra "Om" into the night, the silence hung elegantly and poignantly. Ram cleared his throat, took his small bell from his pocket and rang it beautifully in the stillness. It was time to hear, not to listen, but to hear.

"Once you accept the seer's knowledge that we have already shared, then you need not deviate," said Ram, "the fact that there is a feeling that I am me enclosed in this skin and that there is a power experiencing that which we choose to call the Self, these two things are the seer's knowledge and they can be discovered by those who look. Then there is an offer; either to ignore it due to a lack of interest or capability, or to investigate those two things philosophically and explore them experientially, to realise them in experience."

"What do you mean by capability?"

"An affection for sadhana and the energy to persist, it's there or it isn't. Most are absorbed by the ego and the common mind which has no interest in investigating the seer's knowledge. The course of exploration is the higher path. The culmination of that then rests on the seer's action which is a powerful, single ability."

"What is it?"

"Discernment, discernment is the seer's action. You know the theory, you accept it, you even love it but how do you experience it directly? The answer is through discernment and that is achieved through the clarity of directly perceiving what is constant."

"Where is the constant found?"

"Everywhere and in everything. You see, this power that we are calling the Self is the pure sense of existing and that is already here in the framework of our ordinary experience, it is the intimacy of Being that I spoke of before but because of the crudity of common perception and the dominance of the I thought it isn't acknowledged or recognised. So now we are out of the clatter and clamour of the café and here in the stillness, I am going to tell you more directly, more powerfully and more subtlety, precisely what this power is so that you can know it. It is, as I said, present everywhere constantly but perceiving it directly requires subtlety and benefits from silence and it is for that reason that we meditate and seek out the pure and the sacred. Then, once you know that, even in the clamour of Percy's you have that knowledge. Listen to these words and feel this description in you as I speak. Discernment is the seer's action. There is an undeniable sense of existence present now. It is direct, immediate and intimately close, all-pervading, perfectly effortless in its appearance, it simply is, and it is simply here, always. It is that which you naturally recognise as the familiarity of being awake and aware and you give it a name, you call it I. It is the feeling of I am and I exist, not the I thought we discussed earlier but the feeling of existence itself. Throughout the entirety of your life, this reality has never not been here; across every second, from being one year old to being ninety years old. It is constant and perpetual, fresh and abundant, it is also very affectionate, loving and appealing, it is the true security of what we might call Being. Through its own properties of consciousness, this affectionate power is what is experiencing everything. It does not have a form; it is not located in some position or organ and it is not an object of experience like other things are. It is present right now flooding the moment as 'I am', that which the Upanishads call Atman. This power cannot be watched as a second thing because it is first, the very essence and substance of Being, it is the light itself, the light of intelligence and existence and that light is beaming now in all directions and through all experience. This power you can come to know. Self-realisation is the fruition of this knowing. This does not happen through thinking about it but by acknowledging its presence and going in the direction of that deepening recognition. The action that is necessary for that discernment to be effective, is the unravelling of that which stands in the way and that is the false identity of the I thought. You think and believe that you are a person experiencing consciousness. Actually, consciousness itself is experiencing the rising of this person. Consciousness is the witnessing power experiencing that and everything else as well; dreaming, sleeping, talking, waking, desire, habit, communication and so on. Consciousness is another name for Self or I am. This is the true position in every moment, whether you know it or whether you do not. Self-realisation is knowing it in natural experience. The seer's action is clearly seeing that the I thought is a belief and then losing that belief by perceiving the 'I am' as first and seeing the I thought as an object, as second. You do this through discernment. If the mind is clear and open, then this discernment is merely a matter of intensity and persistence, if the mind is clumsy and confined, then the discernment will be shallow, inconsistent and difficult. Responding to that situation to refine the qualities of your mind is sadhana, that has been your intensity over these years and that is now fulfilled. Sadhana propels the mind towards greater and greater capabilities for discernment. The context in which this occurs is the spiritual karma of your life, which alongside knowledge and refinement must include meditation. Reading, thinking and knowledge are critical factors but these alone will not provide the same intensity or sensitivity. It may change your thoughts but then you will just have a different belief, you won't feel it. When, after meditation a mind has become mature and ripe, then the loss of the belief in the I thought can be enabled by a single piece of direction. It is intensely profound. You can call it advanced yet as with all such things, it is beguilingly simple in its instruction. This is the essence of our Big Conversation; the seer's action, the result of all your tapas and puja."

"Please tell me what it is."

"Everything is happening by itself. Everything is happening by itself. Everything is happening by itself."

Those words, which I had heard many times before, leapt and sang with a reverence and relevance I had never previously experienced. It seemed momentous, gigantic. Later, when I thought about that moment, I realised that for the first time in my life I had heard their meaning. I had literally taken them to heart and felt them penetrate me. I wanted to shout 'Wow!' but I was lost in a profound reverence. My eyes closed. The fire crackled as the glow from the heat kissed my parted lips. I heard Ram's voice as it floated into the moment.

"All fluctuations, all movements, all of it is happening by itself. From the position of the I thought this is impossible to see because it seems that very same I thought is the one doing it. With that position removed, it is obvious. Let me put it like this, you are experiencing everything, including the movements of thoughts and ideas. In the freedom state without the I thought, everything is spontaneously happening, even the sense of person itself. Events take place just the same, nothing has changed except the characteristics of identity and that change in identity is the freedom state; not a change in stuff."

"What do you mean nothing changes, surely it's different?"

"Skin, blood, life, time, actions, personality, character, all the things which you might call the default qualities of this living experience stay put, just the same, they have never been the problem, isn't that an exciting discovery? What has been the problem is something else entirely, something so confining in the beginning but then so shamelessly insubstantial in the end and you know what that is, you know very well."

"Yes, I do know, it's the ego but if everything is the same…"

"I didn't say everything is the same, the qualitative elements of human existence stay put but the absence of the I thought identity enables the state of openness and in openness all that is in you can flourish. This is really what you want and what nature wants of you, it is the natural state, the freedom to live the moment and in that freedom, the natural expression in you is free to flourish. This may well lead to change in life events, or not, but that isn't the point. The dissolution of the I thought identity unravels this natural state amidst the continuation of skin, blood, heart, mind and so on. Life is then an up-swell in that natural openness of heart, which is nothing more than unfettered expression, creativity and love. There may well be change in the direction of your actions but the architecture of what we might call your mode of person is the same, it's just free. Currently, the Self-realised are in a minority amidst a majority which perceives things differently but that doesn't matter, your whole personal world is the projection of your own mind and in liberating that mind, you are a pioneer of the new because you have transcended the old. You have not needed to travel to new dimensions or new worlds to do this, there is no travelling in space or time or even circumstance, the only travelling is a movement in that position of identity and an arising of natural intimacy. Freedom is that unfettered intimacy in which all happens. I am that, you are that."

"How does the sadhak do it Ram, amidst all the duties and responsibilities of life?"

"Faith and sadhana, accepting it's a whole life project of increasing vision and sensitivity. As we said two days ago, you've gotta get determined to push on through, naïve prayers don't work, 'God make me happy' will not work but patiently and persistently unravelling that which is the source of unhappiness will. That is the answer to any prayer you may make and the unravelling is active and purposeful. Its application is sadhana and the power for that is nothing less than wanting it, you have to want it, some do and some don't. The guru is here for those that do and others are in place for those that don't, such is the architecture of spirituality. Where that power is running in a person, it defines a life of spiritual discovery, it's inevitable, it might be avoided for a while but it's inevitable and if that enthusiasm remains prominent then that is a blessing. You do understand don't you, that for you this is the purpose of life?"

"Yes, I do."

"Do you really? I want you to consider it. Others will view your commitment as casual, as something that competes with other life interests but it isn't, it's a central drive. It truly is a blessing and it needs to be acknowledged as that. This is the seer's action, to discern the reality within you and act on what you find. It's there now already and the discernment reveals that truth. Your spiritual practice started in all the actions, all the techniques, all the ideas, all the stuff, now that's finished or is at least reducing and diminishing. Your attention doesn't need to focus on all that anymore, you need to be alone often, experiencing life under your own steam. In that regard there is a disadvantage in having or needing constant access to your guru. It's indulgent and leads to complacency and dependence. Such easy contact keeps you spiritually warm inside, doesn't it?"

I admitted it did.

"Warmth is vital for the child, all children benefit from being embraced, even swaddled but as the child develops there needs to be a change of relationship and if there isn't, then the child never properly matures. It is common to crave the safe embrace of childhood, even in adulthood some still yearn for that but do you know the hazard associated with that?"

I told him I didn't, not because I couldn't guess but just because I wanted to hear how he would say it.

"One of these days you will transform into death and that passage is best accomplished striding confidently, joyfully, not timidly, not seeking your protector or clinging to attachments, no, it's a freedom state. It's best to have restrictions to accessing the guru, this invokes the freedom state. Don't take things at face value Amelia, there is always a mystery to apparently random instructions."

"Like what?"

"Don't drive. You had to walk here, you had to explore and investigate and more importantly, you did not have an easy exit route. As a consequence, you had to be fully in the experience and roam independently in the moment; in the roaming you discovered new things that became growth and resilience in you."

At that moment something happened between us. It was like a merger of sorts; a kind of synergy. I became lost yet also centred at a different point and at the same time neither of these categories seemed important. There was only depth and no boundaries. We gazed at each other; gazed and gazed. The woodpecker drilled, echoing across the hilltop.

"Ram, what do we do now, what do we do next?"

"Create. Live, love and express, act for the art, for the creativity and the beauty, then you will become the teacher of yourself."

"But Ram, you will always be my teacher."

"Yes, I can always be that up until death, but after the seer's action, the teacher stops being a teacher and becomes something else."

"What?"

"Your Self."

"That suits me just fine."

"I will see you in a thousand years then."

"Or half an hour."

"Quite so, a thousand years or half an hour; it's all the same to me, but half an hour would be nice, wouldn't it?"

"Yes, really nice."

"So, let's choose that then. One last thing Amelia, stay alert, once you leave this hill the world will close in on you with rapidity and force. Be vigilant, remember this, put it into practice and stay alert."

"I will Ram, I will."

Chapter Three

Enlightenment
nine months later
in Amelia's house

In The House

It is January 10th and it is time. The frost on the window behind the closed curtains grips the glass; I can sense it and the icy air behind it hovering in the night-garden, more lunar than earthly. I am alone in the dark and everything is ready, arranged. This is my solitude, my hermitage for ten days, isolated and undisturbed. Either I will become enlightened or I will die. I am not being dramatic or indulgent and I am not afraid. My mind, so recently agitated and fatigued, feels strong with determination and purpose. I can feel this purpose like a force.

Before The House

Amelia had last been with Ram on Bowers Hill in April. It had been a remarkable three days; he had given her a powerful instruction - discernment. It had excited her greatly yet somehow the affection for it had faded over the weeks that passed and life had fallen back into old routines. She didn't spot this happening at first, although it was obvious to Ram. She just felt a bit grumpy, knuckling down as usual to her practical responsibilities, unaware of the turbulence that was about to come. It was seven months later in November that she read the passage about enlightenment that would change her destiny. In 528 BCE, Buddha is said to have made a pledge to either obtain enlightenment or die. After six years of austerity and ascetic practice and not attaining the truth, he sat under the Bodhi tree in Bodh Gaya and claimed: *'I will not rise until enlightenment arises even if I die in the attempt'.* Inspiration hit her like lightning, her course was set. How do you prepare for death? Amelia didn't want to actually die because to do so would be some kind of fruitless collapse. She didn't want to collapse, she wanted to thrive, not as conflicted Amelia but as the freedom that she dreamed about and wanted; the same freedom that she assumed Buddha wanted. "Whatever that freedom is," she said to herself, "I shall have it, or face death in the attempt."

To see her situation in such extremes and with such finality had not come from nowhere, it was a consequence of her spiritual crisis. The seeds had begun months ago amidst a period of disruption and doubt that left her confused and unsettled. Ram was her Guru, their relationship was a critical, gigantic element in her life. It brought her intense riches, far beyond the conventional to-ing and fro-ing of routine companionship. Then in summer, something changed. She noticed it first as hesitancy and then a withering, like falling out of love. Aside from common pleasantries Ram stopped talking to her, appearing to barely notice her. Then on the last occasion they had been together, directly ignoring her. How is this change possible, she thought, what can it mean? With the pain of loss rising within her, they met in the Orangery at Bowslip House amidst the bougainvillea and the lemon blossom, when the scent of jasmine was heavy around and the bees buzzed from flower to flower. The Orangery was the place where they gathered, her and the others from the satsang group, on those balmy evenings when the gardens were closed to the public. It was Upanishad in its most real sense, to sit in company and to be in that current and dialogue until the sun came down. But as spring gave way to summer, she began to withdrew and became an outsider, increasingly aloof, distant and not participating. The others understood distance and she was left alone.

On that final evening as she sat quietly under the fig tree in the corner by the terracotta urn, someone began talking about enlightenment. Ram responded with his usual flair and energy but the word enlightenment rattled Amelia. It was the word that described her spiritual objective, unrealised and still seeming so distant despite the Big Conversation on the hill. Intense loneliness came over her like a rising wave, her lip trembling as she stifled the pressure rising inside.

"It is both the goal and the obstacle," said Ram, as he responded to the point, "the sadhak won't accept that it is an obstacle because it undermines the assumptions so deeply held, it exposes the addiction of the seeker, it is a crisis you see. Seekers think they are going somewhere and that gives them momentum and purpose, there are things to learn, things to do, intrigue. Then disillusionment occurs, the thought nothing is going to happen and a plateau is reached of enlightenment fatigue, it's a tamasic state that has the power to possess and consume. The disillusioned seeker may then just wither, giving up spiritual practice and pursuing normal habits. On the upside however, such a crisis trembles and stirs, carrying within it an offer to settle into a deeper tapas, a real depth of discovery and knowing. It is at this point that a seeker could be said to have become mature. The Vedas would say ripe but I prefer the word mature."

The conversation went on becoming animated and playful; people were laughing and making jokes. Amelia thought they were not talking about her directly and she was right. Nonetheless, you know how it is sometimes when teaching just hits the spot so personally that it is uncanny. The words entered her like sparks igniting a fire she did not want to acknowledge or recognise. It was true; the unfulfilled search for enlightenment in her had become some kind of farce. She slipped away out of the open back door and went to sit at the lower end of the walled garden surrounding the Orangery grove, feeling worthless and not sure what to do. Over in the plane tree a squirrel scurried about, jumping from a branch onto the adjacent pitched roof, padding along to the gable and then running back at full speed, leaping onto the slender branch making it swing alarmingly. It was comical but it passed through Amelia with no flavour at all. The chanting started; somebody took up the lead singing a lilting bhajan, the notes of the harmonium reflecting off the flint stone walls beside her "Shivoham, Shivoham, Shivoham".

Ram stepped out of the arched Orangery doorway and made his way up the path. He would leave out of the gate and disappear across the estate to his private hut. The path to the gate wound directly past her seat. Because of how it had been recently Amelia wasn't expecting any acknowledgement, in fact, it now seemed a poor choice of location to have sat here in the first place. Ram strode up, rhythmic and relaxed then halted just before the gate and turned. Amelia felt his steady gaze scrutinise her mind, it was like being tumbled in the surf. She looked up, meeting his deep and powerful eyes. Ram nodded just once; it was a simple gesture yet it contained a sophistication of communication that was beyond analysis.

"You haven't spoken to me," said Amelia.

"That's true," Ram replied.

"It has upset me greatly."

"Addictions require some upset to shed."

"What addictions?"

Ram didn't reply. She felt insulted but didn't show it.

"You can choose to be insulted if you want, it's really up to you now. All I will say is this addiction is the common state. It is not an embarrassment to be addicted, it is a feature of the common state but it is painful when that is seen. I have told you that enlightenment is a movement in understanding and experience. You have thought words themselves were the movement, questions and answers, but even when the answers have been given, all you have taken from them is a new space of ideas. You have needed the words but the power within them only manifests in discovery and conviction. This is what we shared together on the hill. Enlightenment is living in such conviction; being what you are without ideas about what you are not."

"You mean stillness, with an empty mind?"

"No. That is the perspective of novices."

"Being happy then?"

"No. That is the perspective of the attached."

"Being free?"

"No. Unless you know what freedom actually is, then that's a different matter."

"Well, what then?"

"It's up to you now, the talking about the way is over Amelia, and the talking about the goal has become saturated. There can be talking again, there must be talking again but not about the way or the goal. You think enlightenment is some type of initiation event. Well, the true initiation that eludes you is seeing the reality of what you already are and living as that reality in the full knowledge of how that is, but that which is addicted in you wants something other than what is present, you are seeking experiences."

"Of course," she responded, "I am seeking the experience of enlightenment. Being what I am is the whole problem, that is what I am trying to overcome."

"Nonsense. Enlightenment is not an experience and is not dependent on resolving all the apparent concerns in the mind. Why would you do that?"

"Because it is illusion."

Ram rolled his eyes and poked out his tongue like some mediaeval fool. "Words and ideas Amelia, nothing but words and ideas and now that is to stop."

"But then there is nothing."

"That is not true. Then there is direct investigation of what is, then there is discernment and determination, that was your word you identified on the hill. I have told you that enlightenment is not an absorption experience occurring in silence. Enlightenment is a penetrating, living, vibrant knowing of what is, and being as that. At the moment you do not conceive the beauty of that reality and what you want are bliss states, samadhis and ecstasies. You will have already had some experiences like this and no doubt others will come, some of which will exhilarate you profoundly but they all pass. What is the abundant presence in which they arise and pass? It is not nothing. Being the answer to that is enlightenment, I prefer to say realisation but enlightenment is the word you have raised and is the word that captures people's attention. For that you need not wait in the silence for something to happen to you, but instead profoundly discern. The seer's action, Amelia, the seer's action; discernment. Do not assume that is regular thinking, it is penetrating perceiving. But enough of this repetition and clarification, it's all been said before on the hilltop, where is its implementation? Show me. Now it's up to you."

They stared at one another in silence for some moments. Despite the irritation and the challenge of the conversation Amelia knew this was nothing to do with personalities and any reaction from that part of her was childish. The magnificence in those guru eyes was illustrious, beyond time. Ram nodded again, just once. There was some intricate communication in that simple action that penetrated deep within her. Then he left. She watched him go with an ache in her heart. The evening became cool as the sun dipped and dusk began to gather. The sounds from the bhajan in the Orangery played in the air with a beautiful acoustic within the walled grove. Amelia felt upset but it seemed like she was watching a performance or participating in one. These apparent stand-offs with Ram had happened before with varying degrees of upheaval. She had always hated it, often resented it and usually responded instantly to try and recover things back on her terms. Something was different this summer night, some new element played in the air. It was difficult to pinpoint its nature, the best she could do was to label it defiance. The teacher had stopped giving and she hadn't got what she wanted. At that time, there on the summer path, she had no idea that this development was the most brilliant teaching intervention of all. Out of it arose determination.

Preparing The House

In the bedroom of Amelia's house, on the wall to the left of the window where the light shined upon it, a picture of Shiva hung displayed. She had cut it out from a catalogue of ancient Indian statuary that she had found at a car boot sale. It was full colour, showing the patina in the stone and the pitting of the surface that gave the image life and presence. The face was particularly compelling, just simple characterisation of expression but there was a depth of intensity there that was hard to explain. The catalogue had been prepared for a sale of antiques; she had cut out the description note and stuck it to the back of the frame.

'A particularly fine 10th century temple statue of Dakshinamurti, Shiva as teacher of knowledge; the personification of understanding, the God of wisdom and awareness. A rare museum quality piece. Sale estimate: $800,000 - $1,000,000.'

That night in October it was a supermoon, the lunar orb had risen powerfully into the sky illuminating the garden. It was hard to sleep but she did not mind, for to experience the moonlight like that was a rare treat. At 2:00am the light shone through the window upon the framed picture which seemed to glow in response. It was silent, no movement outside, the air still, only breath moving, belly rising gently, falling slowly. It may have been a play of the moonlight, something to do with the shadows of the night as the image in the frame appeared to come forward, seeming to grow, the face becoming three-dimensional rather than two. Dakshinamurti's hands in the form of the jnana mudra quivering, seemingly adjusting with miniscule ethereal movement. Turning her eyes to the face, Amelia held her gaze steady, in intimate contact. Nothing stirred, only presence and timeless potency flowing from those 10th century eyes. Her breathing shallowed even further, a pure, empty clarity replacing the space where thoughts moved like crystal water flowing across smooth stone, the sirens of dreaming. She awoke refreshed and with a new perspective. She had been brooding over the encounter with Ram and her change of status for months, fermenting resentments, about that and all things. Now on this autumn morning, some resolution and determination was upon her.

Perhaps I am addicted, she thought, but to what? And anyway, is it surprising? The Upanishads, the Gita, the works of Shankacharya's teaching was thrilling to know, seeking it had filled her life. But her assimilation and approach had now been challenged by her Guru and she knew it. He had claimed something different; he had claimed she was addicted to experiences and had not achieved discernment, but how does teaching become real like that, alive beyond the words? She knew in her heart that was the challenge she had been given and what a provocative time for it. After all, she was starting to become the teacher herself, the person who explained, the one who repeated ideas about Vedanta and Brahman, she knew about these things. So, was that the climax of all the seeking, to be able to repeat the words, where was the enlightenment beyond the words? This recognition had been depressing but there was a change this day. Amelia wanted to do something about it, she did not know what but she wanted to move. In earlier times when it had been like this she would go off and speak to her Guru to describe her feelings. Ram would respond, reassure her with words and bring her back to clarity but now that was denied. "No more words Amelia, words are finished," is what he had told her on the hill.

As she sat in the kitchen wondering what to do next, the radio alarm came on in the upstairs bedroom, she had forgot to reset it. A haunting piece filtered through the house like a whisper, the tones of cello and violin washing through her mind. Her skin tingled, her heart softened, something released. With eyes closed she appreciated the sublime intricacies of the whispering Bach and thought of her experience in the night with the Moon God.

Far away on the Timecoast where the seeds of things are sown something stirred, just like a sound in the woods when all the creatures become alert; an intensity in the air, some vibration on the ground, some interest. The Timecoast constantly oscillated with a deep shruti note embedded in the breeze; it was the tone of the place. Now a movement arose, you could say it was a desire. In response a complimentary note appeared, gentle, hard to discern as it shimmered and resonated, raising the pitch of the whole just one semitone closer to harmonic 5th. When things are at harmonic 5th there is sattva upon the Timecoast. The very mechanics of clarity and balance where discordant effect cannot be sustained but not yet, not quite, still a semitone or perhaps two away. Nonetheless, it was an important change indicating an intention. The Timecoast was the architecture of the unconscious, the land of potential that becomes conscious life. The Timecoast was the pre-generator of instinct, desire, motivation and possibility and was resonating two semitones below harmonic 5th. As the sun died for that day, the moon over the Timecoast occupied the sky with a power of presence, immaculate in its authority. Supermoons always take your breath away with the portent of new magic.

Back on that fateful summer evening at the Orangery, Ram had watched Amelia leave the grounds from the path that went to his hut. Ram lived in the world of the long game; his responses were acute to the moment but shaped in the context of the long game. The time spans that underpinned most people's perceptions were ludicrous to him, the sense of start and finish absurd. For Ram, it was a limitless expression, a constant, abundant wave and when he said something it was part of that living wave. Amelia was becoming aligned to an ancient instruction. It had been given to her before but like many things a jigsaw doesn't always fit the first time you open the box. It was the Upanishadic instruction; shravana, manana, nididhyasana, to hear the teachings, reflect upon them and then meditate to establish direct perception. What she had not properly absorbed was the deep and accurate meaning of the word, reflect. This was the discernment he had conveyed to her on the hill as the seer's action. It meant to profoundly review, to scrutinise through intelligence and perceiving. The sadhak is cultured not to reflect like this and to pursue experience but Ram had always told her that Self-realisation was a mixture of feeling and knowing, a blended intelligence. She was firmly aligned to the feeling but only superficially to the knowing, falsely assuming that to be dry philosophy and only an idea. He knew this time was a milestone for Amelia, just as there had been points before of passionate volatility, so this was too. Volatility always had some danger within it but he would rarely have used that word to describe it, not danger but provocative potential, it was funny how people mixed up the two. Movement was on the cards now; would she allow it to proceed or would she defend the common state? He knew she would feel as if something had come to a head in her. He expected she would frame it in her own mind dramatically and he understood that but everything was dramatic wasn't it and this no more than that. Nonetheless, to her it would be a precipice; Ram and Amelia had been together before upon precipices. It was quite a homely place for him but he knew that others considered such events as life and death encounters. He watched Amelia disappear around the bay tree.

January 10th

But that was that, water under the bridge, the theatre of beginnings. Now it is that January morning, commitments are made, the course is set, there is no turning back. From here Amelia can describe her own story as it happens.

In The House

It is 6:30am Sunday morning and my eyes are closed, listening to the birds and the early sounds of the world moving, trying to keep my mind free, holding onto that night-space, the space just before all the ideas come. Then with a rush and a whoosh I am awake. Today is the day. My room is neat, very neat; I wanted it clean, nothing to distract, nothing out of place, like a monastic cell. Yesterday I cleared away the ornaments, all the reading materials and the photos, for I will need nothing for enlightenment to arise, only silence, meditation and contemplation. I will be the ascetic living in seclusion close to my God. The only adornment left is the framed picture of Dakshinamurti which I have decided to leave on the wall by the window. My clean, freshly laundered clothes are prepared like a bundle you have when you are a child. Just one set, one large fleece and a big all-enveloping shawl. I take a shower, the last I will have for ten days because I have decided that all my normal, fickle habits are obsessions and distractions and I mustn't be bothered with such things. If I become enlightened then I will wash, and if I don't, well, I will die anyway so it won't matter. I stand under the shower for twenty-four minutes until the water starts to run cool, then cover myself in big clean towels and sit on the edge of the bed. This is it. Minutes tick past. I dress and throw the shawl around my shoulders; it helps me assume my role. Clearing away the things from the shower I make my bed, smoothing it down, smoothing and smoothing and go downstairs. The kitchen is sparse following my clear out the day before and the removal of all the old newspapers and current correspondence, the air smells clean. I make breakfast, clear away and walk through to my room. This will be my monastic temple, my own Bodhi tree. My cushions are already arranged on the floor and I have my plan, I will meditate until mid-morning, have a break and a walk in the garden, meditate again till lunchtime, rest, meditate all afternoon, take tea and supper at 6:00pm, meditate in the evening and sleep by 9:00pm. But now there is something else about my practice, something new. It had become clear to me that my tapas could not only be absorption meditation, for peaceful and compelling as that was, it wasn't enough. Some greater shift was needed, a new intensity if I was to realise what had not been realised before. I needed to approach the mysteries in another way so the truth could become real to me. I wasn't really sure how I knew this now but the recognition had come upon me in recent months as I had reflected and since my exquisite dream encounter with the Moon God had solidified in me. Perhaps it was grace, perhaps it was just time, I wasn't sure but something had given way in that moonlight; I had finally accepted Ram's annoying word, discernment, and had formulated a plan to reflect and discern in a powerful way that had not been possible before. Freedom from the I thought was the goal. I understood that but how would that arise, what did freedom mean? Was it a void or a great happiness, an exhilaration of energy, a sudden rush where all my ideas of self disappeared? I didn't know what the experience of losing the I thought was, there were some things about it that I knew theoretically but did not feel. If I could change that, if I knew them truly because they were within me, then wouldn't that be enlightenment? If I could find clarity of knowing and if I could add that to the appreciation of Being I already had, then that might be something. The idea tingled in me from deep down appearing like a ferocious motivation but how to achieve it? It seemed possible that from the body of the teachings I could distil the key phrases that held out wisdom and at the same time were the cause of my most puzzling confusion. I had worked to identify these phrases and was happy with my selection. They appeared to represent doorways currently closed and if I could pass through them then, well then we would see. But for a doorway to be a doorway you have to move across some threshold and how do you move? I didn't know, I only knew I wanted to, with a passion as great as any I had ever felt, a passion which was truly life and death and which it was to be, didn't matter. On my table are ten envelopes, within them are the cards I have prepared. I had written them all carefully in gold ink on embossed peacock cards, the preparation had been centring to me, giving reverence and ritual to my work. I will meditate on Being in the way I already know, deepening into that silence and openness, feeling that essence and then I will sit on my chair and contemplate the statements in a more penetrating way. Isn't that what the rishis did, meditation and discourse? I wasn't sure but my memory of the Dakshinamurti encounter was fresh in me and I knew that's what the Upanishads said:

'Correct knowledge of Brahman can be acquired by study of the Self'

So that's what I will do, study the Self. I take the first envelope and put it on the occasional table by the chair then sit on my meditation seat, chant Om, ring my bell and enter into the silence, no agitation, no effort; all that had passed for me now. I am aware of the notes of birdsong outside, the occasional passing car, some rumbles in my stomach but no thought, only random movements rising up and passing through like smoke. I do not need to think. Silence prevails.

On the Timecoast the waves this morning were particularly mild, the swell of the deep ocean a mere flicker across the vast expanse of water, a calm day on the Timecoast. In weathers like this nature seems to take on a different hue, with a gentleness in the air and a generous disposition in the light. Sadhu got up from his seat and stretched, a fine morning, he thought. He walked to the forest temple amidst the green of the jungle, smelling the sap from the frankincense trees and honeysuckle from the vines, he breathed in the air, it invigorated his mind. At the temple, the monkeys were skipping around the veranda picking up the forest debris and throwing it over the balustrade with squeals and grunts. "Bravo!" Sadhu shouted, throwing them handfuls of cacao nuts from his bag. They all chattered in response, the parrots joining in. Sadhu laughed as the monkeys scattered, chasing one another down the path dive-bombed by the squawking parrots as they ran. Inside the temple he untethered the great ancient bell tuned by the mystics at the beginning of time, to the note perfectly and precisely calibrated to harmonic 5th. Pulling back the long wooden bell-strike, he released it from its harness and launched it muscularly. The Timecoast was flooded with sound; crisp, bright, the whole day became alert.

Consumed by the harmonic, Sadhu sat in the forest and thought; it was not linear thinking, it was seeing, for he knew how to see through thought.

Towards the end of my meditation a freshness comes upon me, I have known it before, it is a capacity for scrutiny as if some brighter light and intelligence gathers and my memory becomes agile. My mind feels fit and lean, my intellect crisp. I am not sure how this has occurred but it has come out of the silence, it is a welcome arrival. Getting up from the cushion, I sit in my chair. Picking up the envelope I open it and extract the card. With my hands in my lap, I hold the card between my fingers and keep it there. My concentration is profound, no thought or distraction has any hope of intruding; if there is even a glimmer I am ready to destroy it instantly. I gaze penetratingly and read the words on the card:

Everything is Brahman

Day One and I am to contemplate everything! It is such a big word, perhaps I've never fully grasped what it means, what is included in the everything, present now, as this moment? As well as the obvious things that I see, like room and chair, my body and the card in my hands, there are an immense variety of other phenomena, some obvious and others not normally noticed. The pressure points at the back of my knees, the feeling of weight and fullness within my head, the colour of the flowers in the vase, awareness of the clock behind me, tingling across my skin, the temperature in the room, the warmth of my clothes, the glass of the window, birdsong, this memory, that sky, this emotion, that noise, this idea - everything really does mean everything and all of this is Brahman? I knew the idea so well but to realise it there must be something that I had not previously seen. Perhaps I had never applied it to truly everything. It's all very well to include things outside and say, that is Brahman but what about my inner soundtrack, my personal voice, what about that? This feeling I am located inside, watching and commenting on the outside is a real presence, not something imagined. It is not an ordinary feeling like a sensation, it's of a different quality, it has distinction and it feels as real as skin. A sudden crack in the ceiling above breaks the silence in the room. The house is warming up, making its own noises in the morning sunlight. Is this all Brahman, the crack, the sunlight, this breathing and my own sense of a personal, separate inside? A change in my consistency comes upon me, not unlike the flavour of spices being dropped into a pan and infusing a dish. It reminds me of belonging, like when you lose your separation to become part of a team and how in those times you feel supported and secure amidst a common, shared whole and a common purpose. It seems a poor and frivolous analogy against the grandeur of Advaita but there is something in it, is Brahman this sense of common whole? Later in the afternoon, my meditation is deep and it feels different. As well as the emptiness that I am well accustomed to, there is something else. It is hard to discern until I realise it is the appreciation that there isn't a 'me' present waiting for something to happen. That activity is missing from my meditation, this is an ease I am not familiar with.

It's 9:00pm, I am lying in bed, steady and relaxed, the room totally quiet, as I approach sleep. A single thought bursts into my consciousness from nowhere like an inspired voice. If all these Vedanta descriptions are true, all these statements, then they must be true right now, not at some later date when things have changed, when circumstances are more suitable or when I have changed, they must be true now. 'All this is Brahman' is true now, right now; the cosiness of the bed, the freshness of the night air coming through the window, the sound of my breathing, the hooting of the owl outside and the gathering energies of sleep are in me like fragrance. I am up at 5:00am the next morning, fresh after an unbroken night's rest, motivated, excited. I feel a sense of company as if I am not alone, even amidst my solitude. It is a great feeling, very affectionate, the warmth of security. I take my breakfast and tidy things away so everything is clear with nothing to distract and make my way to the meditation cushion. The feeling of not being alone fills my silence; it isn't another presence, just a bigger and more spacious me. I decide to enjoy it rather than analyse it and the silence is deep, infused with Being. After meditation I make myself some tea then go eagerly to my chair. I have jumbled the envelopes and they have no headings upon them so I don't know what's coming next, whatever the sequence, it is undesigned, at least by my ego. Cutting open the envelope I take out the card:

The Self is not an object

I am the Self is something I fully believe so whatever the Self is, and whatever I am, cannot then be an object. What is an object anyway and what isn't? That is the question. The heat from the tea comes through the cup as I hold it on my knee. The cup is an object, as is the heat itself, a thing to see and feel, a thing being experienced but where does the distinction of object end, doesn't that include everything that is taking place? I get up and stretch, feeling the release in my muscles then purposefully walk across the floor slowly, carefully sensing each step as the pressure moves from heel to toe and the softness of the flooring yields to my weight. These sensations are objects as well, something I perceive, as is the colour of the carpet and the aroma from the ash in the incense burner. I want to light some more incense; is that desire an object too? I think I will have to get more matches from the kitchen and immediately realise that just as the smell of the incense and the carpet under my feet is an object, so are my desires, my thoughts, my feelings and my moods. All of these things are objects. This possibility seems immense. I sit back down, look at my card and close my eyes. Everything known is an object yet the Self is not an object, so what can the Self possibly be and how can it be experienced? I sink back into silence; some intuitive intelligence in me knows that this question should not be thought about now because to do so will just create confusion, instead it should be left to dwell in the intelligence beyond thought. For now, the recognition that every single experienced thing and even the knowledge about things is an object, is more important to allow. I spend the rest of the day and into the evening doing all I can to stay steady in this state of allowing. Sleep comes easy at 9:00pm.

It was raining on the Timecoast. It had been torrential for two days across the landscape; in the dunes, on the beach and in the forest. The fall was running in rivulets, some small, some larger, together establishing a wholly original network of re-sculpted channels reconfiguring the surface of the earth into subtle undulations, widening some of the streams, pooling in some and re-channelling others in fresh combinations. It was not unlike the undulations and folds on the surface of a brain and the connections beneath; it was not unlike that at all. Sadhu was meditating in the bell temple sheltering from the rain. Even after two days, the shimmering from that single enormous chime of the bell continued to oscillate. He knew the change in frequency had caused the rain, harmonic 5th resonating as a hum in the air, the heart wave of the bell metal; it was the object of his meditation. The monkeys were in the temple too, quietly snoozing and silently preening themselves. They knew there were more cacao nuts in Sadhu's bag but they were not desiring them. The rain hammered on the roof and dripped through the thatch; it smelled like new day.

Daybreak on Tuesday comes upon me beautifully, one of those gorgeous mornings when you have slept long and deep and all seems optimistic. The house is welcoming and intensely peaceful. I can't think of any better way to spend time than on my cushion and on my chair. When all is ready, I open my envelope with eager anticipation:

You are not the mind

The words stand like a challenge on the card. It is an assertive statement, it almost feels bullying to hear, over and over again this conundrum that I am not the mind; it has been said to me so many times. I believe it but, like a nagging commentator, the belief plods tediously and hasn't effectively changed any of my habits. 'You are not the body' is acceptable; I have no problem with that. It is a little more difficult when there is pain or illness or some vanity playing but it is an easy truth to agree. 'You are not the feelings', that is also obvious, feelings come and go, sometimes possessive, sometimes seductive, sometimes elaborate and splendid and sometimes mundane, but they are not me, they are distant from the core of me, similarly, with moods and events and observations. There is no doubt about this now but what of thoughts and the thinker of thoughts, that is mind too and that seems different. There is something like a platform of person present inside my head, a seat of identity. I am certain it is there rather than anywhere else in my body as sometimes it is as if I can feel my brain and this thing called 'me' holding residence there. It's like it is the ruler of my thoughts and it has attitude. I know the teaching of the I thought, I understand it but the truth is, I do feel the mind to be 'me'. I'm aware I often pretend this is not the case, even to myself but here in my monastery the truth must be faced. If the statement on the card is true, then realising it is my real obstacle and I do not know how to overcome it.

Thunder rattled over the Timecoast at just the moment that the final, subtle tones of harmonic 5th decayed into silence. The great bell would not be rung again; it wasn't necessary now the new landscape was irrigated and the rain had stopped. Sadhu strode out through the temple doorway and into the forest, breathing in the invigorated ozone and stretching all his limbs. The thunder boomed deep, a wonderful energy like a great boon drum beating out a new march and a new voice, the parrots squabbled and squawked. Sadhu walked down across the dunes and towards the beach. He wanted to walk close to the ocean to feel its rhythms and tones now that the swell would be back and the currents would be moving again. The ocean was the very fabric of consciousness upon the Timecoast and he knew the thunder would have reverberated deep within its waters. The monkeys followed him, they wouldn't leave the forest but they could go to the edge of the tree line and if they were stealthy maybe there would be opportunity to grab cacao nuts from Sadhu's bag; stealing them would be quite acceptable.

Outside the house a storm is developing, there are dark skies and it has become gloomy inside the room. I reach up and switch on the table light. The glow flashes into my mind like a shock-wave. Although the light appears just as it always does, my experience of it is completely different. It is penetratingly obvious that the glow is an effect of the primary power of electricity. Instantly, I am fascinated, excited. The bulb is a device; it is the electricity that is the power. This is obvious but I have never before seen it this clearly or this deeply. Of itself, the bulb is inert yet in the presence of the energy of electricity, a living reality is expressed that electricity by itself cannot perform. For light to shine as light, both elements need one another and isn't it the same for perceiving and awareness, isn't that what the Gita says about the Self shining through the senses and doesn't that mean that mind as mind is by itself inert and not I? The body is a device and so is the mind. Suddenly this is vibrantly clear to me. It isn't a new thought; I'm sure Ram has said it to me many times but this intuition this morning is different, this comes with a weight and density of recognition to it, like the 'Eureka!' of the scientist. This is a shift of knowing, different from a belief; it is a conviction and the knowledge sings in me. Perhaps enlightenment is more of this bright and certain knowing, a grand and all-consuming conviction that removes doubt. Conviction is the word Ram constantly uses with me but I realise I have never quite appreciated its proper significance or power. Like electricity, awareness flows, in combination with the senses awareness feels, through the mind it knows, and through the intellect it thinks. Just like the bulb enables electricity to be light so mind enables consciousness to be thought. So, when I experience mind, I experience consciousness as mind. When I feel my body, I know consciousness as skin. Just as electricity agitates and warms up the filament in the bulb, so consciousness reflects in mind and brings about all these beautiful phenomena. Not only is consciousness doing the thinking but thinking is consciousness. This is important. I realise I'm not viewing it as some intellectual point; I am seeing it as really happening in a way I haven't before. Exhilarated, I gaze out of the window at the cloudy winter morning and remember with affection the sky analogy Ram had given in the Orangery last year; it was very beautiful and impacted upon me at the time. Now, in my chair, I hear the words afresh like listening to a recording re-playing in my head...

"Sky is difficult to discern Amelia, because when we look we see objects; perhaps blueness, or cloud, or light, or dark, sun, moon and weather, but we don't see sky. There are many diverse conditions seen in sky yet you always know it is sky; you don't need to think about it. Well, awareness is like that. Just as sky has all things in it and flows as day or night, consciousness has all things in it and flows as skin, mood and thought. In the same way that sky is being the weather, so consciousness is being thought."

A great peace comes upon me. The common tendency in me to think and analyse and question what I have just seen does not arise; it cannot arise because it has been defeated by powerful knowing. Truth is closer, not as an idea but as something present and happening, something real. This power to eliminate doubt through knowing seems very great. Is this elimination an aspect of enlightenment? Wednesday morning seems like no other Wednesday before, ever, even though it's quite ordinary, it doesn't seem ordinary to me. There is something completely staggering about the presence of the day, a continuous 'Wow!' moment. Nothing has changed externally except that I haven't washed for four days and haven't had any contact with people, but my perceiving is different, the beholder is different, there is a greater sense of capability, a confidence and also I am ravenously hungry. It's easy and pleasant to satisfy with a huge bowl of porridge, fruit, nuts and tea; ashram food for my spiritual task. I wonder if I should have a second cup but decide not to and make for my seat and my envelopes. The card when it comes out glares at me provocatively:

It's all happening by itself

What is the nature of experience and action? I sit and observe the intricacy of the moment just as I did two days ago. It is amazing how things arise; thoughts, feelings, sensations and events. The recognition that just as a sound rises outside, so a thought rises inside and they're all being experienced as objects is a beautiful recognition. But what is the generating power, what is making it all happen, who is the doer and can it all really be happening by itself? I think again about my own perceptions which have now become so acute in me. When the owl shrieked in the night I didn't say, "That has come from me". If the house creaks in the sunshine or the smells of cooking appear in my nose, I don't say, "That is done by me", yet if a thought moves it feels like mine and that I have created it or thought it, why? Because it feels as if I am the thinker, that's why. So strong is this understanding that it shapes my every waking moment. Ram had told me this situation is what the Upanishads call ignorance and right now, in my changing state it seems possible to glimpse beyond that ignorance. Suddenly I want tea, hot Tulsi tea. I want it with a power and intensity and I want it now. From where has that thought arisen? Some habit, some thirst, did I choose it or am I only experiencing it? Do I have any control in generating any of my thoughts and desires? And what about this questioning itself, taking place within me now, am I the originator and architect of the thoughts moving in me right now? It feels like I am, especially as these abstract thoughts seem different from the arising of the desire for tea, higher in the hierarchy of thinking, more purposeful and selective but is there really any difference at all in the physics of their experience? Am I choosing any of my thoughts or is it all a great, intimate flow of expression and response, all being experienced through varying modes of mind? Once again I watch my inner events, I concentrate, I try not to generate any new thought, I try not to be the thinker; mind however does not stop. The heating fires up and comes on and I wonder what time it is, should I turn the thermostat down, when is the boiler service due, the strange shoes the boiler engineer wore last time he was here, my mum buying me shoes as a child, my first day at school, studying, libraries, being quiet, shyness and solitude, advent calendars, money, winter storms, maybe I should get a dog. The heating goes off. It is easy to observe in this moment that even though all this thinking feels intimate and close, feels like I am choosing it and doing it, actually it is arising from some unknown place and arising by itself within me. What is necessary for thought? Intelligence, chemistry, senses, perception, knowledge, nourishment of the body; it is all these things in combination and the atomic forces underpinning them that are actually responsible for doing the thinking. It feels like me but now it is obvious that however it may have felt, the phenomena of thoughts are a product of these elements at work and I already know that I am not the elements; I am that in which the elements appear. I have sat through many Q&As and discourses on free-will it has almost become tedious. I feel now that it is no longer necessary to win that argument or even resolve it. Perhaps in the multi-dimensional context of the universe there is no one answer. Nobody knows all the properties and workings of the universe, not even the greatest sage has the full picture and some things do not need to be solved. Beyond philosophy it is as clear as day to me in this moment that the elements are the doer and I am not the elements, they are all happening in me and through me. This is very big indeed. My problem in spiritual practice has been the desire to eliminate the thinker but that has been my mistake, the action of thinker and the functioning of thoughts is a natural aspect arising from the movement and collection of all these physical energies. Just as rumbles and sensations in my stomach are the natural aspect of digestion, so thoughts are the natural aspect of chemistry and karma. It's not the removal of the thinker itself that is realisation; it's the certain knowledge that even though the thinker operates, it is being experienced. Nature is the doer; the device is the doer and all that intricacy is happening by itself. I am the knower, the illumination of the doer. I am awareness.

That night I dreamt of a great snowfall covering all the tracks, covering everything. It was pristine white, fluffy and iridescent in the starlight. A single animal moved across the surface creating a track, there was nothing to follow; I wondered how it knew where to go. Then I saw the animal was me. I watched as it walked very confidently towards the horizon.

I wake on day five feeling fresh and inspired by my dream. My early morning routine comes smoothly and easy as if I have been a hermit for years. I am excited by what I may find on this morning's card:

Satchitananda

I want happiness; I am not alone in that. I am resilient, able to endure hardship and lack of happiness but surely what everyone wants is happiness? I experience happiness often yet it passes and then I return to a regular state of what you might call normal. This is my frustration because I want that normal to be constant happiness. That is what has fuelled most of the desires and ambitions in my life, a search for happiness to be permanent. Permanence has eluded me and that lack has been the source of my sense of inadequacy. The gold ink on the card glints in the sunlight, Sat-Chit-Ananda. The meaning is so familiar to me, Being-Consciousness-Bliss. Closing my eyes, I settle into the easy presence of consciousness, it is pleasant being here in the peace. Being is rich and full, my confidence of yesterday plays sweetly, there is an ease and poise about the moment. Sat is clear, Chit is clear but what of Ananda? I find myself waiting for bliss to arise, expectant, searching. I realise this expectation is often a property of my meditation but what would bliss be? It might be a light, it might be some emotional wave, it might be sensuous or audible. Whatever it is, I want it to arrive to overwrite my normal neutral state. If I can just do that, well won't that be enlightenment? Time passes, the rhythms of the day take their course, I pause for tea, meditate on the cushion, make lunch and proceed throughout the afternoon and evening sometimes meditating, sometimes reflecting and once or twice just looking out of the window but I can make no progress and the day takes on a fateful air. I have lost the vitality of previous days, a despondent mood has started to creep upon me, I know it is an object, I know I have the power to experience it as that, but I allow myself to become it, I can see this happening but nonetheless, I allow it. A whole drama assembles then, waiting in the wings, eager to be brought onto the stage of my attention but that, I do deny. It isn't difficult to do; it just requires the force of will. I spend the evening experiencing this ability of will and watching its power. I understand how not just passive surrender but also force of will or rather, mental organisation is integral to clarity of mind. But as for my mood, that seems beyond my will to affect. I end the day feeling fed up and restless, Ananda still a distant quarry.

At 3:00am I wake, or half-wake, I am not thinking. Consciousness is fluid, there is less structure. I have not come forward fully into the waking state and I languish here in spacious peace. Sleep is calling from somewhere near at hand; wistful images loosely arrange themselves within me, hovering in and out of dream. Then with tangibility, substance and full definition I am suddenly lying on my back on a carpeted floor, in a room with a chair and a window where the light comes in. A sensation of energy occurs, gently at first, then building. My body becomes alive with tingling across the whole skin surface, then inside, everywhere about my person, every cell tingling and vibrating, growing in intensity into an abundance of sensation, a radiance of luscious and ebullient waves flaring and growing. My whole self is alight with breathtaking pulsing bliss, my mind soars and shines. It is out of this world, ecstatic. My body begins to move, potency vibrating my limbs, dragging my body. I slide forwards and then sideways, my feet pressing against the chair, overwhelmed in bliss, ecstatic. Spontaneously I mouth the word "Shiva", a prayer to God to care for me, to take me into his arms and guide me into the experience. Wow! My God!

It is 6:00am. I leap up out of bed, exhilarated, excited, different, immense. I go downstairs, ignore breakfast and sit on my chair. Is it the same chair from my dream? Beaming in the afterglow of my experience, I reflect. A dream? Ridiculous to dismiss it as such, whatever its properties, absurd. It may have arisen in the dream state but that's irrelevant. It was bliss, the experience I have often craved in the waking state, a tangibility of bliss arising and pervading. I am honoured by the encounter, delighted but that isn't the point. All through the experience and while it was happening there had been a knower, that which knew during all elements of the experience. That is more relevant to me now than the spinning and the pulsing and the ecstasy itself. How could such an aroused state possibly prevail in my life, how could bliss of that magnitude possibly enhance my state of Being in these physical conditions? It couldn't. To have the experience itself is remarkable, affirming of a greater power and mystery but here in my chair, my overriding thought is, thank you for this and not that. That form of Ananda is for another dimension, another time but there is something else, something intensely exciting. I see that bliss is an experience and like all experiences, whatever they may be, they cannot ever be permanent. Anything experienced is bound to move, bound to rise and fall, all according to the play of the gunas. This is how nature is arranged. An experience cannot be it; experience can only be that. Enlightenment isn't an experience; it can only be something beyond experience and what is that? The answer is obvious to me now in a way that has never been so prominent before. It can only be the knower of experience. This recognition is so firm that my spiritual practice chasing experience states is bound to be over, finished. I will enjoy experiences time and time again for pleasure and beauty but I cannot be experience and I can never find completion in experience. I need to look beyond experience into the realm and status of the knower. What is the nature of that which is beyond all the movements, the nature of knowing itself? The question is deep but there is power and a clarity in me now that doesn't find depth daunting. It is security, isn't it? Deep, profound security, consistency, steadiness and truth; a permanence outside of and unaffected by time. It is the constant, the ground, the eternal continuity of Being. Isn't that existence itself and aren't those magnificent, stable properties not a joy of greater magnitude and desirability than any possible ecstatic and moving experience? A joy independent of the pleasure of rising and falling happiness. So, isn't that joy itself Ananda? Wow! My goodness! That is what Ananda is! That is the Ananda in Satchitananda, not some passing ecstasy but this very stability and joy of Being. This is gigantic. As I lie in bed prior to sleep, all I can feel is gratitude. A great bedrock of gratitude for this existence and the knowledge which now seems to be penetrating into me in ways I had not before thought possible. My mind, infused with happiness, snuggles into the beauty of the night waves.

Self is already present

Today's session presents with what seems to be the most perplexing statement of all, at least that's what I would have thought before, however, after yesterday, I have a sense that it is in my grasp. What is the Self? Beyond all the questions and answers and reading and thinking, what is that which is already present and is not an object? Present now, here, in this chair and this space and this mind. It is still puzzling but I won't be perplexed because that will just go round and round in me, stifling knowledge like when you ask the wrong question as if you are trying to view one dimension from another. I have no idea how I know this but in the moment it is very clear to me that if I am to avoid old, common frustrations and perceive anew, there must be a different way of viewing. What is that new way to view? I can't say but my mind is not working as I normally experience it, there is a willingness and an intensity to examine and deeply perceive the truth of things beyond common thought and assumption. I will just carry on in that mode like an explorer, undeterred and undefended. So where is the Self, that which is already present? To answer that, to find it, I have to feel it. How do I feel it? Whatever the Self is, it is that which knows, so it must be that which is knowing right now. What is that which is knowing right now? Intelligence yes, consciousness yes, they are the properties of knowing and underpinning them both, the ground of awareness. That is present now obviously yet even though I accept that is true, I don't feel awareness and because of that I don't feel the Self. This is a big insight into my position, it is simple but I know it is big because the hairs on my skin all stand up and I feel a rush of anticipation. This is my problem and has been my problem for all these years; I can't feel the Self directly, I don't experience it and it is that lack of tangibility that means I believe I do not know the Self. I have been searching for it as an experience for so long and have not found it, even though I believe it is in me. Is it in me, is it? And what of that Ananda, so clear to me from yesterday? That is here, Being-Consciousness-Bliss. So what else is missing, what is in the way? What is it that can't be found? My mind stops and I do not try to prevent it; the stopping is delicious, warm and fluid, affectionate space - Ananda.

Sunlight flared over the Timecoast, pure and sweet like an infant's breath, illuminating the sea and the dunes, filtering through the canopy and dappling amidst the leaves on the forest floor. The Timecoast was perfect in its expression, experiencing the great cycles of creation and destruction and taking it all in its easy stride. There was passion and expression on the Timecoast but there wasn't thought, at least not in any lumbering way. What is the need to think when you are perfect in your expression, for isn't thinking secondary to expression? The Timecoast had no need for secondary forces, it was only able to be primary, constantly first, for that which is true can only be first. Sadhu was asleep in the dunes, lulled by the sound of the surf crashing on the beach. His bag was empty of cacao nuts. Later, he would wake and would do something. Nobody knew what, Sadhu had no need to plan, only to act. The monkeys would keep their eyes out for him next time he was in the forest.

Sunlight streams through the window falling upon my skin. Is awareness like sunlight, sunlight without heat? What is the feeling of awareness? What can it be and what do I expect it to be? Is it something felt through the senses, some vibration, some activation? It can't be, can it? Because even if something like that did happen, it would be an object and there would still be that which is experiencing and knowing the object. I am completely clear about this now. So is the Self inert and can't be felt at all? No that's impossible too, because the Self is aware and awareness must be vibrant like sunlight, must have vitality and the property of creating and knowing. Perhaps the answer, as in all my other investigations of recent days, is in what is happening now. Awareness is obviously present so right now, in this second is there anything I can feel? What am I feeling right now that could be awareness? Maybe the feeling is so familiar that I am just not noticing it. Perhaps awareness is being awake, like I am now, so what is the felt property of being awake? Is there a flavour to being awake? Yes, there is, most assuredly, it rushes upon me in an instant each morning, it's big, massive and obvious but how do I describe it, what is it? The answer comes to me immediately, like most things which are accurate and true, it simply unravels instantly in the moment, there in my chair. It is the presence of knowing, awareness is the presence of knowing itself and that does have a flavour, I discern it most distinctly, it's the fabric of what I am and impossible to miss. This natural knowing is happening freely and happening now. Goodness! That is close to an answer, this presence is intimate, it's almost structural, it's the bedrock and whole landscape of Being, it's gigantic. Awareness is something I am. Gosh! Yes, that's right; awareness is what I am now, right now. Awareness is not a thing, or an it, or a that, it is what I am, and I am that now. From this point I do not need to think, I could think but the urgency in me to proceed and explore like that has ended. It seems irrelevant, I feel whole and complete. The remaining cards are superfluous now; I could throw them away but that would be disrespectful, so I put them in my drawer and leave them there, maybe they will be relevant for something, someday. Even though I do not need to think or move mentally, I do want to move physically, in fact, the sense in me to act is suddenly intensely urgent.

After The House

I am on the road to Ram's hut; I think he will be at Bowslip. It is great to be travelling down these roads in this winter state, everything brutally beautiful in its stark outlines and misty airs. The big main gates of Bowslip are shut tight, everything battened down until April. I leave the car in the lee of the flint-capped boundary wall and walk around the perimeter into the beech wood that surrounds the estate. It is quiet and lonely in its hibernation, my footfalls crisp upon the hard ground. Midway along the wall is the gardener's solid oak doorway now sealed for the winter but I have the combination code, it is how we get in and out to the Orangery. There is a sign on it saying 'Private' and 'Closed - No Entry'. I close the gate behind me quietly and walk through the empty gardens and half a mile down the forester track. There is a curl of smoke coming up from the little hut. A brace of chaotic, raucous pheasants crash out of the bracken as I approach. The door opens instantly and there is Ram, rough and wild in woodland clothes, standing solid in the frame of the doorway. I am stopped in my tracks by the potency of the moment, pulsating with spiritual energy.

"They are my guardians," said Ram, pointing to the pheasants, "better than geese, I find." He leaves the door open and retreats back into the hut. I go inside and he is at the stove cooking up tea. The place smells woody and smoky, it's like being in a fairytale or some other realm yet at the same time it is basic, musty and completely ordinary. We embrace, long and deep, it is exquisitely poignant, flooded with honesty. Ram is the magnificent Guru and I am magnificent too, not because either of us is special but because the moment itself is magnificent and that is flowing here freely between us. I realise I have absolutely no requirements to shape the moment in any way at all; it is an amazing, delightful feeling.

"I wasn't sure I would find you here," I said innocently.

"I've just arrived," said Ram, "I will be here for the winter now, would you like to stay?"

I look around the shabby place throbbing with spiritual energy.

"Yes, where have you been since we last met?"

"Sleeping in the sand dunes."

I have no idea what he means and don't ask.

"Something has happened to me." I said softly.

"Good, then it's all right then."

"It's been intense."

"Then it's alright then?"

"Yes, it's all right."

"This is 'Bush' tea," he said, handing me a huge clay cup, "it's my own concoction from the woodland plants."

It tastes of nettles, rose hips and the earth. We sit outside on two damp tree stumps and watch the pheasants as they patrol.

"It's beautiful here." I whispered.

"Yes, people want to build shiny temples to it and create ritual and practice to shape it to some design; all very well, but I prefer to be in the natural places, the woods or the dunes, as well as the odd temple from time to time."

"But there is nothing wrong with comforts and white linen."

"No, there is nothing wrong with that. When you know that the magnificence is already all around and within yourself, requirements for special circumstances fall away but soft pillows are always sweet."

The sun shining through the densely packed beech trees falls as dappled light on to the woodland floor at our feet. Pigeons coo amidst the birdsong and something barks sharply further off, deeper in the wood. This natural presence, honest, simple, poised and open is the freedom I have constantly sought and now I do not want anything, nothing at all.

"Why have I had to live within so many confinements?"

"That is so for everyone, Amelia, just see it as practical. Being is the field, social obligations and the concepts that arise from your character is the fencing within the field."

"What a beautiful analogy, how do you do that so poetically?"

"It's not hard, it's the vocabulary of the mystic where you see things fresh and you speak them like that."

"Can I tell you what has happened to me?"

"Sure, I would like to hear you describe it."

"I now know truly what I am and I know for certain what I am not."

"Nice, and what of the Amelia that thinks and acts?"

"She is thinking and acting most freely."

"Nice, in what does all this play?" Ram asked with such intensity in his eyes.

"The field," I replied as a new excitement rose and moved within me.

"And what is that and all this as well?" said Ram, spreading his arms.

"The Beloved."

"How would you describe the Beloved?"

"Satchitanada."

"And what is the Sat?"

"The presence of this."

"And what is the Chit?"

"Knowing this."

"And what is the Ananda?"

"Being this."

Ram looks at me with a depth of affection as vast and open as the sky. It is a magnificent look, free of any boundary at all. I know that this new position between us is the evolution of relationship I have longed for.

"And how did you come to this state of jnana?" he enquired.

"The discrimination matured in me; I discovered what discrimination really is."

"Good, it is critical that you experience that insight. You see, the Vedic source of the instruction is really two things *neti, neti* 'not this', and *tat tvam asi* 'I am that'. For the wise, this is complete darshan, purely distilled, but it is inadequate for the meditator who needs direction. What would you now say discrimination is?"

"Investigation into the presenting state, direct perceiving and knowing of that which is present. I now realise that 'Who am I?' was never just a question; it is a penetrating and dynamic exploration, something investigated through all faculties. It is a blending of feeling and knowing all together."

"Yes and alongside the silence and meditation, what has been crucial to bringing about that development in you?"

"Reflection on appearance, discernment of what is."

"Exactly Amelia, that is the discovery, the blending of those two properties which you could say is the fusion of thought and feeling. Firstly, the undeveloped meditator thinks about it and doesn't know any other way. Then the developing meditator feels it but becomes lazy and stuck in the feelings. Then the developed meditator knows it as well as feeling it and the mature meditator simply is it and lives it. How are you now?"

"Free."

"What do you want now?"

"This."

"What shall we do together?"

"Whatever arises, but there is just one thing missing."

"What's that?"

"Pillows and white linen."

Ram laughed and put on his boots.

They went out together to gather more ingredients for the tea and to go up to Bowslip House. If there was anyone there maybe Ram could charm them into sharing some sheets and cushions, maybe not and either outcome was all right. They tramped through the forest arm in arm, the pheasants breaking cover, flapping and shrieking in all directions.

"Ram, is this enlightenment?"

"Ah! As I said before I prefer the word realisation."

"What next then?"

"Abundance of heart and soaring jnana, into the advanced Amelia, meeting the Beloved."

He started to speak of it but the pheasants made so much noise it was impossible. We tried to mimic their shrieks and just fell about laughing, sitting amidst the leaves on the forest floor like children.

"Some other time," said Ram.

"Yes," said I, "some other time."

Chapter Four

Transcendence

five months later
outside the hut

A New Offer

Nothing was particularly different yet there was a ripeness in the air and everything was about to change. My daily routines with their various ups and downs had continued just as they were before but since the revelations that came to me last winter in the house there was a new context and smoothness to experience, nothing seemed to particularly matter. Not that I was disengaged, not at all, I was fully present, involved and responsive but somehow everything, whatever it was, was alright. The new insights I had gained played large in my mind. Throughout February and March I thought of Ram all the time. The potency between us that had been awakened in the woods on that day in January had eclipsed all I had previously known and I knew it was not yet complete. Right at the end of our time together he had left me with a possibility *'The abundance of heart and soaring jnana'*. It had just been a mention with no drama or explanation at the time yet it had risen in me with a poignant voice like a secret that knows it is about to be told. Just as pilgrims yearn to return to their places of inspiration so I wanted to return to him and the discovery of that.

Into this state of arousal, spring burst forth. Spring, it was as though heaven had leapt out of the ground and the very air I breathed. We fell in love, the spring and I, and I had to do something for my love. Through a short flash of curious coincidences and a burst of ideas I changed all my annual plans, re-arranging my holidays and squaring off my commitments with work and family. The course was set; I was to have two weeks in June alone with my Guru at his hut in Bowslip.

"You cannot find the best of me anymore with words," said Ram. "Speak as you like. I may respond or I may not, either way you can no longer find me or yourself with words." This was the statement he met me with when I had arrived nine days ago. I came across him working on a stick with his knife. He was sitting on a small hummock of grass in the clearing outside the hut. It had been five months since we had last seen one another and I was expecting some welcoming greeting or at least some introductory niceties.

"Old words are pointless now," he said, "and if that's what you have brought you may as well leave. Explaining yourself no longer achieves anything of value. The line of investigation in you that has been defined by old words and habits is exhausted now." He continued to whittle at the smooth slim stick. "You realise my words of late have been a smokescreen, don't you?"

"Have they?" I asked.

"A smokescreen hides the fire within and shields you from the heat; the fire behind the smoke is the new communication between us."

"But I get so much from your words."

"That was then and this is now. It isn't the words anymore, it's the fire which the words convey and from which they spring forth, the words are the veil of intelligence; it's the energy of intelligence itself that is now upon us. That is what has brought you here, that is what is exhilarating to us both and that is all I want to give you now. I am not averse to words Amelia, by no means, we have certainly shared millions and there maybe a million more but I am pointing out to you that old words are a smokescreen, merely perpetuating your attachments and in the end smoke just clogs up your lungs and makes you cough. What is beyond such words is the advanced state I am pointing you to and for that we need new words and new experience."

"You mean abundance of heart?"

"You have come here for the advanced state. Before it was impossible, now it is not."

I took off my backpack, unsure how to proceed. Sitting on the grass I watched him work, cutting into the stick and holding it in his hand balancing its weight. By his side was a pile of rushes and twine, behind him a fabric pouch. I realised it was a quiver and he was making arrows. It caught my breath as the symbolism of arrows had become very great for me. After ten minutes he got up and went around the back of the hut to the tool store. I could hear him chopping wood and took the opportunity to go inside. The hut was as I remembered it, rough, not uncomfortable but basic and sparse, constructed of solid logs and planks. Three wide steps led up to a veranda forming a porch at the front. To the left was a lean-to earth toilet, at the other end protected by a section of corrugated iron, sheaves of drying oats had been stacked in bundles. Inside, two cots made of willow lay against the opposite walls either side of a small round table upon which were an incense burner, a very large rose quartz crystal, some candles and a pile of rudraksha beads in a wooden bowl. A Tibetan yak wool rug covered the boarded floor; it smelt musky and reminded me of nomads and travellers. The iron cooking stove stood prominent on a slate base at the rear of the hut, its open grate overflowing with mounds of ash. The compact space was a bit feral but clean enough and beautiful in its simplicity. The spiritual potency was palpable, almost tactile. I unpacked my backpack on the unused empty cot and spread out my neatly packaged things. Carrying a basket of sticks for the stove he came and stood beside me, sneering comically at my pile of possessions and the toiletries I was holding in my hands.

"There is nowhere to bathe," he said, "the stream is perfectly adequate for basic needs."

"But I always like to be clean," I replied.

He continued to sneer. "There are many conventional things you depend upon and almost all of them are pampering absurdities, pleasant enough in civilised life I am sure, but here you can leave those behind. You have come for the advanced state not to maintain obsessions; you have come to explore a new house."

"What house?"

"The only house there is around here."

"You mean Bowslip, but it's empty and shuttered up."

"I have the keys to the house." He looked at me then with great affection and I felt that intense wave of inspiration that was the exhilarating effect he had upon me. We embraced long and deep. "Welcome to my Kutir, let's have tea."
I packed my rose scented soaps back in the backpack.

From that moment we had fallen into long silences often lasting all day, not because we had made a vow or anything, that's just what happened. Maybe it was a consequence of that, I'm not sure but all I can say is any perceived agenda in me just fell away. From within that absence I sensed some unspoken new intelligence fluttering at the edges of my mind, just like when an amazing idea starts to form in you, shimmering and pressing. The storm of words which had fuelled my anxieties for years, burying my teacher and myself under a bombardment of projections were absent. Forest routines and the rhythms of the hut became the music of the moment; living like a sadhu, serving, meditating, cleaning, cooking, working together to thresh oats, walking in the forest and playing hide and seek with the deer wandering close to our camp. Amidst the long silences sometimes an intense exchange would spontaneously erupt, an exposition of brilliant ideas thrilling me with their insight and beauty. Sometimes there were jokes, sweet moments with the animals. The hut surrounded me like a true home and I felt I was experiencing perfect living. I knew there was a life left behind and one I must return to but it wasn't pressing, the memory of it unravelling in the presence of these simple, uncomplicated moments, living in intensity with my Guru. Once Ram said to me that he wasn't my Guru because the Guru was bigger than him and was all around and was truly my own Self. I knew what he meant and why he was saying it but I also knew he was wrong. On the eighth morning he told me he was leaving and that he would be back at dusk. I asked him where he was going and he told me he was creating something.

"Shall I come with you?" I asked.

"No," he replied.

Momentarily I felt uneasy, it was hard not to feel resentful at being rejected but it was only momentary. As I watched him prepare his boots and pack I realised the impeccability of his actions. He didn't act to please me or appease me, he didn't even explain, he just acted and I knew those actions were authentic; not selfish but impeccable.

"Today you must go to the house," Ram said as he was standing ready to leave.

"Must I?" I replied, confused.

"Yes, you must enter the house and explore its floors."

"But is there any reason?"

He looked at me then with a sudden and unexpected ferocity. Poignant silence hummed between us. Embarrassment rose in my belly, either that or anger, it was difficult to tell.

"Enter the house and go up, go through the cellar gate and follow the servants' corridors and stairwells. You don't go in the main galleries or enter through the main door. The servants' corridors give you access to observe, the main galleries would just overwhelm you."

I hadn't known then what he was talking about, I had no interest in viewing the house, I wasn't there for tourism or entertainment, it seemed an entire distraction, a waste of precious time. I wanted nothing to interfere with the peace of the woodland and the hut. I stared at him and knew my stare was challenging, we held each other's gaze.

"Before you can know the abundance of heart, you must know the house," Ram said enigmatically. "Here are the keys. Only use the cellar gate, the one behind the railings beside the plain set of kitchen steps on the east side."

"But what am I looking for?"

"Knowledge."

I had assumed then that he meant some facts about the house. It was annoying, I wanted to object and then realised that either I trusted his direction or I didn't. That's the thing isn't it, that point of faith, that place where you realise that you are either directing yourself within your own cautions and boundaries, or you are surrendering to something else that you trust, something in which you have faith and belief. In that second as we'd stared at each other I felt the weight of what mature faith actually requires, there is nothing about it that is reckless, feckless or submissive; everything about it is heroic. He passed me the old keys, nodded and left. The solid iron objects weighed heavy in my hand. I watched from the veranda as he walked away down the 400 metres of visible track until he turned the bend and went out of sight. I prepared for my walk to the house.

As Ram tramped alone through the leaf mulch he felt the responsibility of Amelia. It wasn't unwelcome, neither was it a difficulty, it was just what happened between them. Fire was fire after all and smoke was smoke. What could be better than the clarity of a clear, clean fire, perfect as a cloudless sky, it was bound to blaze and what was worse than suffocating in smoke? The problem was smoke was mesmerising, lingering, heavy as fog. It needed intensity to dissipate it, some power of displacement. When people make great leaps of insight and change it is always as a consequence of intensity. He could no longer tell her about the house; she must see the house now, encounter it and know it. He shifted the weight of his bulky pack onto the opposite shoulder, it was heavy today, there was much to prepare. Let us see how she copes, he thought and how deep her perception goes. Then we will see.

The morning sun as it crested over the treetops instantly illuminated the landscape in front of me, catching the flag pole on the top of Bowslip House, shimmering there like a dance of fireflies. In its heyday Bowslip estate must have been magnificent, nestling proudly within its landscape surrounded by the swathes of beech wood carpeting the lowland for miles around. The estate was huge, thousands of acres of managed land but the old park had fallen back to unused pasture long ago, fences and gates rotted away and the elegant gravel pathways long since sunk into the moist soil. Only the edge of the principal promenade could still be seen amidst the overgrown grasses. At its head the lip of an ivy-clad broken stone urn peeped mournfully over the three foot high ragwort. All that remained fully intact was the huge outer boundary wall snaking mile after mile around the perimeter, strong like a defensive barrier, solid and high. Ahead of me the sweeping front steps of the grand house curved up to the portico porch framing the big solid oak doors. Lines of windows arranged across four floors punctuated the wide façade, each shuttered firm and tight, giving the place an austere look. Bowslip House was seemingly mothballed and forgotten, it had been standing here like this for hundreds of years. A reflection from high up caught my eye. The top windows of the east tower curving around the turret were not shuttered and the morning sunlight sparkled and glimmered off the sixteenth century glass. What would it be like standing in that space surveying the landscape from up high I thought, the view must be magnificent. I found the cellar door around the side of the house. The iron key fitted loosely into the old lock. It was an effort to turn as if it had not been used for a long time but once the mechanism engaged, a simple push on the door caused it to swing smoothly inwards. Daylight illuminated the tiled floor of a long corridor darkening into the distance. It was not inviting. I stepped inside. The door behind me swung closed with a loud clunk, I didn't like the sound of it in that echoing place. Immediately the light dropped to murky twilight filtering in from small grubby windows near the ceiling. It was silent as stone. Sometimes I am really brave in facing and tackling things, I am brave in my sadhana and brave at coping with challenges and people but I did not feel brave now. I was enclosed and I did not want to be enclosed. I knew it was just an empty house but could I be sure that it was truly empty? Maybe if I just went to the end of the corridor then I could get some bearings. I didn't like the noise of my shoes clapping and shuffling against the tiles, it took more than a minute to get to the end. Facing me were two light oak doors, one straight ahead and one to the left, I didn't want to see inside either of them. To my right, a narrow stone stair waited for occupants, one flight going up and one going down. "Go up," Ram had said. I was about to ascend when the light shining through a round stained-glass window on the lower landing threw charming patterns of blue and red onto the descending steps, sparkling invitingly off the dust particles hanging in the air. There was no sound but the shimmering seemed lyrical, I imagined I could hear appealing tinkling bells. I walked down into the coloured light feeling soothed and made to continue down the second flight when the imagined sound of bells grew in intensity. It was no longer sweet but coarse, harsh and clanging like the thud of something heavy falling again and again. The dust in the air came into my mouth and eyes, it felt sharp, more like splinters than dust. The rhythm of my feet continued moving downwards with an automatic momentum, one step, two. I wanted to stop but it was confusing, harder to think. Three steps, four; the bells were loud, the dust was thick, a feeling of dread possessed me. "Go up," said Ram, "go up". The memory of his voice penetrated the fugue that was rapidly clogging my mind. Go up, I thought, turning in an instant and pounding back through the rainbow light and up to the top of the step. Instinctively I pirouetted around the banister post and ran immediately up two flights, pausing on the landing in a little pool of daylight. Should I leave? I knew I could but the thought of walking along that corridor was horrifying and more significantly I was here to do something on the direction of my Guru. No, I would stay my course. I would stay my course in the faith that I was profoundly protected. This simple acknowledgement brought me a rush of composure. It was deadly silent; I calmed my breathing and looked around. The stairs were bland, structural, not ornate in any way and they were very old; strong, ancient stone. As I climbed the third and fourth flight it got lighter, the illumination coming through small, square, thick glass windows set into the ceilings. I couldn't think where that light could be coming from, I couldn't be anywhere near the outside walls of the house. After four flights I came upon a landing and another oak door, beside it hung a long fabric curtain with a drawstring rope. The door was intimidating; the knowledge that it offered an entrance into something brought nothing but foreboding. "Avoid the main galleries," Ram had told me, "they will overwhelm you." Cautiously I pulled the curtain to one side. Before me was a large pane of the same thick glass. As I peered into it, the opaqueness slowly receded and the transparency revealed an astonishing sight; an inconceivable library, immense, millions of books lined floor to ceiling, filling every inch of wall space going back and back; I could not see an end wall. Upon the floor more books spilled out of hundreds of smaller bookcases of all shapes and sizes. Between them stood long banks of filing cabinets made of ornate dark wood. The room was high, broad and spacious in all dimensions, filled by this immense collection of words, ideas and thoughts, spilling out from every surface. Out on tables there were manuscripts, pamphlets, folios, filing cards. The library was arranged, ordered but also chaotic, abuzz with research, opinion, commentary, study, facts, systems and knowledge. It was disturbing and the thought of going in terrified me, not because I was timid, it just repelled me. The idea of all its workings and functions and intrigue looked, to my eyes, like some kind of insanity. I pulled the curtain shut and then peeped behind the fabric. The glass was once again opaque, thick and milky. What was this place, why was I even here inside this structure and was I alone? I must keep control, keep calm, even to get back out now would take a couple of minutes and I did not want to go back to that corridor, there must be another way. Daylight playing upon the rising flight of stairs behind me caught my eye. I thought of the turret room I had seen from the ground, I wanted to go there and be away from here. Cautiously I ascended four more flights and reached a carpeted landing, the carpet was thick and lush. There was a tall window to the outside where the light had been coming from. Somewhere in the woods out there was our hut, and somewhere else Ram was roaming about doing something. I wished he were here now, I wished we were together facing my fears, my Guru was my only true ally in these moments. "You have to experience things alone to truly face your fears." Ram had once said. I knew the state of being alone, I was alone in my sadhana and alone in my life; not socially, my life was full of connections but spiritually in that deep compelling passion, I was mostly alone. Before me was another huge solid oak door with brass handles and a keyhole. The door screamed at me, don't come in; the very idea of the sound it would make if I pushed it open horrified and repulsed me. Kneeling down on the soft thick carpet with the light from the window shining around, I put my eye to the keyhole. The space before me was astonishing and impossibly huge, so brightly lit I could see perfectly in any direction across long distances, everything coming into sharp focus by itself. Was it a studio, a factory, a workshop? I was looking at worlds within worlds; busy, complex and industrious. There were tools, materials, machines, metals, wood, masonry, granite and marble. All surrounded by architectural drawings, art materials, sculpture, cogs, wheels, rods and levers combined in intricate complex mechanisms. Winches, hoists and chains lay amongst huge scaffolding supporting unfinished structures. Fabrics of infinite variety and mounds of unspun wool fed looms producing bolts of fine, delicate and precise tapestry. There were anatomical models, laboratory equipment, chemical elements, astronomical telescopes. I saw long writing tables piled high with notes and the debris of creation, a cornucopia of creativity and industry and the whole vast arena shimmering in intense light, seeming to hover with substance and intelligence highlighting details in the room, moving quickly, gaining brightness then fading away. I knew I was seeing the darting of ideas in that light and I did not want that light to shine on me. I pulled away from the keyhole, my heart pounding; an impossible unreal display existed just inches in front of me behind that oak door.

Moving further up the stairs I climbed six flights, then eight, nine, that's over a hundred feet, more than the height of the house itself, impossible. The landing I was now on was tiled, an ancient mosaic, uneven and pitted. This was a very, very old floor, was it Egyptian, Greek or something else? In front of me was a remarkable door set in a solid frame of eroded stone, the mortar missing and chipped. The door itself was monastic in its appearance; heavy planks of old wizened oak fixed by huge iron nails, rusting brackets and hinges. On either side, stained-glass panels provided a kaleidoscope view into the interior. I pressed my nose up against the biggest panel and through a scarlet hue, looked inside. My heart stopped at the scale, this was cathedral in stature and form, high arched ceilings, buttressed alcoves, fonts and altars amidst tall and domed minarets, huge open floors dotted with cushions and prayer mats, statues of gods and goddesses, fierce-looking brightly coloured deities, temple bells, serene Buddhas, a youthful and strong figure of Christ, candlesticks, bells, horns and drums, a massive tiered fire-pit surrounded by copper vessels, a gigantic golden incense burner hanging from the roof surrounded by a forest of prayer flags. The light from the stained windows high up on the east face fell hauntingly upon the pillars and windows of a delicate cloister but the most striking thing of all was the vast banyan tree in full finery, spreading across the central space creating a meditative shade with places for teacher and students. This was a temple of all the virtues and it was shattering in its power and majesty; I was looking at religion in all its faces. Open-mouthed I gazed at the details of the spaces and objects. Then my heart leapt, all senses hyper-alert, defensive. The door was open. Not fully open, not even ajar but I realised it had no lock fittings and was just sitting there loosely and untethered in the door frame. If I pushed it I could enter and walk into this drama. In that moment I was more certain of my next action than anything else in my life, the certainty possessed me like a force. This invitation was not my action, nothing would make me enter. I stepped back with the impact of this ferocious conviction, my thoughts falling, my mind changing, I had to go up to the fourth floor, to the turret.

The stairs beyond this point were wrought iron and spiral, broad at first then narrowing, uncomfortable to move through. I turned sideways and squeezed, pushing against the metal. Looking up, it was a long way, how could it be so high? I continued, determined, purposeful, counting one hundred and eight steps until I reached a small and delicate landing on which there stood a single white urn upon a pedestal. It was like the broken urn in the garden but this one was intact and exquisite, more than exquisite, ethereal, out of this world. The lines of form, so simple yet containing such expression of symmetry and beauty. Inside was the purest, clearest water, it was powerful merely to look upon. The landing was absolutely silent; my thoughts receded and receded, my ideas about where I was collapsed. There was only the air, the urn, the light and the water. Intense softness of presence saturated my mood. I felt light, then lighter still, with a freedom of movement unencumbered by hesitation or desire. In front of me was the final flight of stairs now broad again, beautiful polished marble, smooth and faultless, empty of any markings or defects. I trod softly up and stood before a doorless archway; moving through it, I stepped into emptiness. I was in a circular arena, neither small nor large, suffused with a halo of invigorating light. The space was entirely absent of objects yet it was the most secure and beautiful complete setting I had ever experienced. Stillness prevailed; I was not thinking yet there was a knowing that did not move. It was powerfully clear that in an instant, brilliant and complex thoughts could burst forth from that simplicity of knowing and it was the most natural thing, the easiest thing, the most welcome thing. I stood in the space moving my fingers to touch and stroke the air, came up onto my tiptoes and moved towards the window, my feet like a ballet dancer pointing through the clarity of the space as part of it, as its agent. Here was the wall of glass I had seen from the lawn, it was clear as day, huge bright crystal panes. I stood before it like a sculpture, like that urn below, an empty open channel for perceiving and sensing. Before me was heaven, a complete wonderland of beauty; sky, forest, parkland, space, light, the detail sang, then sang louder and then harmonised as it sang with a confidence and purpose, displaying the creativity of the moment. I had no doubt, not even any room for a splinter of doubt, it was abundantly, profoundly obvious that this was divine. I moved my fingers through the air, through the divine and cried out in joy.

The grass underneath was wet and the air cool on my skin, here in the shade of the east turret. My shorts were damp beneath me and the birdsong indistinct like a fading soundtrack. I sat on the border of the lawn blinking and breathing deeply. How did I get here? Standing up, I saw the fire escape immediately behind me and traced its track curling around the wall and up to the tower, I felt certain it was not there before. I remembered the room, the joy of it, the brilliance. I tried to gather my thoughts to consolidate the memory; it was hard like trying to pick away at the fading images in a dream. Was that it? Had I been dreaming? My shorts were really damp, maybe I had been sitting here in some kind of trance imagining it all. There was a sharp pain in my thigh, it was the heavy keys, I must have been sitting on them for some time. I couldn't remember how I got here, did I come down that fire escape or have I not been anywhere at all? One thing was certain; I felt exhilarated, lifted up.

If that was a real experience it was peerless in its properties; inexplicable and if it was a dream then it was unlike any dream I had ever had.

Evening light shone beautifully across the park and upon the trees as I walked back to the hut. It was 7:00pm, whatever had happened I had been out all day. The deer were grazing at the tree line and a great commotion was going on above the canopy as a gang of crows harassed a pair of buzzards circling in the air, bombarding them and cawing aggressively. Inside the forest, the pine smelt luscious and vital. A red squirrel ran along a fallen trunk then stood up on its hind legs and called out before scurrying up a high spruce tree and disappearing. Everywhere the birds were in vigorous summer voice; vibrant, singing, chattering, returning each other's calls. Wild garlic crushed under my feet; the pungent notes dense in the air. Ahead, the evening shade hung over the hut. There was no sign of Ram; it was obvious he had not been back since this morning. I ate some nuts and fruit, made Tulsi, closed the door and lay in bed exhausted.

The sound of grinding woke me, it was 5:30am. I had slept solidly in dreamless sleep all night. The door was open. Ram was at the table on the veranda, a blanket around his shoulders, winnowing oats from a pot at his side. Hunched over the table, he was using his roller to grind and split the groats. My mind flashed with the memories of yesterday; a thousand questions. I grabbed my blanket, draping it around my shoulders and stood opposite him.
"Morning," said Ram spreading his arms and smiling, "what a beautiful day for the experience of all this."
"What is the house?" I asked urgently.
He looked at me with a quizzical, mischievous expression, grabbed another handful of groats from his pot and trailed them through his fingers. "The house is a mystery." he said, "All people ask

themselves in various ways, what is the house? There are plenty of potential answers but none of them are good enough because truthfully we don't know what the house is. The universe is unbelievably ancient; the house, civilisations, whole solar systems come and go. The powers from which the house has come into existence are beyond science and beyond any idea we may have about it, however brilliant the idea may be. You know that the name we give to this power is Brahman but any word is frivolous and not grand enough to do justice to that it is attempting to describe. Obviously, the house is that."

I sat down opposite him. Dust hovered in the air as he ground the oats rhythmically against the board. The fresh smell of broken oat groats reminded me of my mother's bread and the water mill I went to as a child.

"You do realise it is perfectly alright not to know," said Ram, "it is also essential for the abundance of heart that you are seeking. You can spend your life searching for the meaning of the house in some investigative way like you may dissect a piece of architecture, or you can allow it and receive it. I am teaching you the second course. It is not stupidity or blind ignorance; it is intelligent openness. The distinction is important, Amelia." He looked up. "All we can say is the house is here and the house has properties; it is furnished, so to speak."

"Ram, listen, I have experienced something inexplicable and amazing, it has happened but it's impossible, I may have dreamt it but I don't think I did."

"Ah, a mystery then like most things."

"No listen, I am talking about Bowslip, what is Bowslip House?"

"A mystery, as I say, some kind of illusion maybe."

"But it's a stately home in the English countryside."

"Is it?"

"Yes, I could trace its history to 1585."

"Oh well, you seem so confident of your facts perhaps that's what you should do then."

"But Ram, I have been in some other dimension or some other realm inside Bowslip."

"So what? Every moment is an impossible miracle, it's staggering that you could ever become so complacent. Look at these oats." He ran them through his hands and the dust blew across my face.

"Ram, please tell me what Bowslip is."

"Bowslip is an appearance of the wonder; just like this hut and this." He threw the oats over me with a comical grin.

"No, that's not good enough, things have order and predictability, physics for goodness' sake, a house is a house."

"A house isn't a house; most things are metaphors."

"How can that possibly be true?"

"Because of misplaced attachment, there is the apparent thing and there is the impact of the house, you are too obsessed with the thing; what about the impact, what is the impact of your experience? Go with that."

I began to reply and then stopped abruptly. What was the impact?

"I don't know Ram, I am perplexed, confused, shaken."

"Excellent, that's a perfect impact."

"But it's disturbing."

"And wonderful as well."

"Yes."

"Ah."

"Well? What can I do?"

"Why don't you tell me what happened?"

This took me aback. I was agitated, I realised I had not told him. I caught my breath, took some water from his pot; it was earthy, tasting of the woods. He looked at me in that open, receptive gaze that demanded honesty without embellishment. I told him what I had experienced. It took some time.

"Make tea," said Ram, when I had finished.

I brought the tea to the table as he cleared away the oats. We sat together looking out into the morning forest. A woodpecker drilled in the distance and the deer rustled in the undergrowth; it was 6:00am.

"The house is a containment," said Ram, "a place of existence and a point of reference from which experience arises. What is a human being other than an instrument for perceiving and expression? This is the house; can the structure of a human being possibly be anything else? The perceiving has limits and the expression has limits, all according to the fabric of the particular house; life is an encounter with the fabric of the house, the contents of the house. What you think of as you, are your thoughts and ideas but these are the projections of the contents of the house. Prominent in those projections are rising instincts, some of them very ancient; forces that come from below the conscious mind, a bit like those cellars, wouldn't you say? These legacies of the past assert themselves, generating moods, responses and hot desires of all types. It's not a linear language at all, it's not even cognitive but a potency of feelings rising in the mind and influencing the movements the mind makes. Fear is present, passion, anger, avoidance, weakness, jealousy and so on. None of it is random, all of it is seeded by the deep past and all of it is calling out, vying for attention, shaping reaction. And then you have the civilised mind, mediating and rationalising these instincts, often in opposition to them. This is what you know, or what you think, what you are told and what you conceive, what you learn and what you assume. Consider that library that repelled you so much, all those records, beliefs and concepts, the trillions of facts, words, images, memories; partly ordered, partly disordered, a constant dialogue of rationalising, assessing, trying to satisfy, trying to conclude. All this together, the instinct and the learnt ideas collaborate into what you want to do, what you want to resist, who you think you are and what you are motivated to explore. It is this dynamic that results in doing. This is action, the output of your life, the work and the art, just like all that industry, that factory of production you encountered. This triad of feeling, thinking and acting is the minute-by-minute world of experience, displaying constantly as the personal day and it is all a consequence of the properties of the house. Absorbing as the character of the house is, it is not sufficient. It may be sufficient for a while, perhaps a long while in some cases, but despite its drama and its draw, it is lacking in the permanence that underpins this appearance. Intuitively people know this but often cannot identify it as anything other than common restlessness. In those that do, a person is led to what you found on your fourth floor; to the inner quest, to gods and goddesses, prayers and pilgrimages, meditations, pujas, yoga and sacrifice and all of that has arisen out of this insufficiency within the house. People then embark on the spiritual journey which you viewed in that temple. Do you know that entering the temple is actually a request to leave the house? You probably don't because almost nobody does. I like your cathedral by the way, especially the tree. So, there you have it, the house is a containment, all perfectly explained in the Taittiriya Upanishad just in case you need a second opinion." Ram laughed at his analogy, he seemed to be able to take these shattering experiences so frivolously.

"Do you mean the house is me?" I said, bemused.

He ignored my question and continued.

"All the intricate phenomena of experience, the desires that rise, the thoughts that come, the actions that take place, are the properties of the house itself. When you begin to suspect this, there arises a conscious drive to transcend the house. Everyone is doing this to different degrees; it is nothing other than karma, that is what we call it, all of it and the karma rising in you now is a momentum to transcend the house and explore the air, the space, the gardens outside the house, maybe even the forest." He rolled his eyes.

"Do you mean the house is me?"

"Ah...and what if it is?"

"I get that analogy Ram, it's inspiring but I am not talking symbolically here at all, I am talking about Bowslip, twenty minutes over there in that direction."

"The thing about gardens, and more particularly, forests, is you are either viewing them from the confines of the house or you are striding about in them, camping out at first, perhaps visiting, then living there. Once you live in the garden the house can no longer be said to be your home. It is still an important place for refuge and storing things, a house is full of valuable assets to draw from, many of them vital and in times of need it gives you great shelter but it's an architecture only and not a principal residence."

"What about the top floor?"

He put his hand over his eyes shielding them and comically scanned the sky.

"Of Bowslip, the top floor, the turret."

"The greatest question is not what is the house or even what is in the house. You can leave that to the archivists. No, a greater question is what is beyond the house? How far do the gardens extend? And then there is a question beyond that, the biggest question of all, Amelia. To resolve it is the abundance of heart but I cannot tell you it, it has to be seen. For now, that is enough." He got up and went to tend to his oat sheaves; it was a deliberate gesture. The conversation was over. I sat there watching him work for some minutes then went back to my bed and lay on my back. Something absolutely extraordinary had happened. Was it psychic, was it a vision? It was so solid, so actual, everything about me was expanded yet nothing had been properly explained. It was agitating and inspiring all at the same time. I closed my eyes absorbed in the memory of Bowslip. The cellar, perhaps I should have gone down? The library, what if I had entered and browsed? The workshop, the cathedral and the turret? Oh the turret... I tried to feel those fabulous sensations of freedom again but the best I could do was to remember them. Remembering was enough. I spent the day like that, on my bed, resting, reflecting, dreaming and drifting. Ram was present in and around the hut occupied with this and that, tending his oats, working his arrows, making tea. I felt he was watching over me. In the late afternoon I made dhal. We ate in silence, spent the evening meditating on the veranda and went to bed at 8:00pm. Being in the hut with my Guru like this, in this mystic wind was beautiful; I wished it could always be this way. Lying in the cosiness I reflected on all that had happened over the past nine days and wondered what tomorrow would bring.

The 10th Day

I am aware of the light; the dawn is up and I can hear Ram leaving. I decide I won't stir for a bit and will stay where I am in this soft, pliable state that has been upon me since yesterday. I hear the pheasant squawk in alarm; Ram will be going around the corner and onto the old forest path to attend to whatever he was doing. I will just lie here, breathing and listening to the birdsong and woodland sounds, drifting for a while.

It's 3:00pm now and I have been up since midday, cleaning the hut and washing our clothes as best as is possible in the stream. I'm rolling oats; it's so difficult sitting at the table on the veranda with his roller and board, trying to copy what I have watched him doing all week. The noise is absorbing, very meditative and rhythmic but the rolling is hopeless, the groats are going all over the place.

"I make the best porridge in the world," Ram says proudly, "I think you need some lessons."

I look up to see him standing in front of me, dishevelled and dirty. There is dried blood on his hands and earth in his hair, he smells strongly of camphor smoke. His hands are on his hips and he shakes his head and tuts with a mock look of concern on his face. It is instantly hilarious and I burst out laughing at his tutting which breaks the mood more expertly than any lengthy discussion could

ever hope to do.
"I want to show you something Amelia, we are going into the forest but let's have tea first."
I brew up some fresh Tulsi and we sip at it as he washes in the stream and bustles about putting things in his pack, I put away the oats. It is 3:30pm. The old forester's path snakes and meanders through the untended woodland, overgrown, covered in mulch and debris but still just discernible up here, closer to the hut. He strides on ahead with his hands behind his back tramping confidently, his shoulder bag swinging back and forth, I am keeping pace behind. It is better not to talk as we walk and I know that's what he wants; it's what I want too. As we gain some distance and the hut is left far behind, the forest becomes more primitive and ancient, untrodden and undisturbed. The pine is powering up through the canopy, fresh, agile and supple. In between and all around massive old beeches state themselves regally as the real landowners of this realm. The forest is bigger than me in all senses; I could easily feel spooked but at least I am not alone.

We have been walking for more than two hours now over rough ground, following a tiny, barely perceivable stream; there is no path at all. We come into a kind of gorge where rocks protrude on either side of a low valley; it gets deeper as we walk further into it. We stop and Ram turns to look at me for the first time since we left. He tells me to wait and scrambles up the side of the slope and over the top. I sit down on a low rock. This is absolute wilderness, deeply ancient and unvisited. A small stream trickles in from the left. I kneel and cup some water in my hands slurping the woody, iron-rich taste and rub the residue over my face. Ten minutes later he is back; "Come on," he says and we continue for another mile or so towards a rocky area at the valley head where it ends in a coombe. On either side moss and ferns sprout from the walls, it's like a cave without a roof, about twenty feet deep and eight feet wide tapering neatly to a bowl-end, partly covered by a huge boulder which probably fell from above and settled itself a thousand years ago. The place is enchanting. I can tell he has been working here as the floor is clear of bracken and scrub and all the growth and loose stone have been stripped out from under the boulder, exposing clear, bare rock. It makes a natural enclosed floor. Spread out upon it are various pots surrounding a single flame which burns steadily in a dish on the rock. From his shoulder bag Ram pulls out ingredients and adds them to the pots. Overhead a cuckoo calls and three buzzards cry in their piercing voice as they circle in the sky, one hundred feet over our heads, soaring in the gathering breeze which gently rushes and snakes through the ferns on the walls around us.

"Ram, this is exceptional. What is it?"

"This is the rock cleft, where no-one has ever been. I have been working on it and it has been working on me. Together we have created your dhuni. I want you to tend it. Keep its fire burning constantly, give it your attention. It is a sacred flame, don't let it go out. Over there is a shelter and inside there are some things. I will return at dawn in three days."

He turns and walks back out without another word or any lingering glance. I am caught off guard, not really appreciating what is happening, a thousand questions and concerns rush into my head. I am tongue-tied, flummoxed, I look this way and that. Shelter, what shelter, the flame, what about the water? I turn to call out to him but he is gone. Some pheasants break cover; there is the crack of a twig and then nothing, silence, he is away. For a minute I am bemused, not certain what has happened, then a rushing and a pulse drive into my ears, turbulence marauds in my belly, gripping and spiking as panic and fear rises up. Where am I? I have been following him for nearly three hours across open ground, lost in my thoughts trailing my Guru - I don't know how to get back. Instantly I begin to calculate and problem solve. I know the estate is vast but it's not endless, if I strike out somewhere and keep going, I will eventually find the outer wall but which way? I have no idea where I am in relation to the whole; I can't even predict which direction the hut or the house are in. If I just start maybe there's a chance but it is late afternoon, what if I get nowhere by dark? Then my stomach sinks even further. I have no torch. It's fruitless; there is no chance of it. I try to revise my plan, re-calculating, refusing to give up until with a sharp intake of breath all my thoughts stop. Open-mouthed, a creeping fatality of dread comes upon me; even if I can fathom a route, my Guru told me to stay. The weight of this recognition unfurls kilo by emotional kilo into my guts until the intensity of it stops me dead, I sink to the ground. This is it. All the years of sadhana, all the years of puja and promises and commitments and tapas have always been my gift to pick and choose; to control, to allow or to avoid. I could always reject, always pull back, always just test the water; I could pretend. But now, my God, this is make or break, this cannot be deceived. Either I take the instruction and stay or I turn and run. Ram is compassionate, forgiving but intuitively I know this is different, a force greater than him is at work here and if I reject this, I will fail and that will break something irreparably, damage some power of commitment between us. I sit down heavy on the bracken, utterly dejected. A light rain has been falling for about thirty minutes, pattering and chattering on the billions of leaves rustling all around me. My immediate destiny hangs upon me hard.

The light has now dimmed. I don't have a watch but it must be 7:00pm, it will be fully dark in three hours and gathering dark in two. I do not feel alone in this space, that's the worst thing, I could whimper just thinking about it; the atmosphere seems alive with watching presence, creeping, sinister. I must watch my mind, contain my mind; I want to pray. There is no point now in bemoaning my state or railing against the actions of my Guru, I am here and I must make the best of it. With my hands to my chest I speak aloud with all the pleading passion that is within me, my voice faltering, my lips quivering, tears building in my eyes. "Lord, help me to bear this, protect me and guide me." A tear rolls down my left cheek and into the corner of my mouth. I must stay calm, I must organise. The dhuni flame itself has to be kept burning, it is the sacred fire and at least that will give me a light. I examine the flame, it is well protected in the cleft, the wick is long and thick, burning in a plentiful pool of oil. It is very pure, spiritual, swaying gently amidst the rock and the ferns. Around it, the three pots of camphor, frankincense and samagri are well stocked. In front of the flame is a second basin built up with rocks and stones for burning camphor and making offerings of the herbs. Some fifteen feet back in a small alcove in the rock is the shelter. A trellis of branches and sticks supports a tarpaulin roof and a second sheet hangs down over the entrance. I pull the tarp across, feeling like a Stone Age woman as I peer into the dingy, earthy recess. Dried bracken is thickly covering the floor, a sleeping bag lays rolled out with two blankets folded on top. An old orange waterproof and a pair of black waterproof trousers hang from a stick in the roof; beneath them is a rope, a few tools, a water container, a battered saucepan and a big square biscuit tin. My spirits lift when I open the tin and find a Primus stove, some tea, lentils, oats, two candles, matches and a little bag of spices. I wish there was a cake, a bun, some distraction, anything. I fight hard to not feel crushing misery. Taking off my damp outer clothes I get into the waterproofs and sit in the entrance looking over at the dhuni. Why has he done this? To expose me like this, it's catastrophic, it's not fair. Resentments brood and build, grasping for my attention. I have enough insight to see that if I give ground, even a jot to these stalking enemies then I will be launched into a morass of emotion and dark thoughts. I must be practical, deal with what is happening. The birds quieten now and the gathering dusk is noticeable. Soon it will be pitch black, just the sounds and the black. There are noises all around from the rain. I know it is the wetness reacting with all the organics of the place but if I let it, it will become chattering voices. I desperately want some comforts to appease the quivering and gripping that rises in my belly. Firing up the Primus, I cook up some oats. Cracking sounds make me jump, is something moving? I can't tell, it's probably just twigs settling or branches falling after the rain but I can't tell. The dark is coming, it can't be avoided. I crawl to the dhuni flame and kneel before it at the little basin. Lighting a piece of camphor, I drop it in and sprinkle frankincense and herbs upon it. I pray; private, intimate, deep prayer. When the camphor flickers out, I look around at the gloom. Feeling tearful and sick, I get into my shelter and into my bag, pile a blanket on top of me, arrange the other one to use as a pillow and finally lie down; still, alert, expectant and deadly quiet. The rain has stopped, it has become silent, just some dripping which I hate. The small light from the oil flame projects a flickering, shadowy glow onto the entrance to my shelter. An owl hoots and I beg for sleep.

Ram knew about fear, all its nuances and pretensions, its origins and its convoluted languages. He knew how damaging fear was and how it possessed the psyche with all its cohorts of allies; defence, timidity, resistance, hesitation, suspicion and doubt. In a free state such discrimination had useful properties but in a volatile state discrimination was never clear, a mere charlatan. He also knew that in almost all instances fear was mental. There were some cases in the practical world when it was essential in the moment to avoid practical danger but these instances were rare. Mostly it was mental, a fantasy world, something imagined; a mischievous story and he knew those stories didn't come from nowhere but were the product of old ties. Fear of this type had to be transcended and the best way to transcend it was to be thrown up against it in a situation that overcomes its power and unravels its ties. He knew a person could never do this willingly and without provocation because they never had the insight. It required intervention to provoke a threat with no way out and to live through it. There was a moment in everybody's sadhana when this initiation must occur, either by spontaneous incident or by design.

It is deep night, I am not sure I can stand this, something is building and I do not know what to do. There is a ringing in my ears, my eyes are tight shut, sleep is impossible and I will have to bear this for hours. At any moment something is going to burst through the tarpaulin and grab me, something will touch me, there is something out there, something brooding and these noises are hell, raindrops, twigs, crackling leaves. There will be animals, lots of them, scurrying around in this blackness. I can hear something in the distance, something large, I am sure I can. I want to cry, sob but I am holding it in, I want to hold it in. I open my eyes in the deep, deep darkness. The glow from the oil flame projects the faintest illumination on the door tarpaulin. I concentrate on it, the gentle motion flickering like living moonlight, soft upon the tarp. With my feet, I push the corner of the tarp to one side and look straight at the dhuni. The little oil flame gives out a subtle, radiant light, the moisture in the air and the shadow of the basin creating a halo around its glow, lighting up the curling fronds of bracken and moss, so small amidst all this forest and rock yet tranquil, pure, compelling. I stare at it, my breathing calms, my body relaxes. Is it cosy here in the bag? This shelter around me, is it embracing? The natural forest, is it peaceful? I watch the flame and feel the warmth of the blankets. In my mind I recite a mantra to my Guru and then whisper it upon my lips. Something large is moving in my mind and I do not know what it is, a sense of otherness that cannot be described.

From his hut, Ram held Amelia in his attention. He had chanted the mantra for her that evening and felt her in his heart; it was a real connection, not something imagined but he knew she would not be aware of it. Ram knew that faith was the only solution to fear, the absolute only one. It was a word he used with discretion these days after having observed how misunderstood faith was. People took it superficially, assuming faith to be some blind hope, some abandonment of responsibility, whereas it was one of the most significant actions that could be taken. Fear relating to an actual threat or hazard is one thing but what of an abstract fear, when confronted with that, what course is there? Either it is endorsed by ruminating upon it, believing in its authenticity, acting upon its validity, or it is seen as the mental ghost it is and not an accurate sense about the presenting moment at all. In that knowledge he chose to trust fate. This is the action and to undertake that action is faith. Fear is a reaction to powers not before encountered. Faith is an allowing of those powers and trusting that it will be alright, trusting in the protection of the Lord, trusting that light outshines darkness. Ram knew from the position of the seer that faith was big, faith was not reckless, faith was advanced and overcoming fear through faith liberates the house. He held her in his heart, willing her to succeed.

Amelia slept. If she had known she was falling into sleep she would have been pleased but she did not know. At 3:05am she woke up; dead silence, damp air, complete aloneness, pitch black apart from the halo of light around the dhuni. A pressing sense of otherness, like a presence, played strongly upon her. In that second she had a choice, just a twitch in one direction and the chemistry of fear would agitate her mind into ideas of monsters, demons, ghosts and murderers. Just a micro-second avoidance of that twitch and the real data present in the experience would present itself to her. Somehow, she did not twitch and things were just as they were. The shelter was profoundly peaceful, the forest all around gentle in its night mode, soft, everything at rest, her breathing felt in line with this rest, at ease in the embracing stillness. The call of the owl was part of the night nature and was the beautiful noise of the woodland night. The flicker from the dhuni brought incandescence to the rock cleft, a subtle warmth and all around the sleeping giants of the great beech and pine stood easy in their night state. It was lulling here, cosy here, snuggly here and that was it, no abstract thoughts moved in her and just because she didn't twitch, neither did she think. I am secure she said to herself and felt it. Amelia did not know how big this adjustment was but the light in the dhuni glowed just a few photons brighter, falling upon her face like moon glow. She fell unknowingly back into sleep and dreamt of the turret room.

Birds began to sing at 4:15am. Could there be anything better than coming awake in the forest on a summer's morning as the light came up so subtlety from out of the darkness itself? Molecule by molecule, Amelia drifted into semi-wakefulness. She lay stock still, lulled in the muse of the night space, experiencing the spaciousness of that, feeling the inspiration of her turret dream. No thoughts moved in her at all, only sensing and appreciation of that sensing. At 5:30am she opened her eyes knowing one thing, I am happy to be in the forest having this experience. So simple was that action that she did not notice its powerful properties. Much later she would come to see this moment as pivotal in her life. Rather than the problem of the forest, she woke to an acceptance of the forest. The world which was previously full of resentments and perceived traumas now became a world rich with experiences. Instead of the forest, her, and her concepts, now there was only the forest and her. The fact that this was the natural state of openness was unknown to her, yet that was the case. Amelia awoke in the natural state. This is the abundance of heart.

Getting up she stretched and yawned, pulled aside the tarp and stepped out in that state, barefoot into the coombe to tend to the dhuni. The stepping changed everything. My foot connecting with the ground is majestic, my heel feeling its place solid and tactile, compression spreading across its surface, flawlessly enlivening my senses; the ball of my foot is altering structure, flattening effortlessly, singing with sensation. The temperature of the ground, the sharpness of the spikes of earth and root, the glorious sound of rustle and crunch, a millisecond of ooze from last night's mud explodes in me like a poem. My foot is divine, this sensing moment is divine. I stop on the path dead still; everything is ablaze with vitality and motion. Light spread everywhere, touching me and touching everything, a billion accents of shade and illumination, shadow and lustre, glinting with the highlight of the artist in the reflection off the dewdrop; the gloss of the variegated leaf rusty in its coppers and browns, coiling in its greens and yellows, sparkling in the light. It's so simple, so exquisite, so beautiful. I want to share and express; I want to flow out. I want to expand to be with my beloved. For a second my heart yearns with a poignant beautiful pain. I do not want to be separate, but in this light and sound, in this sensing, in the vitality of this perceiving, what can possibly be separate? I am not separate; this is the Beloved.

To my right, a squirrel moves across the low bough of a beech tree. I can hear its scampering feet against the bark, the sound is within me; what a wonder sound is and now its richness rushes and mingles with the light. The call of the robin has substance; it is tactile, flavouring the air. The touch of breeze on my face rolls across the pores of my skin and the colour, my God, the colour; it is not possible to exist for one second in this explosion of wonder and not notice these infinite filaments of experience? It is all a glory; the rise and fall of my chest, the blinking of my eyes, the magnificence of each molecule of hearing and seeing and feeling. I am expanded yet completely, profoundly stable. This is not hallucinogenic, it is not imagined, nor is it embellished, this is as it is, moment by moment. How could it have been missed, how has it been possible to not notice this? The dhuni is fragrant in its camphor notes, that spicy pungency, sensuous against my nose, the freshness of the flame flickering on the old stone with its shadows and undulations. I am delighted by the vitality of the glow of the light against the deep, lush and moist green of the fern, whose young leaves curl and fold more delicate than lace. I bring my hands to my face in a gesture of prayer, my Lord, you are great.

From a distance Ram observed Amelia, although she didn't know it. He observed her through his sensing. This was not some clairvoyance; it was quite natural, it could be called instinct or intuition, a closeness of knowing. It was a product of the state of openness in which his world moved and the affection he held for her. He felt her expansion but more importantly, felt the reason for her expansion. Amelia wasn't thinking; she was receiving. He knew this was the secret; that which is written about so complexly, that which whole theories were constructed around. It came down to this simplicity; abundance is receiving not thinking.

Amelia had left the dhuni and was strolling amidst the undergrowth, hearing the birds, experiencing the light, feeling her body as it interacted with the space, touching the textures and fabrics of the foliage and humming. The forest was supremely enveloping, as was the sky and the earth below. She hummed louder and developed a spring in her step, jumping over the logs playfully and walking along the fallen tree trunk. Amelia was in happiness and that state continued to shape her mind, establishing a platform for enthusiasm and exploration. She became naturally inspired, not about anything in particular, just inspired to be alive, inspired to walk. After an hour she returned to the shelter with a desire for morning tea. She came into the coombe and with a gasp, stopped dead in her tracks.

"Tea?"

"Ram, how beautiful to see you! But I thought you were returning in three days!"

"Today is better don't you think?"

"Oh yes!" she said, "Oh yes!" bursting into tears.

We brewed tea on the Primus, ate some oats and did puja at the dhuni as the full morning sun came out. I sat there with my Guru amidst the ferns and the rocks, shattered by my experiences of these incredible days, eager for him to speak.

"You brought those fears into the dhuni Amelia, they were not in there, they were in you, in the house and as for your sense of otherness, that sense is God inside. You are continuously at one with God within, in all situations and in all places. You see it as other now until it becomes apparent that it is the Beloved, this is abundance of the heart, the abundance of divine intimacy and expression."

I was mesmerised by his words, they exploded something in me. A force like liquid burst in my chest and I cried tears of release and passion for six minutes; I knew it was six because as it eased and I sat poised and calm before him, he told me so.

"Ram, what happened to me in the house, was it a dream?"

"Not a dream, an event. It was the darshan of the I thought, displayed rather than spoken. Call it a vision if you like; the perceiving of new eyes Amelia, experience rather than words. It doesn't benefit by being understood in conventional ways, only the impact of it demands attention. The absorption of that attention is the knowledge you are here for. Bowslip is a strange place, full of powers, a good place to live wouldn't you say?"

"And the dhuni, Ram, I was terrified when you left me."

"I know."

"And then something changed, that little light in the dark, I can't explain. It's still changing now I think."

"It's enough to know that the world is magical and divine, both the dhuni and the turret are experiences of that. You now know that the house is this body and mind. The house has content and that can be transcended, that is what you have seen."

"That is what I want, the transcendence of all those habits, the lustre and the joy of it, how can that become stable?"

"It will if you let it and if you strive for it, striving only means establishing irrevocable knowledge. True knowledge is not belief you see, it is like the proof of an equation; it is true because it is seen. That is what we mean by knowledge, that is what the Upanishads mean."

"Ram, it is pulsing in me now, my time here this morning has been magnificent, I feel beautiful."

"You look beautiful and it is beautiful here and now."

"So, tell me what is it that happened."

"Nature happened as a result of your diligence and your sadhana. That moment in the night alone, your terror was penetrated by a powerful and simple purity, it moved in you and it changed your mind. You came to a position free of old mental movements and old reaction and it was blissful, peaceful, true and accurate. The sanctity of the turret propelled you beyond the legacy of the house into that same freedom. On both occasions there was a falling away of old identity, an absence of attachment and in its place, easy natural awareness of what is. Your experiences were enhanced because they were provoked and accelerated, hence the lustre you describe but whether there is lustre or not, it is all magnificent when experienced just as it is, without an identity trying to evaluate or add something to it. You saw that and that is what happened, that is the change. It had some drama to it because being here in Bowslip with your Guru is powerful; it is nature Amelia. It is transcendence, the experience of realisation, the living of it."

"What shall I do Ram?"

"Love the house; I want you to love the house Amelia, because at times you have not, it is truly the treasure of the Lord. You need the house; it is a beautiful house, those who reject the house are fools."

"You mean me, the body and the mind?"

"Yes, yes, we don't need to say it again, the body and mind is what I mean by the house. Accepting the house and knowing it for what it is brings you great peace. You must realise that every rising event that comes to you is the property of the house; I want you to know that too. The way you feel, your desires and the reactions that arise are the projections of the house, even the motivation for change, the sadhana itself. This is what we mean by karma. Everyone in the world is experiencing the outworking of their karma. Call it chemistry if you like, call it physics or call it soul, it doesn't matter, the content of the house produces the moment by moment activity which fills the mind."

"But do you mean it isn't me? How can that be? I can think my own thoughts can't I, go my own way?"

"Something thinks the thoughts obviously and that something has great familiarity, a certain flavour. You feel it most keenly, that's the big question I referred to at the hut, the biggest question that you have not yet conquered. What is that something which feels as if it is thinking the thoughts? Who is occupying the house, having opinions about what the house is and does?"

"Me."

"No Amelia, not me, that is the spiritual revelation and that is the knowledge you are in this dhuni to see. If it is realised then the impact is the natural freedom and abundance of heart, just as you have experienced. That is why you are here and that is why you have been so challenged and provoked over these days. It's not so difficult. In an earlier time you would have had to live with tigers and take tea with murderous bandits, or serve a tyrannical guru to achieve similar ends. Fortunately none of those are here in Bowslip any longer for that is all in the past."

"So who is this person that I know so well, the me who has done all the sadhana?"

"It is the functioning of the house and only that. There isn't a personal me, Amelia."

"Ram, that's absurd! I remember every moment of it; I am talking to you about it now, what I did, what happened, how I felt, my achievements, my problems."

"To whom is it absurd? It isn't absurd Amelia, it is liberation."

"You mean the Self? I worked out its meaning last winter in my hermitage."

"We are beyond the winter. Bowslip of this potency cannot be visited by theorists, only by heroic and passionate explorers. To live is complicated Amelia, to exist is simple. Can you see how important that statement is? That which lives is full of effort and force, that which exists is full of freedom and peace, even though events are the same across both states. One is conditioned by the house, living in it, reacting to it. The other is free of the house, viewing it and knowing it, constantly enjoying the gardens like the Lord and Lady of Bowslip, enjoying their domain in security, letting the staff get on with the work, staff that they treasure and develop, treating with great respect and constant kindness. There isn't a personal me at all, there is experiencing and knowing. That is the whole summary of the darshan and the summit of the discrimination. This is the seer's action that was revealed to you on the hill. That is what I want you to see now."

"Ram, look, I get it and I don't get it too and I am fed up with the conundrum. So, what is Amelia, who am I?"

"You say it with such exasperation because the effort to get it and solve it for yourself goes round and round. It's no good anymore, that effort, which is why we have stepped off the roundabout of old words and old eyes. Seeing it is living beyond the house. That is what you need to do now, give up the management of the house. You are being promoted Amelia, you used to be the housekeeper, now you are the Lady of this fabulous estate, the goddess of your realm surrendered into the greatness of it, just as it is. So let me tell you what that surrender is because it is a deeper and more subtle surrender than you have previously attained. Up to now your house has seemed occupied. One of the principal properties of your house has been the feeling of an agent, the sense there is a person generating ideas, something making decisions, something having opinions, something with a need to assert and defend itself. The agent is called many names; Jiva, or I thought, or ego, that is what you mean by the person of Amelia. You have believed that is you but this sense of agent is not you, it is a property of the house. The sense it is you is the veil shrouding the abundance, just as darkness shrouds the sun. This is the advanced knowledge of the sadhaks, the darshan of Shiva, the revelation of the Upanishad and the mystery of Bowslip. Knowing it is Self-realisation, the freedom of this estate."

"You mean I am not the doer?"

"Yes, that is true, you are not the doer but this has been said to you many times with little effect as it is only words. It is how the spiritual texts describe it but inevitably it has brought confusion into sadhana because you have expected the feeling of doing to disappear and it cannot disappear, for it is the mechanics of common mentality, decision-making, concentration, reaction, etcetera. How could that possibly disappear? These activities are how the mind works and thinks, they are functions of the instrument. Realisation is not a change in the functions of experience, only the knowledge of experience. There will always be doing."

"So Ram, right now I know I am here, I am wondering about this conversation, remembering last night, having feelings about it all. What is all this that is happening so keenly if it is not me?"

"It's thinking, intelligence, observation, motivation and concentration, functions, the cellars and the library of the house interacting. To date, that activity has appeared in you as a personal voice because you have allowed its identity and believed that you are doing it but that is the ignorance. What you are experiencing is the movement of perception and attention, the workings and functions of the house. When you are dreaming at night there isn't a me that is generating or controlling the dream, it is self-generating. From where has that generation come? From out of the house, a reflection of the house. Waking thought is like that as well."

"You mean it's all a dream?"

"No, not a dream but an appearance just the same. In the dream you allow it for there is nothing else you can do, you witness the whole drama, you know the experience most intimately; watch it happening including all the actions the dream protagonist takes. Abundance is living that same position in the waking state. Allowing and receiving whilst all the doing goes on."

"You mean witnessing?"

"That's the common word, yes. It's okay but it carries a certain austerity to it. This is not austere Amelia; it is not possible to be austere in this, it is only possible to be abundant. Receiving is my word, not witnessing. The grand recognition that comes to you as a culmination of the discrimination is that there isn't a personal I at all in the way you have previously imagined. What there is, is the beautiful vastness and intimacy of all this existence being known, being received. The turret was its demonstration, as was last night and this morning and now we are clarifying it, so as well as the experience you have the knowledge because it is only knowledge that will free you, not the memory of the experience:

- Becoming aware that it is possible to perceive without thinking is its first recognition.
- Seeing you are not that which is doing the thinking is its second recognition.
- Seeing that all the projection is a product of karma is its third recognition.
- Seeing that the sense 'me' is truly nothing other than an idea is its fourth recognition.
- Then the ability to let that idea go, rather than cling to it, is the fifth recognition and that is the abundance.

You realise that you do not need the sense me for either your well-being or your welfare? Nor have you ever needed it; it is the stranger in the house and has been the burden of the house. As if somehow you have been kicked out of heaven and isolated in separateness but it is only the I thought which makes it appear like that. With that ignorance pierced, the house expresses and perceives spontaneously, radiating capability, love, compassion and generosity of spirit because it is no longer occupied by an intruder, only by the intimacy of God within. Then the content of the house itself changes; old habits recede because there is no structure to support them. It is freedom, it is evolution, it is Self-realisation."

"So, if am I nothing, what can I do now?"

"If you have taken in anything that I have said, it must be obvious to you that you are not nothing, there cannot be nothing, not in experience, nor in existence. There are powers prior to experience but I must tell you a vital truth. Such realities are not worth considering now, they confuse and place a strain on freedom. You are fullness, all this divine presence, knowing and Being, experiencing and receiving. That is happiness; the intimacy of Being from which Satchitananda radiates, just as it is. Dwell upon this, take inspiration from the teachings. See it gain stature in you as a living experience, give it your attention and permission, engage in the passion of jnana and let's engage together in the passion beyond that. Find the way Amelia. Also, observe yourself and be constantly alert to the day because this abundance happens to you frequently in life, not necessarily with that lustre you enjoyed so much but in ordinary moments when you are absorbed in something and happy, when there is free-flow of activity and ease of experience. In those moments you are without the ego-mind and it is apparent that everything is happening by itself but it is temporary and you do not know it consciously. When that is sustained consciously and continuously, the experience rises in intensity and status."

"Can I live with you Ram?"

"No. It is critical you live apart."

"I miss you when I am away."

"I know, maybe a time will come but not now."

"What is left for us here?"

"Intense communication, the seer's action across all means, exploration into the subtlest, profoundest nuances of this recognition and then, the glory of the passion beyond."

"What is the passion beyond?"

"Devotion, the purest love. Did I tell you there was a temple in Bowslip, an amazing one, incredibly ancient?"

"No, is there really? I had no idea."

"Bowslip is full of mysteries."

"Can we go there?"

"Some other time I think, some other time."

"Okay, some other time."

"Shall we go back to the hut now, roll some oats, shave some arrows?"

"What will you do with the arrows?"

"I have been using them Amelia, all through your time here. Now there are none left, we may need some more. Arrows that pierce."

"Ram, which way is the hut?"

"Ah, that is a good question."

Chapter Five

Devotion

eleven months later
on the forest ridge

To be alive is amazing. To take it for granted is a disease. To follow your destiny is unavoidable, to transcend is sadhana. The events that took place in Bowslip had become my passionate delight. Within its territory was the thrill of truth, an encounter with advanced sadhana. It was not so much a place, more an experience within a place. Its physics were mysterious and variable yet it had dimensions, architecture and substance, not unlike a dream I suppose. Getting to Bowslip used to be an ordinary thing, a question of roads and gates, time and space, diaries, making arrangements with others but as I penetrated deeper into the interior alone with my Guru, arrival was no longer a question of travelling and distance but more a question of being present; experience was of a different order. Ram was Guru and I was student, or shishya as he would come to say, a term to which I knew he gave the greatest respect. Together we progressed a timeless equation in this mystery. I asked him for the address, the actual location so I could rationalise it more. He had just replied Bowslip is @ Ram.

As I stood on the ridge that evening looking down into the valley I knew that my life was perfect, not a random incident but perfect in all its features. This realisation had been so elusive even though Ram had been telling me for years. The reason I had found it so hard to accept is because I interpreted the word 'perfect' as meaning always nice, problem free, how naïve I was. I realised now what he had meant all along, it was karma that was perfect and karma was all of it, the motion, the change, the momentum for growth, the incidents, the setbacks and the learning. Perfect didn't mean nice, although it often was, perfect meant inevitability. How many years had I spent struggling within my own self to push away movements and experiences that were simply part of my humanity, in an impossible effort to make everything fit my expectations? Mad, isn't it? The faculties of thought, feeling, ideas, responses, sensations and actions are normal and will continue to take place as long as this life exists;

whatever the heights of spiritual maturity there will always be the function of Amelia. This had become so clear last year in the dhuni, knowing this and accepting it deeply had changed my life. Amelia was my intrigue and my pleasure, not my pain. Ram sent me a note after my last visit and it had such an effect. It was quite stark, there was no *'Dear Amelia'* or, *'I hope you are well'*; in what proved to be his style, the piece of torn notepaper bearing his illegible, handwritten scrawl was completely absent of punctuation.

'As you read this text you are experiencing consciousness as it looks through the lens of the senses and the particular mind that constitutes your individual life this produces all that you feel to be me and mine character personality attitudes feelings wants desires and a hundred other things you are always complaining about realisation is new knowledge Amelia and new perceiving not the loss of this ordinary humanity which is itself an expression of God that which changes is identity not function - get on with it R'

The winter had been such a fruitful time and now here we were on the cusp of spring. I had set my resolutions and knew I was at the start of something fresh. I cannot say what these resolutions were because such things are between me and God but they were based on the extraordinary experiences I had with Ram last time I was here; the encounter with the house and my profound night alone in the forest. Putting those teachings into practice had transformed me. I felt excited and eager for this new visit even though I had no idea what was ahead, I knew it would be something big and I was ready. The primary instinct that moved in me to find God was the life-blood of my mind. Whenever I could I strove to be with my teacher and with others in whom these same passions were arising. To be together in that field of truth was the finest intimacy and my greatest pleasure. Superficial worldly things had become tedious to me now; not the world itself, not life and relationship and people but the superficial content which was so prevalent in routine affairs, had

become like an alien language and it was such a contrast. Being with my Guru in the
potency of Bowslip, doing tapas and having spiritual adventures was sublime, then on returning back to activities, old stresses returned burdening my mood and well-being. I had always dreaded leaving because of it but last summer after we had returned from the dhuni and my mind was expanded, we had an outstanding conversation on happiness and since then things were very different, remarkably different. I remembered it keenly...

"You don't have to experience happiness to be happy." It was a typically provocative statement from Ram and it had annoyed me. I thought it absurd, especially when he said nothing else about it for the whole morning. Happiness was happiness; surely I either felt it or I didn't. He continued "You have a mind and you don't like what the mind does, that's your burden, that's what makes you restless. What does it matter if you feel sad at times, why is the experience of sadness a problem? What you want is to experience constant peace and the feeling of ease, you like it when you have it and you feel unsettled when you don't. What an entrapment. Get beyond it."

Hearing it put like this annoyed me further because of its rudeness. I couldn't help the way I felt, could I? The various ups and downs of my feelings were a frustrating reality and I was pretty sure it was like this for everyone yet he was talking to me as if I was an adolescent. I knew he was provoking me.

"Overcoming the burden of unhappiness is not changing the feelings themselves but accepting that experience is never always going to be positive or pleasant and that is alright. It is not because things have gone wrong, it is nature. This is such an important teaching, Amelia; do you see its significance? Rather than becoming absorbed with the feelings and lost in them, you live through them steadily and with patience. You have heard it before yet you keep getting caught out, it requires an effort of remembering. Why don't you remember? If the body has pains or gets injured, what do you do?"

"Sometimes I fret about it I suppose but mostly I adapt, take action if needed and get on with it."

"Perfect, I like that. So why is the mind different, can you tell me?"

"Well, it makes me frustrated Ram. If I am unhappy I am not myself, not who I want to be. No one wants to be unhappy surely?"

"You should, it's a most fruitful experience. Your trouble is every time you have some dip in mood it possesses you, you are a hypochondriac of the mind Amelia, an addict for resentment. The wise understand the mind is variable and absolute consistency is not going to happen. Just as weather occupies the sky and is variable, so mood and concerns occupy the mind and are variable. Why don't you just accept this?"

"But the mind is so intimate Ram, it bites deep."

"No, it isn't. It is not intimate. It is immediate, that is true and it is close but it is not intimate. The mind is an event. It does not bite deep."

"But we all like pleasant events and we don't like unpleasant events."

"Exactly! The whole of humanity is in this drama but the sadhaks are out of it. My teaching is these movements are natural, the drama isn't. Rather than sadness or difficulty being a new disaster every time it occurs, it is just nature moving, unpleasant maybe for a time but so what? It really is a bizarre thing that you expect stability and do not notice that all around you, in every direction the minds of people are in flux. The human mind everywhere is not steady and is experiencing variance, in other words, shifting moods and changing thoughts. You see, this is nature. The shishyas see beyond the common impact of that nature and have the capacity to flit amongst it and be unconcerned. They constantly know and remember that everything is temporary and everything is an experience taking place."

"So, what can I do about it?"

"Do the same as you do with the body just as you said, adjust, take action as needed and get on with it. These are the actual tactics that you apply moment by moment and you need to remember them to stop being constantly caught out but I will give you something more now, a kind of magical device, an upgrade - Faith."

"You mean hope that it will be alright?"

"No, not hope. This faith is far bigger than that. This faith is knowledge and evidence for that knowledge; it is supported faith."

"What do you mean, knowledge?"

"To know. Knowledge is not hoping or speculating but knowing that the default of your mind is already just what you want. It is constant, stable and happy, the positive enjoyer. This truly and accurately is the state to which you naturally return when sattva prevails or rather, when rajas and tamas subside; in other words when restlessness and dullness subside. It is not a fluctuating mood like other things, it is the default. You must realise that. The distinction is important and changes your understanding. In other words, it is always there because it is how you really are. Just as the sky is space but weather moves, so mind is happy but unhappiness and moods move. This is the knowledge and once it is steady in you, then rather than bemoan the temporary loss of happiness and fret about it, you just get on with whatever is happening and see it through, acting accordingly, whatever its duration. You are certain that the default of mind has not been defeated or lost; it is only covered for a time, all depending on the circumstance of your incident. Faith means proceeding in this way through any hardship and remembering it, as that hardship happens. The remembering is your action and where the power is. Then you no longer have to feel happiness to be happy because the happiness is in the knowledge itself and not in temporary sensations that are bound to rise and fall. This is not imagination, this is fact, natural order, how could you become so deluded? Why don't you remember Amelia? It is a spiritual resilience to remember, it changes everything to remember, give it attention and don't fall back."

"So, what is the evidence then?"

"Proof. Look at your life, reflect on all the incidents and encounters, what has been your experience? Has it not been recovery from setback to a default 'you', which is happy and at peace? Never mind how long

that may take and how difficult it may have been at times. In those who have some accomplishment as you obviously do, it is as natural as magnetism. This default is ananda. It is a state not a mood and it doesn't matter if that state is temporarily obscured because it is the nature of things that that will happen. If you have the capacity to truly investigate this, you will realise its truth. And more beautifully, the more you take this approach, the greater its effect; it is a powerful sadhana for unravelling ignorance. You cannot lose the default condition because it is your nature. You realise what this means Amelia? It means you can then say that I don't care if I am unhappy because I never am, there is only an experience of unhappiness happening to me. Because I know this completely, unhappiness itself is very, very rare for me and is not something affected by event. It can be the same for you."

"That's amazing!"

"I told you it was magical, obviously not everyone can do this, it is not the right advice for all; it would be meaningless for many and dangerous for some. If a person is in the grip of the common mind and dense vasanas, then entrapment is strong and such people need to be guided towards all the basic yogas and skills which promote well-being and equilibrium. However, we are not talking about the common mind are we? We are talking about your mind; we are talking about you."

"I know the mind is not my enemy, Ram."

"Fantastic and that is a mark of your attainment, for when we first met, you were fighting with your mind and burdened by its random waves. The mind is a difficulty for many but this is the nature of karma and awakening. For the wise, the mind is a peerless tool of friendship. To overcome the grip of the mind's reactions and movements you need tactics. I have given you many, you are accomplished in most but now you need some advanced tactics. The time is ripe Amelia, when you come again we will explore them. For now, apply what has been shared with you, investigate it, manifest it in yourself and also know that despite any grumbling about unhappiness and the challenge of living in the world, you do not want to be anyone else."

"What do you mean?"

"Think about it. You only want to be who you are. You don't want to transpose yourself and become someone else, you don't want to be anyone different, you only want to be you, which means all this has to happen just as it is. Your karma is perfect."

After my return home I thought deeply about that exchange as its impact began to filter into my life. It was a revolutionary thing to come to understand and implement, so simple yet so revealing. He was right, I had criticisms of circumstances, desires for change in situations, frustrations sometimes but fundamentally I wanted to be me and not anyone else, even in times of hardship this was true. I may have wanted the events to change but I didn't want to not be me. I began to see the real honour in the experience of my life, how it had a momentum all its own and how I could trust it. The whole thing was my destiny in all its flavour and nuance. It was simple really and now because of it all, here I was in Bowslip once again standing at this incredible spot. Had you been standing on the ridge beside me you would be relieved to have completed the trek following Roly as he plodded though the dense, tight yew forest. Some of the yews were 1,500 years old, stoical and leathery, warped by a millennia of rain, frost and sun, standing packed and close together like ancient Chinese warriors. You would be looking out on the levels below and see how they broke the geology of the landscape, forming a small valley like a flattened bowl with coppices of spruce and silver birch standing elegantly amidst the grasses. The valley was about half a mile long and a quarter wide, surrounded on all sides by the hills and the yew. Large willows border a little river flowing across the glade, fed by a waterfall tumbling down directly below me. It had been epic arriving here at dawn eleven days ago and had felt almost biblical; Ram forging ahead throughout the night with Roly on the leading rein, carrying all our supplies on his wide donkey back and me following up behind. I had been overwhelmed by some tumbling shakti spilling out in streaming tears; it wasn't just the natural beauty of this concealed jewel in the forest, the lightness of it, the sparkle that moved me, it was what I saw on the valley floor. Before me, reflecting in the rising sun stood the Temple of Ram.

In the first three days we had set up camp in the stone-roofed roundhouse that sat close to the river and about one hundred metres from the temple. A certain isolation of ideas had come upon me and mostly I had sat in wonder and pleasure at being here in this extraordinary place. The temple itself was mysterious and prominent, as if a third person occupied the valley with us. Its circular stone walls of ochre sandstone were pitted and rounded at the edges by the wear and tear of time, a lot of time; the place looked tremendously ancient. It wasn't at all large, a single, low, four-tiered tower like a gopuram rose from the squat and solid building. There were openings around the structure, all shuttered from the inside. A single door, low and arched made of rock-hard, iron-black wood, tempted exploration. Simple carvings circulated the tower, their detail and edges softened by erosion. The third tier seemed to be open to the sky. I imagined how the light must pour into the interior from this opening. The building radiated status just like a great ring of Sarsen stones does, potency shining from its confident, faded walls. It was masculine in its shapes and feminine in its energy, like a great goddess dominant in the landscape, the erosion enhancing her magnitude, making her more of nature than any other built structure I had ever seen. I recalled visiting very ancient trees and Neolithic burial mounds, powerful cathedrals and sacred mountains, all of which had affected me with wordless awe. The temple had that same impact yet at the same time projected life and vigour. It was an incongruous mix; I had never seen anything like it, immense authority and levity all together at once. It was humbling and I was humbled before it.

The moment we had arrived Ram told me that we would not enter the temple for twelve days. I had not objected; I had not even questioned. A beautiful, spiritual rhythm quickly established itself, punctuated by the dawn and the dusk, the joy of watching the rabbits tumble around on the mound, the glory of the nature, washing in the river, doing our puja, attending to the cooking fire, feeding and grooming donkey and meditating with Ram. We hadn't spoken much except to address spontaneous spiritual points and the occasional practicalities as they arose. I served my Guru and he nourished me with his generosity of spirit and his strength of presence, brimming with affection. At times I felt I was his object of worship, not because of any specific actions but because of the atmosphere between us; it was very beautiful. The days passed in great peace but not the nights. Sometimes I was heart-pumpingly terrified. It was hard to understand so I stopped trying and allowed it to happen as best I could. The place was so full of acceleration and spiritual power that it ruffled and threatened some order within me. On the one occasion I had called to him for help, he had told me that it wasn't threatening, it was only purity and that which was threatened by it was a ghost in me we were here to transcend. It trembled in my guts and prickled upon my skin for six days. I could not have stayed there alone; I would have run, even into the yew forest, the thought of which also made me shiver. Each evening we took donkey and sat under a large reed canopy set up directly in front of the temple, chanted the Vedas and read the Upanishads.

Roly seemed to enjoy being there as much as I did, standing steady by my side. Birds chattered in the bushes beside us, a breeze swayed the silver birch like temple dancers, the river murmured and the frogs croaked in the gathering dusk, it could have been 10,000 years ago, a timeless communion with the spiritual nature of things. I knew the Upanishads but sitting here with Ram and voicing these majestic phrases in the presence of the temple brought out a renewed potency. As we were lying in our beds in the roundhouse one evening after Roly had been settled in his stall, the lights were out and the silence was total, I spoke to him in the jet-black darkness.

"Who could have written such original insights as those in the Upanishads, what moved them, Ram, who were they?"

"The Upanishads are considered shruti, not inspired by humans but exhaled by nature and then recorded by human hand. They were heard, which means experienced directly and that experience was then described. That is what shruti means. It is direct and not acquired knowledge."

"Are they true, then? Do they have accuracy?"

"The Upanishads are the best mystical authority we have. They are considered as the truth of nature to be verified through experience, just as they are by sadhaks across the world. As your experience is true so the Upanishads are true. They verify one another in the end."

"Then why do they vary so much? Some parts are stunning and clear, other parts are cluttered and obscure, difficult to absorb."

"They are not intended to be consistent, they are a collection of stand-alone revelations, brought into a whole for convenience and are the source upon which teaching is based. They were also articulated in an ancient culture when minds and words were different. For consistency and clarity in ways that speak to you in a clear voice, you need the organised spiritual texts that have come from the Upanishads and you need interpreters, teachers. It is like abstract art; you love it but don't understand it. You are moved by it but you can't explain it. Being moved is the point. They are cryptic and are not meant to give you all the answers, they are the prompts from which your own enquiry comes, they are the inspiration not the explanation."

"So how do you know what is right and how to proceed?"

"You don't need to worry about that. Beyond a certain point, once your motivation is unleashed and followed, your sadhana steers itself. Realisation is a natural progression; it comes about in you all according to your karma and intensity. For a long time you have to study, investigate and be told, then just as the Upanishads were revealed in the minds of seers, so realisation is revealed in you. You discover what is. In the beginning you are chasing after your concepts and in the end you find what is actually there. A point comes when your only tutor is God itself and your own realisation supersedes the statements in the teachings. God is your Guru all along, speaking through the teachings and the teacher, then speaking directly to you in the freedom of yourself. This is how it is and this is how it is experienced. The Upanishads are the ground of that awakening, the prompt from which it springs."

"What is God, Ram?"

"That is what you are here to discover Amelia and once you do, your life will change."

The dark was deep black in the hut, no light chinks anywhere. Nestling into the darkness felt timeless, just as these encounters were timeless and the Upanishads were timeless and the current in which I was immersed was timeless. The atmosphere fizzed with purity and maturity. I listened to the sound of Ram's breath as he went to sleep and felt open to anything.

As the dawn rose on the twelfth day, Ram was at donkey's stall feeding Roly some apple peel and stroking his back, whispering to him and making soothing noises. His mind was on Amelia and the intense commitment he felt to her. Nothing else was required to be the teacher other than that commitment. The expression of that had taken over from any calculation. That's the thing about being the teacher, to really be the teacher, it's best not to teach. Common teaching is mere show and tell, the sharing of archetypes and prepared ideas. The real teacher is empty of curriculum and abandoned to the moment, free of anticipation, full of brilliance but without plan. The teacher is only the real teacher when he meets the student at the exact point of her poise and receptivity. He was here with Amelia now because it was natural to him to engage with her intensity and fire. She was not Amelia though, not to him, and was not even student, she was becoming shishya. To have someone of Amelia's capabilities was exhilarating and enhancing for them both, which is why he was devoted to her and why this day was happening; it was like an equation finding its own proof. The trouble with equations is that maths, despite its accuracy, is perplexing for some, boring for others and terrifying for a few. It's something to do with the perceived difficulty. Ironically, once grasped, maths expresses the harmony of the physical universe in numbers. Ram was not concerned with numbers however; he was a mathematician of a different order, a mathematician who didn't do maths.

After three days Ram had sent me back to the hut saying we needed time apart before we entered the temple. I had left with Roly just because it was lovely being with donkey but also because I didn't know the way. That was the thing about Bowslip or at least these new areas I found myself in now, there were no paths at all, not even faint ones, there was just the bracken, the heather and the forest scrub. I didn't even see way-marks although Ram said they were there for those who knew what to look for. Roly however, didn't require such things, he plodded along, resolute, strong and gentle with a gait that affected me like a lullaby. I had come to love donkey very much and leaned against him as we walked with my arm around his neck, his coarse hair against my skin, my eyes closed and my mind filled with the sounds of the forest and the scents on the wind, mingling with his lovely musty smell. It was a long walk and dusk was about to descend when we got to Main Track. After ten minutes the hut appeared around the bend, looking cold and forlorn, all shut up with no smoke coming out of its pipe. There was something on the door. As we got close I could see it was an envelope pushed into the space between the door and its frame. Post! Someone had been here. It took me aback and made me uneasy. It felt like an intrusion and a threat. The envelope was sealed with the single word, 'Ram' written on the front in big letters. I turned it over in my hands, feeling it, inspecting it. There was nothing else to indicate what was in it or who it was from. Someone was trying to get Ram's attention, to occupy him in some way. This is my time! The idea of anyone else intruding upon that felt like an assault, as if I had been attacked. This is going to ruin everything. My guts tightened. It was a familiar feeling, forlorn and anxious, a threatening anxiety wave building in me, creeping upwards to splinter my mood. I knew it was irrational, there was nowhere good to go with these thoughts, they were unwanted and nothing but destructive. I knew that if I didn't get some grip upon them immediately, they would turn into a deeper and more disabling fantasy. So I stopped it in its tracks, I removed permission for it to be and sent that wave packing. No! Shivaya! It was just my way, my method, like a mental stamping of my feet or a stabbing of my finger. I am not doing this, I don't want it, I don't believe in it, I won't allow it. It was decisive. I watched, retaining vigilance and attention as over several seconds, that creeping pathway of thought, which was just straining at the reins to possess me, declined, reasserted itself briefly, declined again and petered out. The feeling stuck around because that's what feelings do but I didn't mind that, I knew from experience that a groundless feeling would fade fast, now that the thoughts that supported it had been denied. It was successful and in that instant, without any evaluation or drama, I simply moved, the incident was over. This was a tactic I had been taught for managing the mind. It was powerful, effective and strong and had brought me freedoms. It was a culmination of an evolving knowledge and tapas that had all become clear when I was here once before at the fire table. He had put it in such penetrating words. I remembered the experience there and then, the memory of it still present in the breeze now blowing across that same fire table here on the veranda.

"Who is in charge of your mind Amelia? Is it you or someone else?"

"Shakti is in charge," I replied.

"Yes but whose mind is it?"

"Mine, I think."

"Of course it's yours, so be more direct. Never mind shakti, these thoughts moving right now, this mood that is upon you right now, whose mood is it?"

"Nature's."

"Look, there is a time for high Advaita and there is a time for the mechanics of life. Both are important. Don't give me Advaita answers now. In this conversation I don't want you to tell me it's all a dream; I want you to talk about senses, feelings, skin and blood, about actions, okay? Are you in charge of your own mind?"

"No."

"Why not?"

"Because it arises of its own accord, it is all happening by itself."

"Do you think you have understood this teaching?"

"Yes, it's all just happening, I am not the doer and it's all being experienced, I just let it be."

"You haven't understood it, Amelia. Your misunderstanding is a tragedy and carries a constant risk."

"What risk?"

"Passivity, an inability to overcome samskaras so that you cease to apply volition. Your mind becomes timid, your actions become small and you are at the mercy of random and intrusive thought waves."

"But you have taught me to live through experiences and not fight them, my sadhana is to experience and allow. Isn't that what surrender is?"

"At times, but that is an inadequate understanding and is neither complete nor applicable in all situations. Such a blanket approach is not surrender, it is defeat and that is your risk. To live through experiences is unavoidable and must be done with forbearance and faith as we have discussed but sometimes the mind needs to intervene upon itself. You need both abilities. There is something mind can do about any situation it experiences."

"But I am not the mind."

"But there is a mind and that mind has capabilities. The fact that it is not what you are, doesn't mean the mind disappears, does it? Mind continues to move and some of those movements require attention. You always need guardianship of the mind, Amelia, even when there is faith, even when there is realisation. This is darshan of the will; it is the essential companion to faith. You must understand them together and apply them both. Go and make tea. Bring those biscuits."

I followed his instruction and cooked up some Tulsi tea, feeling agitated. I would prefer not to think about this today, it all seemed too intellectual. Actually, I would prefer not to think at all and just be in the peace of things. In truth, this was causing some problems in my life, as so often there would be some event or self-doubt that ruffled my peace. I wanted to avoid those things and not experience them but I couldn't and that troubled me. It annoyed me that he had said "Bring those biscuits". I had brought a packet of chocolate biscuits in my pack, just as a treat, something nice amidst the austerity of the place but since his scowl on seeing them, I never had the nerve to get them out. Back at the table I poured the tea and put the packet of biscuits down between us. We sat with the steaming cups in silence over the fifteen minutes it took to drink them and toss away the dregs. Ram stood at the veranda rail looking out into the trees. I felt tense as he started to speak.

"The meditators seek tranquility of mind, good for them. Tranquility is an attainment and a pleasure but it is not freedom. Tranquility is a soothing and beneficial wave within your mind but how will you act when it is ruffled or invaded? Faith and recovery is one thing but what about intervention, what about action?"

The question lingered in the air and I felt that anticipation of energy as the atmosphere seemed to deepen, my senses became keener and distracting thoughts ceased. Sitting back at the table he looked straight into my eyes.

"Philosophers say there is no free will, nonetheless there is a real mental faculty of determination at your disposal. If the doctrine of no free will is poorly understood, it confuses action. The mechanics of mind are mobile and not fixed; your experience can be changed. You cannot choose which thought will arise but the progression of that thought and its impact is not pre-determined and the action you take influences the next thought. This is how mental mechanics change. Think of a habit, any habit."

"I don't know... Eating chocolate biscuits?" I said, mischievously.

"Good, a truly pointless habit I am sure you will agree but it is a good example."

"It's not pointless," I responded defensively, "it's just a simple pleasure, it tastes nice, I like chocolate biscuits."

"Ridiculous. You are not eating it because it tastes nice, it is eating you. You are eating it to avoid the discomfort of not having it."

"It's just a biscuit Ram."

"I know and they look so lovely don't they?" He opened the packet, took out a biscuit and ate it noisily. "It's just an example, eat it if you like. But similar examples are happening throughout your day, like an automaton within you that has been wound up and is going through its cycle. For small things like biscuits you may say, so what, pleasure is good and it doesn't really matter. I would agree but what about the bigger things that come to claim you; unwanted and invading, debilitating moods, unwelcome reactions, inhibiting ideas and restrictions, all these things that make mental life burdensome, aren't they habits too, and who is in charge of that? The truth is, most of the time nobody, because the moods have become in charge of you, just like chocolate biscuits." He offered me a biscuit. I shook my head.

"How much of your daily thought is new, fresh?"

"I am not sure; it depends on the day I suppose."

"Almost none of it is."

"That can't be right."

"It is right. Your mind is repetitive Amelia, the cycling and recycling of old reactions and it is like this for most. Maybe you have a familiar experience of feeling inadequate, it's just an example. It will manifest in you as a bundle of depressing mood and critical thought. Various incidents will trigger it and because they are all different you will pin it on the incident as the reason, but it's not the event itself that is being unfair to you, it's something stuck in you which is repeatedly unleashed by these triggers. Where is the new in that? Where is fresh experience? Where is the openness? It's all old habit. The absolutely new is rare and when it comes you know it as inspiration and exhilaration, you can feel the freedom in it, it's very thrilling. To enable the new, you must make space, making the mind spacious is essential for Self-realisation. Really all sadhana is about this and now I am giving you something big, it is an ally of the surrender and faith we have discussed but it has very different characteristics. We call it will. It is a sword of discrimination and determination to be wielded under your direction and at your command. Without the will, if you fancy a biscuit you would just respond to the impulse and get it. With some awareness in place you can objectify the desire but you might still get the biscuit because you choose to have pleasure. Then some intelligence in you becomes alive, you desire change and if you really commit to that change the will is how it happens, then biscuit has no chance. The mistake you could make because you are passive by nature and want to go with the flow, is to neglect that ability as being too forthright or mental. My teaching to you is don't go with the flow of oppressive habits, create new flows. This is not resisting event; this is changing the waves in the mind that respond to event and thereby bringing that same mind to spaciousness. Do you see the difference? People are doing it all the time in small ways but our conversation is nothing to do with small ways, this is about big ways. Giving up biscuits is one thing, changing mental states themselves is another. You are not in control of the events of your life but you can intervene in your thought and alter pathways of reaction; you can delete biscuit. The will is your agent Amelia, it deserves to be honoured, promoted and utilised in the greater purification of this mind, as I said to you, whose mind is it?"

Just as many things he said to me this took some assimilation. Could it be right? Wasn't it too simplistic? I felt he was saying to me, pull yourself together and I could feel myself resisting, I was still annoyed about the biscuits. But it was true, invading moods and worries were a nagging hazard. I seemed so susceptible these days, so sensitive. Was it possible to alter these events? I decided to try and not be defensive.

"Are you saying I can control my moods and feelings?" I asked.

"Let's not say control," he replied, "let's say command. You can't control but you can have powerful selective influence on what reaction you allow and what you do not allow; and not just reactions, memories, patterns of thought, redundant attitudes, in that sense you are in charge."

"Are you seriously saying people can just change their moods?"

"Not people Amelia. You! People are of all shapes and sizes. Obviously what I am giving you is entirely out of range for those entrenched in the common mind but that is not you. Because of your sadhana you have achieved those abilities described in Vedanta as detachment and dispassion; these words only mean objectivity, distance. You are capable of it Amelia, not people, you. I am giving an advanced sadhana of the mind to you. This is upgrade."

"But how on earth is it done? I can't imagine just changing my mood. How is it put into practice?"

"It is not complicated; it is the common sensation of being determined and acting on it decisively and with conviction. Often that simple capacity is neglected and cluttered by all kinds of doubts and hesitancy. Through this sadhana you honour that ability, recognise it and strengthen it, make it agile, make it fast. Instead of being a simple receiver and follower of the mental waves which come, you select which waves are allowed and which are not. It's thrilling isn't it, exciting, it's the vibrancy of sadhana, don't let a moment go by. This is darshan of the will and not the heart. You must be supple and capable in both and ignore neither. If you choose to feel and enjoy the pleasure of chocolate biscuit I will say nothing about it, eat ten if you like. But if you choose to not eat biscuit, then next time you want to pick one up, don't prevaricate, intervene instantly with your intent, don't do it and move on quickly, that is the action of will. A weak mind will continue to eat it anyway and feel bad about it. A strong mind will not pick it up but will miss it and regret it. A vital mind, a freedom mind, won't really care either way but will act in line with the will seamlessly. Be decisive in action Amelia; be vital, not for me, not for my pleasure but for you, for the continuing project ahead. You will face some challenges, biscuits are easy, moods and emotional responses are not. The insight is to not care, command over the thoughts is enough. If chemical agitations are running in your veins, bear them with good grace until they recede and they recede quickly if they are not supported and endorsed by the thoughts that created them. The thoughts are the target, remember that, don't worry about the feeling."

"But Ram, I am confused now, does that mean I am the doer then, after all?"

"No, you are not the doer but forget that, it's distracting and over-complicating. Every moment is full of the actions of doing and I am speaking to that intelligence in you which is the agent of that doing; that part of mind which can wield the tool of the will. One thing at a time Amelia. There is a higher sadhana beyond this which truly knows I am not the doer and is the ultimate solution to all experience, it is darshan of the witness, the doorway to Self-realisation. I will give you this master sadhana but now is not the time. Prior to it you need spaciousness and the discipline to create that spaciousness. You are doing that anyway through your tapas and other aspects of your sadhana and now I am adding to that and giving you an advanced tool. I am telling you straight that the witness will not work in the demands of an engaged life unless you have established greater command over the movements in the mind. Your mind is magnificent, its properties are immense, it deserves to be your constant friend and inspired companion, not your critic and not your enemy. Are these just words for you or are they invitations? I do not know if you understand the power of the teachings you are being given here today and I do not know what you will do with them. I believe you will apply and I pray for that application to flourish in you. Start small, give something up, change some habit, cease some attitude, next time a recurring negative memory attempts to rise or some regret tries to claim you, deny it, refuse it, send it packing. Achieve this and if all else fails, well just get upset with me and gorge on biscuits until you are sick."

He left the table and went around the back of the hut to the earth toilet. I took the biscuits along to the tethering rail and poured them on the ground for donkey. He sniffed at them, pawed at one or two and then went back to his hay, leaving the biscuits to the ants.

Despite the incident with the note on the door, my two nights in the hut passed peacefully and quickly. I was keen to return, rising early on the third day. Walking back through the woods I felt playful and full of energy, talking to Roly, thinking of inconsequential things, picking up sticks and calling to the birds. After an hour or two when there was some distance behind us, my mind fell into a pleasing introspection upon itself. This thing we call mind was the whole issue; the thoughts and feelings, moods, reactions and ideas were really where my life experience appeared. And what was this mind? It was a tool, an instrument, a set of abilities and faculties. It wasn't me but it was mine, my mind, my instrument to use as I pleased. This had seemed a revolutionary idea but now it seemed so simple and obvious. How could this have been missed? I knew now that movements are natural, that is what mind does when left to its own devices. Just as my muscles ached after a hard day's work in the garden, so my mind fretted when responding to some unwelcome or perceived provocation. I knew now that sattva did not only mean tranquility, it meant neutrality and that wasn't dependent on no movements but on something far more powerful, freedom and transcendence. These were my own words, the teachings described it differently as detachment and dispassion but I preferred my words, they were more meaningful to me. I knew it wasn't finished, it wasn't all done but my everyday state now had a new and exciting inner security, some real wisdom, resilience and capability. Ram's faith of the heart and darshan of the will was advanced and I had put it into practice with energy. It wasn't fighting with mind, it wasn't force, it was discipline and command. To fight is like a diplomatic negotiation, a dialogue of appeasement, pleading with mind for it to behave differently, railing against it when it doesn't, complaining, asking for mercy. Command is decisive, positive action. Just as the mother gives her definite boundaries to the child and does not yield because they are definite, so the commander directs the mind and does not yield. I was capable of denying unwanted thoughts, gathering myself and mastering my mood. I was capable of making choices and moving on quickly. I was capable of fast and new thought. I was capable of deleting habits. These were amazing things, wonderful things. I watched the world around me and noticed how rare these attributes seemed and what a treasure they were for those in whom they were established. Coming to this knowledge and experimenting with the teachings that had been given to me in everyday life had been challenging, revealing and exciting. Sadhana was a joy and a wonder, the miraculous amidst the ordinary. My life is perfect.

Since before dawn Ram had been on his knees burning camphor in the temple and watching the flame. This was his only preparation for the days ahead. Intense activity was taking place all around the valley, in the animals and the plants, the river, the air and the earth but not in the heart of Ram. This is what he had to convey to Amelia when she returned, the spaciousness of that motionless heart in which activity and thought moved splendidly and with affectionate ease. His task now was to show Amelia what God is. He knew it was what she wanted and it was what he wanted to give to her. It was the purpose of the sadhana. So much of their history together had been husbandry of the mind, explaining things, tackling things, responding to things, clearing things. This was inevitable but she had gained knowledge now, she had some ability to be the ruler of the mind rather than its servant and he knew she had sufficient resilience to continue with what was left to be done. Her milestone had been realising her mind was an instrument rather than being her. Just as with all instruments, mind needs to be tuned and mastered; such had been her sadhana of late. The simple fact that mind was an instrument and not me was a revelation to many and a revolution to some. Life after life had to be dedicated to this discovery and now because of her intensity and maturity, the time was ripe. He could show her the space in which mind moved, he could show her God. They were in the valley for that purpose alone and he was ready for her. As the camphor smoke curled upward, Ram did his solitary puja. There was no content to it and no sounds to convey, his puja had evolved to be only joy; the enjoyment of the feeling of existence.

Donkey stood at his rail. He knew it was home and he was pleased to be back. Walking in these woods had been his whole life for twenty years. He hadn't liked being away this time, the lean-to at the forest hut was not his home now, not the place to be and he hadn't felt safe there. It was good to return last night. There was something new in his blood and being in his stall was best, by the river with the sound of the water when he closed his eyes. Sleep was good here; he wanted to sleep and to be with the river, not to walk through the woods again now. The pain in his belly was a fire, he wanted to sleep. He watched the two figures as they moved from the roundhouse to the temple, her in the lead and he following behind. It was early morning; they didn't stop at the canopy as usual but went right up to the entrance. He watched with gentle eyes as they approached the door.

The wooden door of the temple moved easily on its hinges, it was wide, like half a barn door, a big opening for such a building that seemed small from the outside. There was a little vestibule with a water bowl cut into the stone and in front a curtain of plaited reeds. I felt apprehensive. This was an exciting moment. I stood still before the curtain waiting. Ram said nothing and made no move. I knew he was behind me and could hear his breath. The curtain rustled slightly from the breeze coming through the open door behind. Parting the trailing reeds with my hands I stepped forward. Instantly everything within me stopped. The atmosphere was physical. I was unsure for a moment what was happening but nothing was happening. It was a peerless, powerful peace and serenity and it was exquisitely shocking. A whimper left my lips, a puff from an unknown recess in my heart, responding to this space of such profound depth. A layer of purity previously unknown to me vibrated my mind. I turned to Ram for an instant with pleading eyes. He was tall, massive in his body, steady and stable, kindness flowing from his gaze and the purest affection in his soft, easy expression. He did not move. The room was completely empty; there was nothing at all, a small round chamber filled with light from the open space above. The roof went up through the hollow tiers above and into the apex, beautifully symmetrical. The floor was spotless; smooth, light stone pitted and aged, alive to the skin of my feet. In the centre, a raised circular platform protruded from the floor just a metre in diameter. I walked into the interior, a slow pradikshana around the small circumference, slow, stopping, slow again. The sounds of the valley outside floated through the space; the crows, the blackbird, the murmur of the stream, breeze rustling in the silver birches, just audible in the distance. At the platform I came naturally down to my knees touched it with gentle, hesitant fingers and closed my eyes. Time passed. I felt myself to be in a conscious fullness, vital, immense, intimate, beatitude. Time passed.

"What is this place, Ram?"

"The Cave of the Heart."

"You mean that which the Upanishads describe?"

"Yes. Hridayam."

My mind raced. Is it possible, could this really be some Vedic jewel of mysticism and mystery here in this old forest, was this actually 'The Cave of the Heart'? Was this Hridayam?

"This is the cave from the Upanishads?"

"Yes."

My goodness. The Cave of the Heart, this temple, my goodness. I looked at him, astonished. What did it mean? Is he the guardian of this place, the keeper and now he is revealing it to me like Galahad? My mind began to spin with excitement. I looked around more forensically at the stonework and the architecture, studying the space. Incredible! I must record this, describe it. This is a world-class treasure, who built it, how can it be used? I ran my hands over the central platform scanning it for marks. Wow! This is fantastic! Sitting down on the platform's smooth edge I turned to Ram ready to shower him in thanks and ask all my questions about the provenance of this place, but one look at his expression stopped me in my tracks, just as effectively as if I had been knocked down. A simple, tiny amused turn of his mouth and a little boy amazement in his eyes spoke a whole language instantly.

"It's not true, is it?" I said, deflated.

"It's absolutely, wholly true and these last few moments are its perfect confirmation."

"So this is The Cave?"

"Yes, The Cave is real and The Cave is here but it's not the room, it's you."

My breath came in a big wave, long and deep. My belly heaved, sobs fell from me, falling and tumbling. Prior to the mind, before the projection of thought, in the purity of the spacious natural radiance that was so present moments before, that, and that alone, is The Cave and it was my own Self.

The days that followed were perfect living, full of bright simplicity and abundance, puja inside the temple, being with Roly, tending the garden, cooking for my Guru and meditating in the moonlight. Each morning the early air enthused the space with a fresh vitality. There was a clarity to it, cleaner than I had ever experienced. The sharp cold of morning prickled my skin and expressed in the out-breath of donkey, mists steaming off his coat and dispersing into the hugeness of the space. Even though the valley was quite modest in its length and breadth, it seemed so big now, growing in dimensions. The very molecules in the air seemed excited as if they were chattering sacred mantras, whispering in my ears. To move my fingers and my face through this open sky, to flex my limbs and place my feet was as if responding to a lover. River murmured with constant voices, splashing, burbling and singing a raga to the day in joy of its own motion. The light graced each second with a show of such exquisite subtleties, such shades and nuance, such sparkle and mood, such brightness, its depth astonished me. At night even the blackness held this same richness, there was nothing empty about it. I didn't think of myself at all, that was the thing that was so very different, I only enjoyed and experienced in generosity, gratitude and such gaiety, laughing. The crows were hilarious. A red squirrel had been scampering hesitantly each afternoon by the rhododendron hedge near the roundhouse. I gave him oats and sat with him, talking to him, tempting him to me. This morning he sat on his haunches no more than a metre away, chewing the oats and flexing his elegant pointy ears with a cuteness that brought giggles bubbling out of me with a force. It startled him and he sat up so abruptly that I burst with laughter, sending him scampering back to the cover of the bush. My-oh-my! This moment is fabulous, divine, a peerless perfection of fullness and presence. I knew it was me; there was something here happening in me that was knowing differently, seeing differently, something wonderful.

Each morning Ram sat by himself for an hour on Swan Rock by the waterfall. On the fifteenth day I went and joined him. I wanted to speak to him about my enthusiasm and perception.
"This is so lovely," I said, poignantly.
"Yes," he replied, "everywhere is like this in its different ways, you just have to know it and have some capability to see it. You have some freedoms now Amelia, as a result of your sadhana and you have knowledge. It is a powerful combination and as a consequence there is expansion and openness in you."
"What's happened to me?" I asked.
"This is the spaciousness I have been speaking to you about. You

stopped. It is deep and meaningful to stop and when you do, spaciousness is there. To really stop is profound and rare. Everyone feels the routine benefits of stopping in times of happy relaxation, that is simple stopping. You have gone beyond that; you have ceased projecting yourself and are therefore relieved of that weight. Because you have stopped the projection, The Cave of the Heart which is the Self becomes free of its walls, then it is no longer a cave at all, it is space, all this. It can be understood as love."

I sat beside him in silence with the water bubbling around us and thought about what he had said. How rare it was to stop, even superficially. From the moment I woke up, my days were either taken up with some stimulation, desire or pursuit, or my mind was dull. My mind was always engaged either seeking activity or wanting distraction from the dullness. Some of this was a consequence of a busy life but how much of it was also my own habit? I knew I could cease activity when I had the chance, I was good at relaxing but there was something more here that was being revealed. He was talking about a possession of attitude that I carried around with me, like a weight of differing density, a thickness of mind, a state of mood and thought, me. This is what he meant by projection. I didn't notice Being because I was preoccupied with this content of mood and mind. It was this that had coarsened my nature, it was this that was my burden and now that the content had fallen away, my mind was not the same; some underlying and long-standing tension had dropped. I understood what he meant by the word, spacious.

"What has been in the way of this space Ram, what has been obscuring it all?"

"Habits and attitudes of mind, commentary and concept, all the things we have been discussing, that is the projection. To experience as you are now can only happen when you have transcended the possessive stream of attitudes, concerns and persistent habits that otherwise claim your reality. You need to think differently and see differently, it requires subtleties of sadhana just as you have been experiencing. It all arises as a consequence of your efforts when you are capable and when it is time. Now is your time, Amelia."

This was my time. I felt it as a thrill. Since those sadhanas of the mind had become so central and effective in me, something new had been happening and this was its impact. This was a real shift in the architecture of things. I had stopped allowing the invasion of my mind, amazing. I had never before thought I could do that. Never before had I known such ongoing, natural ease and I could not think of anyone I knew who demonstrated it quite like this. How could we have come to such a condition of ignorance?

"How can it be like this for people, Ram, why is it like this?"

"It is Kali Yuga, Amelia, the age of density is prominent when minds are thicker, more distracted, the world is complicated and demanding but never mind the age, you can extract yourself from anything, even the deepest entrapment and such is sadhana. The levity is always there, spinning in the physics of things. It is the dense quality of the common mind that doesn't see it but there is always hope and possibility. The radiance of God is never diminished, even in the darkest of circumstances there is always and forever a light to reach for. The most crucial thing is to constantly pursue the potential of your perception, to use this life and your time for that, rather than spending decade after decade in distraction. Did you make any spiritual resolutions Amelia?"

"Yes."

"Good and are you remembering them, living them out, fulfilling them?"

"Yes."

"Then that is all that is needed, a continuous liveliness and enthusiasm for sadhana and spiritual discovery, constant freshness, always enquiring and developing to greater subtleties, greater knowledge. You should not see your goal as some transcendental samadhi which rejects the interplay of the world, you should see it as increasingly clear intimacy whereby God is known within and expressed through a polished and clean lens. The goal is to constantly walk up to your edges, explore those edges and push beyond, to keep walking forward towards knowledge of God."

"Ram, what amazes me here is that my sight hasn't changed, it's the very same looking, everything is familiar and quite ordinary in that way. My body hasn't changed, my senses haven't changed but there is a new property here. I feel it most keenly."

"You are not experiencing separation, that is what feels different. Don't see this as an esoteric mystery. It's oneness, openness, no sides. It's ordinary for you because you are ready for it. It would be extraordinary for others who would be threatened and afraid of it, disturbed by it because for many, the walls surrounding the cave are territory they do not want to relinquish. I know you can't understand that but that's the way it is. You need sadhana to transcend the content, see beyond the habits and stop the projections. This is the radiance of ananda Amelia, I want to be sure you understand that. It is integral to life just as the senses and awareness are integral to life but perception of it is not constant. Ananda is only reflected in a sattvic mind. The evidence of your own spiritual practice is proof of this; ananda does not reflect in rajasic and tamasic states. You cannot eliminate these gunas and that is what you have been learning but you can gain sufficient command to diminish their prevalence so that they become weaker, less frequent and lose their influence. The default condition of your mind is sattva, then ananda is experienced naturally. That is how you feel God, through the ananda. Let devotion become your sadhana now, it won't be an effort, it will be natural in the presence of this. Bring the Bhakti to the Jnana. This is the Beloved, Amelia, this air, this sky, this place and time and skin and mind. Find the real meaning of devotion, that is what to do now. The fact you have strived for this and pursued your goal with persistence is very beautiful to me and deserves honouring."

He cupped his hands and took water from the pool, dribbled it over my head, touched his wet index finger to my forehead, formed his palms into namaskaram, gazed into my eyes and bowed. It was an action of exquisite purity that trembled my heart. That night I stayed in the temple, sometimes sleeping, sometimes not. It was utterly silent, the only sound being in my own ears like the rushing of the sea in a conch shell. This temple was full of forces, the witness of billions of memories, incidents and events yet she radiated a pure and childlike lightness of being, that was peerless in its kindness and security. And she was a she, I was certain of that. I rested with her as the mother, nestled amidst that. We were good together, temple and me.

Meeting God

It was 7:00am and Ram was cooking the porridge on the open fire outside the roundhouse. The morning was cold, the air dense. He had predicted a storm the previous day saying that the wind had changed and the moisture content in the air was high. I was full of energy, feeling exhilarated after my refreshing night. The world was awake with natural beauty despite the gloomy sky. I was inspired and eager and had a big question on my mind. We ate the porridge, cleared away and sat with Bush tea by the fire watching the mists as they cleared.

"Ram, what is God?"

"That's a very big question. There are many easy and contrite responses but none of them are applicable for you anymore. We must share an original and full answer between us. Let's walk."

We went up to the ridge where I had first arrived and sat on the rock that formed a small cliff looking down onto the temple, the roundhouse and Roly's stall. It looked like heaven to me even though the skies seemed to be darkening. We chanted the mantra 'Om' into the space; tears filled my eyes and my lips quivered. There was nowhere else I would rather be, not anywhere in the world.

"Look at all this Amelia, how can it be explained? It is said that this entire cosmos with its multiple universes stretching everywhere, is only a fraction of Brahman. What you are seeing before you is what we mean by God, all this variety, expression and abundance, the whole manifestation; above, below and all around. God is the entire appearance."

"You mean nature?"

"Call it nature if you wish, it is better to call it existence or reality and better still to name it, Beloved. The power of this appearance is immensity beyond your comprehension and at the same time shines within as living presence, closer than your own thoughts. God is the majestic potency that creates and destroys stars and also that which vibrates as your very Being, sweeter than the most touching human kindness. We can say some very confident things about this experience but even our finest understanding and our deepest feeling is only an aspect of the vastness. What God is, must be left as an open wonder in your mind."

"But then who is God, does God have a face, is God a person?"

"Such a naïve question for you Amelia but a question well put nonetheless, a question that occupies the minds of many. God is not a person but the power of God is deeply felt as intensely personal. God is pure consciousness, the source of the entire universe which means the source and essence of you, it is impossible for that to be impersonal. The significance of this is so great that human culture has a deep need to understand it and reach out to it through religion and science, ideas and investigation. As such, God has many faces and many names. But whether you conceive of God as a particular form or as formless, this intimacy is definite, tangible and perceived, full with affection, familiarity, closeness and love, purity is its character. Even a sceptic would not deny these attributes are accessible within the best of human experience. The difference is, a sceptic would say these are my feelings and my attainments, whilst the sadhak would say they are divine presence. That difference is big; it is the difference between ignorance and realisation. The great spiritual discovery proclaimed in the Upanishads and verifiable through your tapas is that the being that you feel as yourself and the Being that you perceive as God is the same Being. Not the thoughts, Amelia, I don't mean that, not the habits and attitudes and all the things we have been discussing relating to the little mind, that is not God but the Being itself is. That is Atman and Atman is Brahman. Do you see the significance of that? Coming to know this as absolutely real, through your sadhana and realisation, is the most beautiful life-changing spiritual reality. The intimacy is then known as so present and full that it becomes unreasonable to call it he or she or it, except for convenience of grammar or to enable devotion."

"So how do I name God?"

"In awe and wonder, in delight and reverence, calling upon any of the revered and established names or aspects of nature, just as you choose. It is all one God. It's all a question of what you see, your spiritual qualities and what your capabilities are; it's a journey of maturity like a road. Before the starting point, God is rejected completely with suspicion and even distaste. Then a signpost comes into view and God is acknowledged but neglected. Then God is up there somewhere as a person in the sky or contained in an external deity. Then God is inside within the heart. Then, God is everything. From form to formless and then form again. You cannot say any of these modes is right or wrong. It is a framework of spiritual maturing and it is a progression from distance to nearness, separation to oneness. Knowing the Being within and without to be all God and to also be what I am, is the experience of Advaita. This is absolutely real. Not knowing it is ignorance, knowing it is Self-realisation. The space between those two states is sadhana, awakening and Self-discovery."

"So is it impossible to actually define God?"

"No, not at all, the Upanishads provide the definition, it is deeply profound."

"What do the Upanishads say?"

"God is existence, consciousness, infinity. Not finite Amelia, just dwell upon that word 'infinity' and feel its weight. It means all-pervading everywhere in and as everything, limitless in space and limitless in time, without boundary, not confined in anything yet reflected in everything. And the power of existence, what is it? Well, we don't know, we can't specify it but it is apparent all around and cannot be denied. Every particle, every motion, everything, everywhere has this power of existence as its nature. You may say this valley upon which we look exists but it is better to say, here is existence being a valley. Do you get that, Amelia, do you feel its excitement? Existence is an unfathomable power, generating everything and that existence itself is what God is, both the creation and the created. And then there is consciousness, knowing and awareness, constant and flooding everything; including you, the dynamic eternal nature of your very Being. This consciousness is what God is also, shining in all sentient things. Isn't that amazing and isn't that beautiful? Every object exists and that existence itself is God. Every object is known to you and that knowing itself is God. These arguments can be flawlessly made using shining logic and intelligence. If you were a sceptic you may want to raise all kinds of arguments but that has been done in philosophical debates of the highest standing for thousands of years and this Upanishadic definition stands up to challenge. It is sensible to take doubts no further so as to not waste time and to accept deep in your mind that God is existence-consciousness-infinity. This is not a religious proposition Amelia, this is nature. God is big."

"Ram, that is inspiring and I do see its magnificence; it is big, so grand, it seems too distant to reach. What about me and my life? Where is God for me now, sitting on this ground, breathing and thinking and feeling and wanting? Infinity is frightening."

"Some may say frightening; others would say inspiring, even comforting. What is it about this that feels distant to you? Existence and consciousness aren't distant, how could they be? It's the most intimate and immediate thing possible, do you see that? You are this same existence. It's you here and now, everything you sense and experience but you are right, the definition is grand because it's the essence of the whole cosmos and to stop at that point is not the whole story."

"Oh good, so what is missing?"

"Taste. You may know a strawberry is made of existence and consciousness but in addition to knowing that, there is experience. The taste could be described chemically but that would not convey strawberry, it would not describe experience. God is feeling, Amelia, not a thing out there. It is felt experience within that, that brings the tangibility of God, intimate, personal and close. All this," continued Ram, spreading his arms, "the Beloved, is manifest here before your eyes in all these forms and in the seeing and knowing and feeling of it."

"But that is true for all, everyone exists and sees nature yet God is not seen by all."

"And there you are, that is your answer. A tree is either a tree or it is the Beloved expressing as a tree. The difference between the two is a difference in perception and sensitivity, this is sadhana. With perception awakened and knowledge in place, the tree still appears as tree visually but the experience is not the same. There is a flavour to tree, a taste; a vibrant beauty. It is not contained in the tree, it is in you, in your experiencing. The experiencing itself is the Beloved and becomes known in you as divine. This is a very high mystical point Amelia. You must dwell upon it, meditate upon its profound and revealing meaning, for I tell you this point is a true doorway. It isn't something you can make happen through your will. This is not darshan of the will; this is the realisation of the heart. The capacity to see anything at all is existence, the capacity to know anything at all is consciousness, but the capacity to recognise the taste and experience that taste is the glittering property of ananda. That is how God is experienced, through the ananda. Just as the taste of strawberry communicates the essence of strawberry so ananda communicates the experience of the Beloved. Then your vision is awake and then the rocks, the trees, the air, the temple, the night and day, the sun, moon, grass and the river, you and me, is all the shimmering Beloved. You haven't changed the nature around you but you are seeing more of nature than you saw before. Once you grasp that and begin to see the wonder in it, then you are able to experience God, not view God but experience God. Truly knowing this Amelia, seeing it as so, is how oneness is experienced. It is the very definition of oneness. Coming to that position with obstacles transcended is sadhana and that you have done."

I looked out over the scene before me. Mists were now gathering on the opposite side of the valley and the air was cold, the damp air settling on my skin. The whole experience fizzed within me and around me in all its detail. It was as if I was in the finest, purest current of meditation yet with eyes open, mind functioning, thoughts moving, senses alive and enthusiasm running through my mind.

"How do you feel here and now?" Ram asked.

"Wonderful, beautiful, happy."

"And what do you want to do with that wonder?"

"Enjoy it, be with it, express it, communicate it, stay with it."

"And that points you in a direction."

"You mean something to do?"

"Rather, something to be, but yes, doing also."

"What is it?"

"Devotion. As I said to you, the direction of your sadhana now is devotion. From knowledge to devotion. Jnana and Bhakti are inseparable as if they are married and living in one another."

"What is my devotion then? Is it ritual, is it prayer, how do I apply devotion?"

"Prayer and ritual are actions that express devotion but they are not what devotion is. Devotion is an attitude. Gratitude is its character. You want to give gratitude and you want to give it generously because you are filled with affection and excitement about the wholeness and beauty of this; the day, the moment, the space, the air, the speech, the face of the person in front of you. You are feeling the power and presence of the Beloved because you are noticing it. Devotion is noticing; it is natural worship. Do you see Amelia? Puja is your song to God, prayer is your communication with God, sadhana is alignment to God but I am giving you something else now, something very powerful and precious. I am telling you what enlightened devotion is and it is noticing, seeing the beauty, appreciating it, knowing it, and praising it through your recognition. If that sounds simple then look deeper and realise how rare that is and how often that is not how it is in you because of defences and thickness and all the concepts of the mind that we have been discussing. Devotion is an attitude; it is the attitude of the enlightened. Look around, see how amazing existence is at every turn, see the abundance, feel the power and the beauty, see the expression and the creativity. This is all the Beloved. Nature is God and nature is everything."

"Including pain?"

"Ah, yes, including pain."

"And suffering?"

"Ah yes, and suffering."

The storm itself began to build around 4:00pm, just as the daylight was due to change but this change was not regular at all. It had been thickening all afternoon, darkening, blacker and blacker over the eastern tree line, the air heavy with threat. Donkey had been restless for a while but was now calmly standing at his post inside the stall. The birds had quietened and there was no sign of the deer. I had experienced storms at Bowslip before but this one did look pretty black. Ram was cautious; the meteorological portents were troubling him and he had stopped communicating with me other than giving orders.

"If the wind comes in strong it will power down the valley and if the stream goes in flood, it will make a route down the spillway over there, so make sure everything is out of its path and all the structures are tied tight."

We worked hard clearing away all the unfixed objects and implements from around our area, bringing them inside. The roundhouse itself was very strong but even so we had put tethers over the finials and had spent two sweaty hours with the mallet hammering in ash stakes and tightening tethers. A thick heavy tarpaulin that was normally folded away on the roof of Roly's stall had been unrolled and secured with its eighteen-inch metal spikes into the earth. The skin had created two solid walls facing the wind and seemed as strong as masonry. All the hammering had hurt my hands which were fizzing and throbbing as I leaned on Roly's rail and massaged them. I stayed with Roly, talking to him, sweeping out his stall and soothing him. The rain started about 9:00pm as we were preparing for bed. It was noisy on the roof as I snuggled up and thought how nice it was to listen to the rain from the safety of this place and the snugness of my bed. When I looked at the clock again it was 12:30am. I had been awakened by the most offensive, violent, rending sound and a shattering, piercing light that bolted me out of sleep as if I had been attacked. Violence, flash and crash, volcanic crack after crack exploding everywhere, dominant and vile, as loud as agony above the already deafening attack of the rain pounding, spiking and hammering on the roof and walls. I sat up in acute fear and threat, lightning searing the space as bright as the sun. Ram was up, positioning cooking pots under the streams coming through the roof; it would be only moments before they were full. Above all the cacophony a new sound built, quickly forming itself, groaning in decibel and prominence, possessing the air with grinding, splintering violence.

"It's the river!" said Ram, shouting at the very top of his voice.
"What about Roly?" I cried, standing up and going to the door. Outside it was a solid sheet of water as if the waterfall was upon us.
"Roly!" I cried out and could barely hear my own sound.
The walls were moving now, the pots overflowing. Ram was placing buckets and all the vessels we had to try and contain it but it was overwhelming.
"Roly!" I shouted and looked at Ram.
He came to the door and grabbed me, shouting in my ear.
"You cannot go out, it's impossible. You will die in this; you cannot go out."
"Roly!" I screamed into the unyielding anger of the night.
The walls were vibrating, oscillating like drum skins. I couldn't move for fear, I watched Ram rushing about picking up things and throwing them on the table and the beds. The roar from the river increased to a constant thunder, the roundhouse was shaking. I grabbed hold of Ram tight as tight and screamed at the top of my voice. I couldn't even hear it against the onslaught, demons were upon us.

The clock said 6:30am and I was exhausted. The rain had been dying down for an hour and was now softening by the second. Six hours, we had experienced six hours of this hell. The roof leaks had stopped and for the past hour Ram had been dealing with the pots and sweeping the water out of the door. It was a muddy, broken mess. When he was done he came to me and sat in front of me tenderly; it was obvious he knew what I was thinking.
"You could not have gone out Amelia, you would have died. That is the most violent storm that we have ever had here, it's bigger than weather, you could not have gone out. Come on."
I didn't speak. We went together to the door and stepped outside. The temple was as solid as ever and unchanged, the copse all intact but the section of land between us and the hillside was destroyed.

The river had swept through the spillway and smashed the meadow in-between to mush, it was a devastation of stone and earth and mud. My heart was exhausted like dying embers and a clawing, stabbing feeling twisted in my chest. The stall had gone. There was nothing, no posts, no stakes, no railing, the whole structure had vanished. Oh Roly!

"Where is he?" I asked, pleading.

"He will have gone with the river."

"But he might have gone to the other side, behind the temple for shelter."

"No, he will have stayed by his stall; he will have gone with the river." He gathered some tools and rope and strung them between two poles along with his mallet. We positioned the poles between us like bearers and picked our way through the stones and mud onto firmer ground and then made off down the river. The waters were calming by the minute, the difference between now and just a few hours ago was hard to understand. Things were coming back. The birds were singing, the sky lightening, the cloud dispersing. We walked for fifteen minutes, the load was heavy and I had to keep adjusting the pressure on my shoulders. As we turned the bend I stopped. Up ahead was Roly, prone and still, bedraggled amidst the sunken river bank, his limbs all angular and askew. My body trembled, I was traumatised, assaulted.

"Put down the poles Amelia."

He went ahead and knelt with Roly, I followed and came to his side, squatting down and placing my face into the coarse and soaking fur of his lifeless body. Roly. We sat there in the mud in the morning as the sun broke through the remnants of grey, dark skies and I wailed, deep and shattering.

The next two days were lonely ones in the valley. My grief and anxiety were big. It was hard to see any beauty at all or have any motivation; something just seemed broken, ruined and jagged.

There was only despair, there was only pain. Ram left me mostly alone as he busied himself down at the creek, building his platform for Roly. At dawn on the third day he instructed me to forage, sending me for specific plants and various grades of wood, getting me to fetch tools and hold timber as he tethered it. I just wanted to lie down somewhere and sink into nothing but he did not let me, giving me constant orders. By midday the main work was done. He had built a ramp and a contraption of hoists and pulleys over a tall A-frame connected to a raised platform, standing strong about a metre above the meadow. It had been industrial labour. Beneath it were the piles of stick and brushwood that I had gathered. He positioned me on the second rope and counted down. Together we pulled in sequence. Roly moved, sliding along the ground which he had cleared of stone and made smooth. Donkey was heavy and large, his dead-weight unyielding but the pulley structure took the strain and the effort was small. His body slid onto the platform. Ram disconnected all the ropes and contraptions tidying them away, making the place clear and neat. I was given the broom and rake and swept all around so that the earth was smooth and clear. We spent the afternoon in the temple. Ram was meditating and saying his mantras, I just sat nearby, sometimes laying on the floor, sometimes snoozing, just being quiet with my sadness, drifting in and out of sleep to the sound of the mantras and the silences in between; it was comforting to not think.

I awoke feeling brighter; it was 6:00pm. We ate nothing, washed in the river, changed clothes and went to the platform. Ram gave me the herbs to sprinkle on Roly and I climbed up and spread them over his body, then we crushed kilos of camphor and piled mounds of it on top of the herbs, then flowers on top of that. It smelt beautiful. Roly was transformed, he looked like a garland. Ram said the sweetest prayer in homage to Roly and the tears flowed from me like a stream. They were not jagged now but flowing more freely, honouring the passing of beloved Donkey. Ram blew the conch and began ringing his bell and I lit the kindling under the platform. It took quickly, the flames built and washed around the structure. The bell was continuous, deep, loud notes. I threw more camphor and flowers until we had to step back as the platform and Roly were consumed in the intensity of fire and heat, illuminating the darkening sky like moonlight. We cast our mantras and prayers into the roar and crackle.

Ram was not there when I woke in the hut the following morning. I had journeyed through contented dreams and felt refreshed. When I went to find him he was waiting for me at the funeral pyre. He had tidied things up, cleared away all the remnants and created a large pile of crushed ash. We gathered it with our hands and transferred it onto a fresh orange cloth. Picking up the four corners, we moved to the river and sprinkled it onto the water. It was a big pile and our sprinkling was slow. Nothing was said. The murmur of the eddies and the sunlight reflecting upon the ash in the water were comment enough. When it was done Ram cut up the cloth with his knife and we threw the shreds into the water, moved back to where the ash pile had been and worked the residue into the earth with our feet.

"Breakfast?" he declared.

"Yes, breakfast."

I hadn't eaten since yesterday morning and was hungry. Sitting by the fire replete with porridge and fruit, I made tea and we talked about Roly. He had been Ram's companion for twenty years and they knew each other like closest family; they had cleared the valley together. Ram explained to me that Roly had been ill for a long time, was tired and in pain. He wanted to sleep, he wanted to move and change. The walk back to the hut with me had been his final expedition and was the purpose of me being sent away.

"Do not feel sorry for Roly, he was the greatest master of acceptance I have ever known. Do not be afraid of the drama or the violence of his death. Neither of us knew how it would be but we knew it would be something. To be consumed by storm and flood and thunder and water would be like a mass for him. You may not understand but I know that Roly would have found joy in it."

It had been five days since the storm, things had been very quiet. There had been very little communication between Ram and me. I had spent my time in and out of the temple and wandering around the valley like a rootless child. A depression was upon me and I had chosen to allow it, rather than trying to understand or change it, I was aware this was my choice. I sat on the hillside for many hours so that the deer came to accept me, coming closer and closer each day. I fed squirrel and the crows and cooked in the evenings, all the time reflecting on this reality all around, my life and all that had happened. A principal question was present in my mind and had gained force and urgency. It was early evening in the roundhouse with supper cleared away and the air humming with spiritual intensity that I broke the silence between us.

"These days have been hard, Ram."

He looked at me so sweetly before responding.

"Yes, these days have been hard."

"The vision you have given me of God is magnificent and wondrous. Just being here with you and in this place it is apparent to me that this whole manifestation truly is the Beloved. But that is everything and there is nothing outside of it. If that is so, it means God is the flood, the destruction, the fear, the death of Roly and these miserable hard days. How can this be understood? Where is God in this sadness?" "The sadness is your own, Amelia, it is a state of mind and not a living thing and you now have a lot of intelligence about states of mind but because of what you have been through it's understandable. As caring, compassionate people, we reach out to one another in such times. Would you like some chocolate biscuits?"

It seemed such an inappropriate thing to say. I looked up expecting to challenge him for being so insensitive but he had such a mischievous and playful expression and a lightness of being, that all I could do was smile. It broke the mood profoundly. He looked at me quizzically and I chuckled in response. I wouldn't have thought it possible as my dense mood had seemed so tight but there it was, I felt released, it was a magical and real shift.

"Don't underestimate your abilities Amelia, because I never do. You are really asking me the great religious challenge. If all this is God why is there suffering in life?"

"Yes exactly, how can it be like this, both glorious and terrifying? How can there be such contrast?"

"It is how nature is. Suffering is inherent in this existence; it is the common experience of all. Pleasure and pain are one of the dynamics we experience in this world. Just as there is light and dark and beginning and end so there is pleasure and pain. Sukha and dhukha have always been humanities' experience and no one is exempt from that. It's not a mistake, it's inherent in nature. You ask why, as does everybody at times. We cannot answer the question conclusively in a way that would satisfy you because we do not have the big picture. Do you understand that? It's such an important context. For you and for all, life is an experience amidst the unknown. You want things to be a certain way, to conform to your values but why should they? The fabric of nature is vast; it is not an experience subject to your design. Across the whole of the cosmos from atoms to stars, birds and bees, mountains and human beings, the forces of creation, preservation and destruction are the web of nature. God is explained by some as those very forces. Instinctively you want to gravitate towards preservation but instability, pain, disease and death is a biological given at times, storm, volcano, hurricane and flood will happen at times and anxiety, doubt and fear move within human experience at times. You must adapt to it, not it to you. You could ask why isn't nature configured differently so that it runs smoothly, without hazard? And I say to you, because this isn't heaven Amelia, or at least, not your conception of what heaven should be. If the nature of the cosmos does not fit with your expectations, then who is at fault, the universe or you? The ignorant rail against these things, complain and become indignant about the unfairness of God. The wise accept it as the drama of the world, look to their own actions, respond as needed and move forward quickly. Suffering is a teacher and a motivator; it gives impetus to your life and opportunities for change; it is a cause from which growth is an effect. This life is a place for living out your karma and suffering is a component of that in certain moments. You don't have to understand all its details."

"But some suffering just seems cruel and deeply unjust Ram, pain is such a burden, it is hard to accept that is also part of the Beloved."

"It is true that cruelty seems to be the character of some suffering and where you come across it either within others or in yourself, flood it with your kindness and compassion, your positive and loving thoughts, act spontaneously to aid and help. We are not passive, we are active, we can respond as I have been teaching you. But also know that suffering is a consequence of actions even if the causes are unknown or inexplicable to you. Suffering points out the nature of things, that there is impermanence and unpredictability, that there is selfishness and restlessness in the human mind, that there is obstacle and hardship to endure and overcome. Seeing these things spurs you on to bring out the charity in you, to transcend selfishness in yourself, to adopt generosity of spirit and reach out towards greater and greater spiritual discovery."

"So God is the suffering then as well as the beauty?"

"Ultimately yes but thinking that too literally will confuse you and is not the way to know it. Notice how strongly the motivation is in you to align with positive and loving forces. Those forces are stronger, more massive and more eternal than apparent suffering. The suffering is temporary, the eternal is not. There is no suffering in pure consciousness; there is suffering in body and mind.

Alignment to the light is to be faithfully followed even in the presence of destructive forces. The more you do that, the more you free yourself. Throughout human history people have characterised this duality as the battle between good and evil, or selfishness and selflessness, there is nothing new about it. You cannot change that in the environment but you can change it in yourself. The little mind of man is not God, the Being in which that little mind moves, is. For the purposes of sadhana that is the way to understand it. Perhaps we could say the hardware is God, the operating system is God, the electricity is God but the programme running within that is a mixture of God and you. Sadhana is deleting the inherited content of you so that it is all God and you and God are the same. If you shine a light through a rough diamond it will be murky and dense, if you cut and polish the diamond and shine the same light it will sparkle and glitter and reflect beauty. The same light is shining in both scenarios and that is God. The changing structure of the diamond that reflects the light is Jiva, the polishing is karma sadhana. You are the diamond Amelia, polishing yourself as are all human beings, either knowingly or unknowingly. One of the agents that stimulate such polishing is suffering. Take heart in the face of setback and pain, nature is not your enemy but in this life you are part of nature and amidst its physics. Change, storm, death and loss are part of those physics as are stability, beauty, birth and life. This is the knowledge that Roly knew. It is all the mysterious abundance of God. Don't let these concerns distract you from the very real experiences you are having in the reality of your own heart. Focus on that, focus on the cave, focus on devotion, this is the direction to take."

For the rest of the day I got on with things around the roundhouse, fed the deer and pottered about in the rhododendrons looking for squirrel. In the afternoon I visited Roly's cremation site and threw some flowers into the water. I knew I could not be in control of the movements of things and that was alright, it was really alright. A great peace came into my mind as I squatted by the river, a deep acceptance of what is. Just as the water flowed, I was content to be with the river of life. Tomorrow I would leave, all that needed to happen here for now was done. I had an enormous amount to assimilate and my place for that was amongst the circumstances of my life and the people of my life.

"Thank you." I said out loud to the space, "Thank you for my life, for all its parts, for the people, for the experience and for you. It is utterly amazing and utterly perfect."

Just as the sunset radiance was beginning to build in the sky Ram came and joined me at the riverside sitting silently beside me. I closed my eyes and was acutely aware of the sound of the bubbling water, the taste of the air entering my nose and the presence of my Guru by my side.

"Describe how you are feeling Amelia."

"Open, happy and unconcerned."

"And how is your mind?"

"Spacious, free and content."

"And in your body?"

"Alive, fizzing with subtle ecstasy."

"How does the space appear to you?"

"Bright, magnificent and fresh."

"And how is your heart?"

"Loving and full, not alone."

"Where is your edge, Amelia?"

"I don't know."

"What is your biggest, most overriding sensation?"

"Intimacy."

"What is the river?"

"This intimacy."

"And your skin?"

"This intimacy."

"And your senses?"

"This intimacy."

"What do you want to do now?"

"Whatever happens."

"This is God, Amelia, this is God. You need no Samadhi beyond this, this is God."

For the last time that evening we sat in the temple and chanted. Ram had brought garlands and told me to sit on the platform as he sang and rang his bell. There was nothing serious about it and it became hilarious and wonderful fun.

"The temple has been waiting for a new goddess and you are my goddess after all, Amelia."

He threw flowers over me, sprinkled me with water and then drew me into his skipping, gyrating, clapping dance. We hugged, laughed like children and then walked along the river in the moonlight and talked happily about little things; my feelings for him, his feelings for me, funny memories from all the years of sadhana, anecdotes and adventures. Back at the roundhouse there was one last thing on my mind; it had been catching my attention at times over the last few days and now came forward like a footnote to my whole experience.

"I have only one question now Ram."

"Wow! Only one! What is it?"

"If my mind is an instrument, whose instrument is it?"

"Beautiful Amelia, that's perfect because the answer to that is the only answer I want to give you now. It is darshan of the witness, the master sadhana that I mentioned to you. For that, you need some more life to pass through you and we need some new arrangements between us. Bowslip is very large, you know, there are landscapes you have yet to see. When you are ready to come again we will travel and discover new things."

"Okay, that's fine by me."

And it was, it really was; I was content.

Chapter Six

Sakshi

twenty months later
approaching the forest gate

Self-realisation was the reason for my eager footsteps, that and happiness. An excited joy leapt in my chest as I approached the isolated perimeter gate and the two stone lions gracing the gate pillars came into view. Almost two years had passed since I had last been in Bowslip, a time of working, engaging with life and also longing for this. My richest and most exhilarating moments were enmeshed in what happened here and the astonishing encounters with my teacher. The gap had been at his insistence, I didn't want to accept it at the time but I had learnt that in such matters it was best to just apply faith.

"You don't know what you need," said Ram, "and neither do I but the actions that take place between us freely determine it. I am acting in that freedom and you are not, so whose voice do you think is the best vehicle for change? Free your mind and come to me in two Februarys, watch out for ghosts."

I knew his parting command to "Free your mind" was not a flippant remark, it was purposeful. I had taken it as a direction to be vigilant against negative thoughts and suppressive habits. The tactic I had learned from him of using the will to assert permissions over mental and emotional states was effective but it was not faultless. Sometimes I just didn't have the energy for it as I lost myself under some old cloud. I had noticed that where there was a new incident, it was not difficult to organise my thoughts and feelings positively and as I chose but where the mood was more pernicious and long-standing, clouds were thicker, habits seemed more persistent and harder to overcome.

Brambles curled around the mortar of the lintel framing the Lion Gate. The paint had peeled around the hinges exposing the flaking rust. Pulling the ivy away I inserted the key into the iron lock and turned the heavy handle pushing hard on the gate. The metal scraped over the ground squeaking and grinding, cracking the ivy curling around the frame. It seemed the gate could not have been opened at all since my last visit. I stepped inside. To get into Bowslip estate is easy with open public access off the main grand driveway, there are events and organised tours, people visit the Orangery, listen to lectures, attend yoga classes, walk in the formal gardens and have tea in the café. But that was somewhere off to the east where there were signposts and regular opening times. Walking through the Lion Gate, I was entering the wilderness of Bowslip; open grassland, ancient wild forest, a landscape of hills, valleys, rivers and streams that I now knew was truly vast. Although there was no hard boundary between the public gardens and where I stood, it seemed to me that almost no-one came here. It was like the hidden areas of mind ignored by most and explored by a few; I was proud to have the key to the Lion Gate.

With the gate closed firmly behind me I was alone and exposed. Immediately a feeling of being watched rose up sharply like an odour permeating a room. My eyes widened and my senses sharpened, something was not right. Is there someone here? A squirrel came onto the centre of the track fifty metres ahead and stood like a gargoyle on her haunches staring at me. Crows rustled in the high oak tree, cawing and arguing amongst themselves in mournful tones. My head shot up as squirrel screeched a primitive alarm call directly at me. Pulling tight on the straps of my pack to settle its weight, I hitched it up and stamped my foot, catching some of the leaf mould and kicking it into a cascade. Squirrel darted into the undergrowth; it was an easy conquest. Some of the other encounters ahead of me may not go so well. Above me the leafless skeletal canopy of the trees came together merging and twisting themselves into gothic, interlacing fingers like a procession way, a tunnel down which I must travel towards the hut sixty minutes away. Pacing out I made some distance giving my attention to the trill of the songbirds, the scent of damp forest, the tall trees, fallen boughs and fresh new saplings, displaying their vitality in the austere winter air. My belly trembled and my heart beat with a growing pressure of palpable unease. Looking back down the path, the perspective of the long walk funnelled into a mournful distant opening. Is that someone? Could I hear someone? The crows cawed hauntingly as the wild wood brooded. Fear rang in my nerves like a quivering bell. I must overcome this, distract myself, there were so many memories here of earlier times. I was on the very same track at the very same bend where years ago Ram had taken me by the shoulders, thrown me down onto the mossy bank and covered me in leaf mulch. He had met me by the Lion Gate when I was full of myself and my life outside. I had been talking in a long monologue, trying to impress him about how my life was devoted to sadhana, how I had organised my routine for daily practice and how well I was doing and he had just pushed me over with what amounted to a war cry.

"Get beyond it Amelia!"

It was an exciting memory now in retrospect but I remembered how insulted and angry I had felt at the time. The memory was intensely vivid like a lucid dream. Sitting down on that same mossy bank, the sounds around me blended into one as the memory replayed like a film on the screen of my mind.

"Get beyond it Amelia! This pride is stifling all the wisdom in you. All this experiencing is for children, the naïve and the weak. You assume you know yourself yet you have no idea how poor your insight is. You think your inner thoughts and intentions are private yet they move on you like chess pieces in a spotlight. I see you Amelia, I see all of you. You are like the actress who has become so consumed in her role that she thinks others believe she is real."

I was shocked and upset by his harsh words, rattled and put down; sitting there in the mush that he had physically pushed me into.

"But Ram I just want you to know me, I am not pretending, this is how I am."

"I might accept that statement from those who visit the Orangery on a Sunday afternoon for a yoga class but not from you striding here with me in the Brahma Vidya. Where is your discipleship Amelia, where is that plain gaze into the mirror unadorned?"

The damp had seeped messily into my trousers, the musty smell of rotting leaves rising around me. There was a second of anger, a second of indignation, how dare you! A fighter in me wanted to stand up and defend myself, I put my hands behind me about to push myself up but in that exact moment, just as my fingers were tensing, an immense wave of grief flooded my heart, possessing all the spaces in me, filling me with a dejection that crept so fast and powerfully. I pulled my knees towards me, bowed my head, squeezed my chest and fell over onto my side in the foetal position. Ram plunged into the mulch, grabbed me with two strong arms and pulled me onto the path and onto my feet with a speed and power that startled me. I stood there shocked, upright as a spring, gripped and held firm at arms' length. My mind was not my own, my eyes stared straight ahead into his intense face, radiating potency and power and the immense sanctuary of those compassionate eyes. It was impossible to move. He spoke, slow and deliberate.

"This is not real."

The sobbing came deep and insistent then, an emptying of all the forces. We embraced on the path for a long time, then walked to the hut in a thought-free space reminiscent of speechless moonlight. It was a forty-five minute walk and the rhythm of our synchronised steps didn't falter once.

"Make some Bansha tea," said Ram on arrival.

I went around the back of the hut to prepare some fresh twigs, fill up the water, light the fire and organise the pots. The work rebooted the doer in me and things took on an easy familiarity again.

"Beautiful morning." said Ram, when I put the tea down on the veranda table, "Great day to be assaulted." He seemed to find this statement hilarious and the infection of his laughter cracked any reserve in me, we giggled together in the morning sunshine as the blue tits chattered on the feeder.

"What happened?" I asked.

"Never mind what happened, it's what's happening. It's an initiation of sorts."

"An initiation into what?"

"Realism. The spiritual life you are about to enter is based entirely upon it, upon discovery of what is real rather than the manufacture and continuation of the imagined or the projected."

"That is what I want, the real," I pleaded.

"Then you must review your method of getting to that."

"But I am devoted to that; I put so much effort into seeking and sadhana."

"For experience, Amelia. You are seeking experience to make you feel better, it's understandable, you are doing what everybody does but it's a preliminary stage and here in this place we are beyond preliminaries. There is a scaffolding of primary powers that supports the Brahma Vidya and brings you to realism. If they are not in place sadhana will continue but little real change will be made even though you may have any number of experiences."

"What are the primary powers? Tell me Ram."

"They are not news to you, you have heard them before in various ways but they haven't sunk in amidst the noise but now Amelia, after your experience there is a new receptivity about you, can you feel it?" He brushed some remaining leaf mould from my fleece.

"Teach me," I asked with all the sincerity I could muster.

"Viveka and Vairagya, Amelia. They are primal powers, integral to spiritual realism."

I had heard the words often, I had read about their properties as I had read about many other spiritual categories but truthfully even though they were in plain sight, they had never stood out for me as being particularly important.

"Viveka means discrimination, like a ray of intelligence to which a mind attunes. In the absence of this attunement, a person will be having experiences and moving through life like a seed in the wind, chasing sukha, avoiding dukkha. Discrimination is intelligence at its best; to discriminate is to enquire into the nature of what is, to look and to want to look, to see things as they are. What is all this, in whom is all this taking place and how do I know? This is Viveka, the vichara of the wise. Such pursuits may be lofty but Viveka is also every day and practical; what is this desire that moves in me, what is this behaviour, whose thoughts are these? Viveka is a constant, exciting vigilance that keeps you alert to the vrittis in the mind and enables you to see what is, rather than what appears to be. Seeing into things and grasping the essence of them, seeing beyond the limitations of appearance into the heart of the matter is Viveka. Vairagya is the natural consequence of Viveka. It is translated as non-attachment or dispassion but that description conjures up an austerity and a disinterest which is inaccurate. Everything is a rich experience of constant motion; phenomena appearing, whether it is the pinpoint of light in a distant star trillions of miles away, a ladybird landing on your skin, a feeling of love or a thought about what I will do today. As well as the sensory activities themselves, there is also a force of attachment that accompanies them, a bit like density, some experiences you are strongly invested in, they stick to you, you become their effect. This is attachment, it is observable everywhere in the cycles of repetition that drive people and the resistance to change. At its worst, a person is trying to rewire the universe to make it how they want, at the mercy of their desire and reaction, rather than surfing through the inevitable highs and lows with acceptance and good grace. Vairagya is responding to the knowledge that experiences, whilst magnificent and beautiful in the moment, are non-eternal and ultimately there is no enduring value in that which is impermanent. Once you have this knowledge then it is irrefutably apparent that true happiness, or meaning, or security, cannot possibly be in that which is impermanent and to invest your meaning in any assumed, fixed position is insane. Vairagya is joy in the impermanent and at the same time transcending dependence or attachment. It is not a forced spiritual state; it is natural, vital, passionate living, in speed and flow. Examine yourself against these aspects; they are not to be taken lightly."

The memories of that time were so fresh in my mind. I had now been walking now for an hour, my heart pumping with the anxiety that was gripping my mood. I was trying to be rational and sensible, to apply the Vairagya that I had been reflecting on but the threat of presence behind me seemed so strong and close. I turned around sharply several times, half expecting to see someone right at my side reaching out to touch me but there was nothing. The morning sun filtered through the canopy, casting kaleidoscope shadows upon the track. I turned the last corner onto the straight that led to the hut, stopped dead and caught my breath. Something was terribly wrong. Even from this distance I could see the hut was cold and shut. It was obvious no-one was there or had been there. Had I got the date wrong, had something happened? The breeze picked up and the woods rattled in the air gloomily. I looked back down from where I had come peering into the distant shapes. Either I am alone here or someone is watching me right at this moment. At the hut it was as if something had died. I thought I could smell decay. Was it Ram; is he dead, has he gone? I gasped at the thought. On the veranda there was nothing, no artefacts, no utensils, no sign of usage at all. The front door was sealed tight; someone had added a metal bracket on the top and bottom, both padlocked, they looked ugly and aggressive. Why would anyone padlock it, were they afraid of intruders? I remembered last time I was here with Donkey, when I had found a letter pinned to the door. I had never mentioned it, never asked Ram about it but it had always bothered me. I noticed the pin hole in the door was still there. Walking slowly around the hut I looked for any detail that would explain what had happened here, trying to see into the cracks around the shutters sealed from within and firmly closed. Ivy was curling up and enveloping the walls. The wood shed was bare except for a residue of decaying sticks. A soggy dark stain crept over the back wall where the corrugated roof had burst its nails. Donkey's lean-to was empty except for half a sack of rotting silage and a sorry blue leading rope split at both ends hanging on a nail, covered in a dense brown cobweb. I sat down on the unswept and neglected veranda steps looking down at my shiny boots, my new pack resting against the rail and sighed.

What is the default state of a person? Amelia wanted happiness to be her default state, she believed strongly that it was and she knew that's what the teachings declared but the state she was experiencing now was contrary to happiness and was all too annoyingly familiar, it came upon her often. Life was bound to be filled with ups and downs, not everything could be easy and smooth but agitation and dejection like this felt intrusive, something parasitic, like it was infecting happiness. How regularly in life some problem or issue preyed upon her well-being, disturbing her mind and the balance of things. Perhaps happiness was not a primary state but merely a temporary mood just like all the other moods she experienced but that wasn't what her instinct told her. Biology books would explain anxiety confidently as perceived risk, fight and flight and she knew that she was experiencing a biological instrument for that was what was flushed and tensed in these moments. What was at the heart of these movements, were they just the human condition or could they be conquered in some way that she had not yet discovered? Even though she had made great progress in the Brahma Vidya, there was something in her that remained stuck. The task to sustain happiness felt like a burden and everything seemed up in the air. Could it all really be only an issue of Viveka, Vairagya and what was the application of those powers here and now? Was there something else she wasn't seeing?

I didn't notice the deer until she was upon me, right at my side three metres away, she didn't move at all. I looked directly at her and she held my gaze, dominating me with her stance until she snorted, turned and walked slowly away. My skin prickled as I watched her in disbelief, deer never behave like this. Standing up I turned and stopped still in an instant, the weeds were crushed down on the side steps. That wasn't me and it wasn't like that just now. In these moments while I have been sitting here staring at my boots, something or someone has come up to these steps right behind me. The breeze picked up again teasing and swaying the grasses as I looked around anxiously. I am fed up with this, I am not having it. No! "Namah Shivaya!" I called out defiantly, stamping my feet and standing tall. The shout echoed like a crack off the big beech tree, a pheasant burst chaotically from the undergrowth and flapped noisily across the track. Where was Ram, how could it be like this?

At the other side of the clearing the trail path wound its way further into the deep wild wood. Perhaps I should walk along just a little way to see if there were any signs of what might have happened and then I should get out of here, go home, just turn around and leave. The winter detritus on the path added to the remote and abandoned feel as I trudged for half an hour down the solitary neglected track. A deer barked up ahead and then another in response disturbed by something unseen, something moving. A glint of light caught my eye, shining off something on the sycamore tree about fifty metres ahead. There was something attached to the trunk and an irregular lump in the ground at the foot of the tree. As I got closer I could see it was a plastic wallet nailed to the tree, green at the edges from damp and mould and sticky with slime trails. Someone had nailed it there and it had been here for a while. There was a second plastic wallet inside sealed with black tape around all its edges. The lump at my feet was a large dirty tarpaulin weighted down with stones and melded into the forest floor. Pulling out the internal plastic wallet, I rubbed off the condensation from the surface and my heart jumped, *Amelia* was written in black ink on the sheet inside. I sat down on the grass beside the tarpaulin and struggled to peel off the heavy fabric tape taking care not to tear the paper. The note unfolded in my hands.

Follow the beech trees for 5 days x Ram

What? Heaving at the tarpaulin it squelched free and I lifted up one side. It was a pack, one of his. Inside I found a tightly-bundled bivvy bag, a stove, matches, a foldaway lightweight aluminium pan and a vacuum-sealed bag of oats. Travelling gear. He meant me to travel into the unknown forest on an unmarked and dangerous trail alone for five days. It was impossible surely, how to even start, no map, no coordinates, no-one knew I was here and no-one would be looking out for me. This note had been here for months, maybe a year. What if whatever arrangement this pointed to was all long gone, maybe there had been a misunderstanding about when I should come, and five days? I stood on the track and studied the wood. It was sycamore and ash, some oak, frequent pine clumps but beech was rare, seemingly randomly arranged and scattered throughout the forest. Even if I could track them and find the way, what would be ahead and what about my stalker, was it safe to even be here? Maybe that's what the padlocks were for, some trespasser from the Orangery not willing to show himself until we were deeper in the woods. I looked again at the note. I was the only one who could make choices, nothing could guide me now. It was reckless, it was perilous, yet right then in that fizz of the moment I knew I was going in.

It was the nature of Stag to dominate, to roam and to survey. He had a low opinion of humans, often he wanted to fight them but he never had. When he roamed up by the house, especially when the summer was up and the days were warm, he would watch their behaviour; noisy distracted things, insensitive to the forest and prouder than the peacocks. What was their purpose? It was mostly noise and scattering mess. If another deer behaved like this he would kill it, or at least send it cowering with bowed head. The humans never saw Stag concealed in the undergrowth; any forest creature would have sensed him but not them, preoccupied with their random movements and scattering their sharp, sweet smells. But this human was different, she was on the deeper paths, solitary and alone, penetrating the wild forest into his domain. Stag remembered how creatures moved, he remembered their smells, where they gathered their food, where they slept and their poise, he especially remembered that, it was like a marker telling long stories. He had seen this one before and he remembered her poise and how she had been with Donkey in those days. This was a different human, she was a follower of Him, the dweller in the hut, the only one in the forest that Stag could not dominate for he did not wish to dominate that one, his poise was too grand. It fascinated Stag and mellowed the stresses in him. He had watched the dweller in the hut leave and had followed Him for a long way until he crossed the border to that other place. Now this one was looking for Him, Stag could tell that from her movement and her noises. He would follow her too for a while, he would keep a watchful eye and just keep her in sight, he would grant her passage. It wasn't only he who surveyed her, the forest contained scores of eyes and ears, horns and quivering whiskers, sensing this human's motion and her impact on the wood. That night Stag settled, silently watching her glaring light and stumbling gait as she spread herself onto the floor and made her horrible fire. They were at the edge of his terrain now, where the earth changed to peat and he caught the first aroma of that other stag's scent. Just before first light he crept stealthily to one metre from where she slept, his breath creating silent plumes of steam in the first teetering glimmer of dawn. An instinct leapt into his mind at that moment, he raised his hoof and positioned it over a strong dry twig, it would make a great crack here in the silent dark night. This human would wake and look up to see his huge, fifteen-point antler, his thick broad head, his black eyes and his big, wide towering stature looming over her, two metres from her face. That's when he would breathe out his best snort on a cloud of steam and spittle. Stags are not good at resisting instincts; it is not in their blood but there in that moment, something changed and for the first time in his life, Stag did resist. The experience fascinated him, he would think about it for a long time. Turning his back on Amelia, he walked silently away, urinated on the big beech tree which was just the other side of his boundary line and headed back to his hinds.

For two days and nights I had been wild in the woods struggling to follow the marker trees and becoming more feral with each hour. My hair itched, my skin was slick and clammy. I had never slept rough in a forest before and it was shocking, the adrenaline in my mouth, acrid and tight. On the first night it had been a moment by moment struggle to just get through to the dawn. My body ached from the hard ground but I was afraid to turn over because of the noise it would make in the silence, a noise that might attract attention. I fought with my mind every minute, longing for sleep just to escape the tension. Any small sound was a demon or a strangler, the danger of my situation seemed insane. Around 2:00am I thought I saw lights off in the woods and heard the cracking of sticks, the sense of another brooding presence became so strong that I spoke to it, whispering so that I didn't get its attention, praying and pleading to be left alone. But now on this new morning I was feeling better. Last night had been surprisingly peaceful, I had rationalised some security from the fact that I had been alone and vulnerable for thirty-six hours but nothing had actually happened. Whatever was in the woods I was so far unharmed, so if I could just get a grip on the fear itself, I would probably be all right.

After porridge, I scanned the horizon looking for the next beech and noticed something different. There was a large humped shape alongside the trunk, was it a rock or a fallen mass of old wood? As my steps got closer it clearly had structure, a stone wall blending into the mosses and lichens of the forest. It was a building with a wavy undulating roof of stone tiles, green with moss. The beech was massive, a ten-foot girth at least and a height of a hundred feet, it must have been there for two hundred years, its roots erupting in bulbous nodes like gnarled fists, encircling the building and protruding out of the stone blocks. Its structure reminded me of the entrance to Neolithic barrows. I walked around the circumference of the great trunk, stroking its bumpy surface with the palm of my hand and came to a stop. Ahead of me was a closed, low arched door with a single cross cut into its upper quarter. The cross and the angle of the arch caught my breath. I know this, I thought. This has happened before. Moving my hand over the darkened split planks, I curled my fingers around the rounded edge, pulled open the door and stooping low, stepped over the portal letting out a gasp of surprise. A chapel! The bright bone-dry interior smelled of camphor, not the fresh smell of rituals just concluded but a steeped engrained smell, the pungency of centuries. The little oval room had pastel painted walls upon which ochre, yellow and blue mosaics faded into formless erosion. I was standing upon a smooth black stone floor about twenty feet from end to end and no wider than two reclining people. A clear glass window in the roof above my head gave muffled light to the entrance and a second larger round window in the far wall spilled morning light onto a lumpy stone altar, with a little side table next to it and a row of three short, backless benches. In the centre of the window ahead of me, a single diamond-shaped panel stained deep, dark rose sent a spreading beam of soft coloured light through the centre of the chapel. Dust particles ascended and descended in it as if they were the musical notes of a soulful and touching hymn. The coloured light fell directly upon my face. On the side table sat a large closed linen-bound book, curled at the edges and stained. It was clearly very old but in fair condition in this moisture-free air. Inside on a thick hide flyleaf, lines of language were embossed, beautiful, captivating Sanskrit characters branded with great elegance and confidence. A few sparse flecks of gold showed they were once gilded. On the thick paper page behind the flyleaf someone had written English text, a translation. My heart leapt. I was looking at the Mahavakyas of the Upanishads, the four greatest sayings of the Vedas:

Prajnanam Brahma
Aham Brahmasmi
Tat Tvam Asi
Ayam Atma Brahma

The remaining pages had close handwritten Sanskrit characters. I passed through them, understanding nothing and wondering what text this could be, there was no way to know. At points someone had written random English annotations in the margins:

Shantam Shivam Advaitam. Manas Buddhi - Is not I
Vijnanamaya is Jivam - The Lord is Sakshi. I am that

They were the personal marks of a reader from some earlier time, a sadhak just like me probing Advaita Vedanta in this isolated place. At the back of the book were several blank pages with entries in different hands and in different languages, some were dated, there were several in English.

1509. May I have freedom from disease and poverty and all the blights that affect me
1612. Protect our prosperity Lord for it is all we have to share and give
1695. Forgive me Lord protect me from myself and these jealousies of mind
1728. May I endure this working life and then be blessed to renounce into holy orders - Mary
1881. May I find you my Lord may I know you I pray that you show yourself to me
Undated. I cannot continue any more of this tasteless tireless bittersweet so I lay all this longing and yearning down at your feet

The weight of what I had in my hands trembled my skin, it was a

melody of human spiritual desire. Here in this little chapel and across the centuries, amidst the entries asking for recovery from illness and assistance for those in peril, there were also the deep questions of seekers, seekers like me. Who were these travellers? I closed my eyes in the peace of the strange little place and realised that they were all me, not me exactly, but like me and I was like them, the sisterhood of seekers, the tribe of spiritual explorers, different bodies, different histories and minds, but a common purpose. I looked at Mary's poignant entry for 1728, it was the only one signed. How would her dedications be rewarded; how would such prayers be answered by a benevolent God? They would be answered by being granted a more stable life, a more secure life with access to teachings and opportunities. Well, that's what I have here and now, I cannot know my history prior to this life but now, here I am with a passion for God, access to the Guru and the motivations to pursue sadhana. Wow! I am blessed and I have to do this justice, I have to do them justice, to do Mary justice. This was it and I had to act now, not wait, not postpone, but act. Ram had said exactly this to me four years ago when he had outed what he called the foolishness of waiting for evidence and clarity and perfect circumstances, I remembered this so vividly as if it echoed around the chapel.
"People underestimate themselves Amelia, hold themselves back through some kind of modesty, waiting for better guidance, waiting to be pushed, waiting for it all to be clear, waiting for permission, it's madness. Do not be the person who says in their final days, "I wasted so much time". Claim the moment, trust the future, amidst any and all circumstances that come to you. You do not need particular circumstances; you just need intelligent, spiritual action. Don't be attached to fixed outcomes, be reliant instead on sound action. Action will save you Amelia, opinion will not."

My couple of hours in and around the chapel had been like a balm of peace and security amidst the challenges of my daunting experience but my goal was still three days away and I had to move on. After walking for a tiring four hours, it was now late afternoon. Ahead the forest floor began to thin, brush and scrub giving way to a flatter, sparser strip of ground, peppered with small clusters of exposed stone protruding through clumps of nettle and thistle. Kicking away some of the thistle exposed a smoothed surface. This was laid, it's cobbling, its line curving and creeping upwards to the crest of the ridge; a roadway. How could that just exist here in rough woodland with no apparent starting point? It must be a fragment of something very old. Following this curious stone surface up to the top of the hill I stopped dead in my tracks, my heart in my mouth, my breath caught short and sharp in my throat. Below me, some three hundred metres away on the side of the opposite hill stood a village. Some twenty stone houses with clay tiled roofs undulating in a hotchpotch clump like a family of wild creatures sleeping in the afternoon light. The remains of the cobbled street curved through them to a complete dead end. There was no other roadway anywhere, no obvious paths and no exit track. Impossible, what is this in the middle of nowhere connected to nothing? It made no sense and it was immediately terrifying. I dropped down onto my haunches crouching low like a prey animal. I wished my Guru was at my side, I wished I was not alone but he was at least two days away. Shit! Concealed by the grasses I peered at the village examining what I could see of each little house. There was no sign of life, no people, no animals, no objects or possessions visible anywhere. It's dead, I thought, abandoned. I listened, nothing stirred, this is eerie and it's soon going to be dark. What if this is where my stalker came from, what if I have been lured here by deceit? What if the whole thing was a ruse, a trap? The vulnerability of my circumstance beat into my chest, pounding my heart and drying my throat. I stared wide-eyed at the village, wishing it was not there. Smoke! There was a trail of smoke rising from the one large house at the far end of the village. It billowed out of the chimney stack as if it had just been lit. It was not there just now; I would have seen it. Someone is in there; someone has just lit that fire. Shit! Shit! Shit!

I pitched my bivvy in an enclosed little clearing below the ridge and five hundred metres from the cobblestone track. I walked through the undergrowth in the lee of the hill ensuring I was out of sight for anyone who would be looking up. It was the worst thought, the very worst but it was obvious that I needed to go down to the village. The unknown nature and the weirdness of it coiled in my mind like extended talons curling in upon its prey. In the hour it had taken to settle into my camp I had gone through an acute state of indecision and inactivity. I felt wretched; I didn't know what to do and just wanted to avoid everything for this not to be happening and for me not to be here. The inertia squeezed in me, tense in my head, heavy in my chest. I hated this. Then I realised a simple thing. Something had drawn me here just as something drew me into every encounter of my life. I could turn away but I would not, there was opportunity in this, I did not know what it was but the new never comes in familiar packaging. This was an offer, a destiny. I was not naïve but neither was I timid. I had to act; I will act. In the lengthening evening light I crawled up from the bivvy nest and peeked over the ridge like a periscope in dangerous seas. The smoke column from the big house rose vertical in the still air, a glow of light just discernible from the lower windows. Who was there? The only way to know was to descend and I would do so in the morning. Shit!

It was more than the uncertainty of the place that was causing Amelia's mind to quiver. It was the memory of another place and another time, always lingering beneath the surface and now newly triggered. The house alone in the village below with its clay tiled roof nestling amidst the trees reminded her of Duncan. She had been trying not to think of him just as she often tried but it was impossible now, the thought of him was out. Those four years together, twenty years ago in the house in the forest, a romantic dream spiraling into a disaster she did not expect and could not avoid; sticking at it, trying to make it better until she realised it never would, and it never did. They had behaved badly to each other, Duncan and Amelia, two spirits desperate for approval, connection and meaning, floundering in the issues of the young. The olive grove had been so exciting then, rustic living, trading crafts in the market, no electricity, cicadas and moonlight; it was the way out, an escape from the sensible and the dull. It was to be forever and it was hard for her to say how the vision became so broken and how they lost each other in anger and deceit. It wasn't his fault, it was mine, or it wasn't my fault, it was his. These were the thoughts that moved through her mind persistently, thoughts that had repeated and repeated five thousand times and never been resolved, always ending in the same dark mood and irritability. Feelings of guilt and regret gathered tight in Amelia, like a chorus of vipers creeping in those channels in her blood, sucking away all the joy in her. She couldn't turn it off, it was a force field of sadness and embarrassment and it always ended the same way. I wish it hadn't happened; I am bad, life is hopeless. She lay down in her bivvy in the damp moss, knowing she would feel troubled and tight with visions of Duncan knocking at the gates of her dreams.

It was 6:30am, I had slept for most of the night and it felt like an achievement. The light was rising as I got up, trying to stretch out the aches from my night on the forest floor and moved over to the high ground to look down upon the village. There it was, quiet and stable just like all these huge trees around me. I packed up my gear feeling decisive and clear of my action. I did not want to do what I knew I was going to do but I also knew I had to. Passing through the little street I kept my eyes dead ahead until I was outside the big house at the end, resisting the desire to constantly turn around with ferocity of will. The village was silent and unmoving, empty. In front of me were two closed wooden gates shaped like the lintel gates of a church but much larger, eight feet of weathered oak. There was no latch, only a hole in the gate where a mechanism would once have been. I felt frightened but strong. I knew I could focus on the fear or focus on the action. Gripping the rim of the hole in the gate, I pushed it open and saw before me a small courtyard sealed by a second pair of doors about twelve feet ahead; they were rotten at the bottom creating a small gap. Kneeling down, I tried to see through and was shocked rigid by a bell toning in the space ahead of me. I stood up sharply. Was it a warning bell, an alarm? But its notes were sweet and soothing like a temple bell. I waited for its resonance to recede to nothing and trembling, pushed the door ajar and peered in. Ahead of me was the ivy-clad frontage of an old, country cottage with two chimneys, its angles oscillating and wandering with the subsidence of age. Rose bushes weaved through the trellis surrounding the door of old oak, turned white by the thousands of seasons that must have come and gone. There were two windows downstairs and three above and what looked like a stable extending to the side. A small cottage garden separated me from the two red tile steps that went up to the entrance, dominated by an extraordinary tree, spindly and buoyant with bright yellow leaves shimmering in the morning light. To the right of the tree, an old bronze-coloured temple bell hung in a rickety frame, still lightly swinging from the action that had rung it moments ago. Someone was close. My heart pumped, my mouth dry and acidic, I moved through the gates and up toward the steps where I stood timidly and uncertainly at the doorway. I could not move despite my resolve. A raven perched on the roof tiles directly above looked at me with silent intensity, clicking its beak. Suddenly a bearded, cloaked and hooded figure burst out from the doorway like a wind, scattering the raven that cawed in complaint and flapped off over my head. All vitality drained from my guts, I wanted to shrink but could not. The figure moved past me to the bell stand and pulled the rope, toning the deep soulful bell. The figure turned to look directly at me, pulled down the hood of his cloak and stood proud and upright in the decaying notes of the bell.

"Morning, beautiful day."

Ram, Ram! I fell at his feet and burst into racking tears. The morning passed in a joy of tea and breath and hugging and chattering, questions and tales, jokes, exclamations, affection and the leaping warmth of relief and security that drenched me. I told him everything and he let me babble, it was the most healing and freeing conversation I had ever had, from terror to abundant delight in a million words. I told him about the unseen stalker and my time in the woods, he listened with patience, interruption, sarcasm and the most riotous wit as I emptied myself. To be here, back with my Guru after all that had passed, together again, was perfection. After a couple of hours Ram said he had to shave his beard off because it was only suitable for him as the hermit and now I had shattered that experience into bits. I went to bathe and then lay down to rest in a small cute room with a tiny cottage window and lime-washed bulging walls on a padded up, sumptuous bed, covered in a floral quilt that smelt musty and it was the best smell ever. I could not sleep; my mind was dancing. To be held in security after what seemed a great ordeal was like expanding in sunlight even though the weather had darkened and rain now pelted upon the thick window glass. Ram made lunch, some old dhal that he heated up with home-made goat's curd and barley, shovelled with a scoop from a three-foot earthenware jar. We spoke about Bowslip and this place, the hut, the woods, the beech tree walk and why he was here. Ram was cagey in a hilarious kind of way; I knew he was not telling me all. He explained that he had graduated from the hut and now lived here in the village and his instruction for me to walk for five days had been placed a year ago. I asked him why he had moved and he just spread his arms and said "Upgrades". He had left the five-day instruction because it tested my resolve, both to take on the challenge at all, and then to act courageously in uncertainty when I came upon his actual hideout two days in advance of what I was expecting. I told him I thought that aspect was a cruel twist at which he comically feigned being hurt and replied it was not cruel, it was deep. I pushed him on the village and the chapel but he said no further explanations could be given now because it wasn't allowed; only that I should appreciate that the place I was in had intense and powerful history. The afternoon passed perfectly and when the rain stopped he showed me the garden and the stable where two goats were beautifully kept with clean hay and a second stable which was equally clean and all prepared with a stall, he said it was for Donkey when he returned. There were four chickens of a breed I had never seen and a rooster of such strident and handsome plumage, standing proud in the yard and stretching his neck like a conquering emperor. "He keeps me in my place," said Ram, "just in case I remember what I am."

It was a strange comment and even stranger when I realised he wasn't joking. We looked at the tree which he said was a very old Golden Honey Locust. He said the original tree had been brought here and installed by a predecessor in the 14th century.

"I have taken four cuttings, they are thriving in pots, I am thinking of planting them to revive the village; it all depends on some movements which are currently not materialised."

It was as if he was talking to himself and I knew I could not probe this point further. What was this village, what had it been and what could it be? A thrill of possibilities radiated through me. We sat on the doorstep in silence; the feeling of his body next to mine was as an ocean of stillness, strength and stability. In the early evening I cooked for us, dhal, curds and barley again, which was all a traveller needed according to Ram, "Except for broccoli", he said wistfully. Later on we meditated and sang lilting bhajans before I went to my lovely musty cocoon to be enveloped in the wonder of the house of

Ram. "In the morning, to business," he said, as I climbed the creaking and slightly mobile stairs.

It was 6:00am when the garden bell tolled. Ram had been busying about attending to the goats, preparing oats, stoking up the range and was now settled in the wooden chair opposite me, either side of the old round table where I had been sitting peacefully watching him for half an hour. The steaming kettle on the stove whistled sharply. I made the tea and served him, sitting contentedly in silence just absorbing the atmosphere of the place and meditating. Thirty minutes later he went outside to toll the bell again before stoking up the fire, settling deep into his chair and clearing his throat noisily.
"One day, one fine day, maybe tomorrow, maybe in four thousand years, you will stroll and stride around the entire landscape of Bowslip in joy and ease, taking any journey in any direction in exhilarating freedom. To be like that Amelia, you have to be empty because only an empty vessel has the space and capacity to accommodate those powers unconditionally. Meanwhile Bowslip invokes a few challenges and reactions in you, just maybe there are one or two intruders hanging around the place, skulking in corners of your mind. What of this stalker, what has been stalking you?"
"You mean who Ram, I don't know, I never saw him."
"So how do you know anybody was?"
"It wasn't just a feeling, it was tangible and real, I heard noises, I watched the pheasants get startled and I felt watched, I knew I wasn't alone, it was horrible, hour after hour."
"So did you see a man?"
"No I didn't but I felt him, definitely. I have been here many times and never had this experience, I don't normally feel ill at ease like that, it's different."
"Well, it's not really normal to be alone in alien woods without bearings and not knowing the way out, maybe you just got spooked. It wouldn't be unusual."

"No, it's more than that, even before I got to the hut, right back there on the gate path, he was there, I sensed him straight away and so did the animals."

"Perhaps you brought somebody with you?"

"No I didn't, I came alone but someone may have followed me, I suppose from the public gardens, like a sneak?"

"Are you alone now, apart from me?"

"Yes of course."

"You don't look it."

"But there is only you and me here."

"That's not so, Amelia."

He watched me with that vital gaze that had swamped me many times before. It was as if all my secrets were suddenly out in the room under a spotlight, not only the secrets I was intentionally guarding, but secrets I did not even know myself. As if some bow strings that had been held tense and tight within me were loosened from their mounts, and all my protective weapons defending and guarding my image and sensibilities became useless. He wasn't doing anything particular, he was just sitting there, implacable in that easy pose but a probing intensity was upon me and there was nowhere to hide and no way to pretend. It lasted as long as his gaze held my face, then he smiled, screwed up his eyes and moved off to feed the chickens. I felt woozy, a subtle activity fizzing around my heart, the boundaries of the kitchen seeming other-worldly and indistinct. I sat down at the table and stared into space trying to even out my breathing.

"Fancy an egg?" said Ram, as he peeled off a boot with the heel of the other, placing a trivet of eggs on the wooden boot cupboard by the door.

"What's happening?" I asked.

"Nothing much, I just found your stalker that's all."

"What!" I said, jumping up and moving to the window, "Where is he and who...?"

"Where, is easy, who, is trickier."

"You mean you didn't see him?"

"Yes, I looked him right between the eyes."

"But who is he? Did you capture him, challenge him?" I was making for the door, "Where is he now?"

"In the same place, he hasn't moved but you shouldn't go out."

"Why not, is he dangerous? Let's go, let's confront him and find out who he is!" I knew it! All this time! Indignation rushed upon me like surf on rocks. How dare somebody oppress me like that! I wanted Ram to be like an angry farmer seeing off intruders with his shotgun or imprisoning them. I wanted him to defend me and call this person to account. "Let's go and get him Ram."

"He's imprisoned already, right here in this kitchen."

I turned to him, startled, and the energy drained from my chest. This isn't what I thought it was. The sensation around my heart returned, stronger, pulsing as rising and falling waves, I felt unsafe, not sure of my bearings, anxious.

"Where is the stalker, Ram?"

"In your mind, Amelia."

"What do you mean, who is he?"

"Not a he at all, not even a she, not even an it. The stalker is you. What is stalking you Amelia, are ghosts of the past."

I felt anger and shock like a rising wind. I wanted to scream at him, I felt so horribly exposed; it wasn't fair, what is this? I wanted to run. Trembling, I came back, slumped in my seat and burst into sobs. Ram left me alone and got on with cooking his eggs. In any normal situation that would have irritated me even more but this wasn't normal, by no means. I was used to that neglect from him now, it was his way of constantly putting all situations back upon your own resources, back to the centre of you and his way of letting things out rather than stifling them or softening them. Only the guru can do this and I had learnt to allow it. If it was anyone else, I would have thumped them or would have smiled nicely, then gone away and fretted and seethed for days.

I stayed in the chair by the range and watched him work at the stove, unpretentious, domestic and natural, just doing things, not embellishing or exaggerating, not trying for any effect or putting on any performance. I stayed silent as he served up two plates of eggs with toast from the bread he had made and brought it to the table with fresh tea. He held out my cup, the one with hares on, I had left it behind last time I was at the hut; he must have brought it here. It was touching and in that moment everything was somehow perfect, even though I was feeling embarrassed and all at sea, had red eyes and no idea what was going to happen next.

"There was no-one in the woods Amelia, at least no-one physical but that doesn't mean there was nothing. The sensation you had was a solid sensation. I do not say it wasn't real because I know you will have felt that there was a physical stalker prowling five hundred metres behind you. You heard things, you saw things. That did happen but the experience was a projection out of yourself. You will have other incidents in your life like this, everybody does. A dark mood may come upon you for no reason. A setting that you find yourself in makes you uncomfortable and provokes a resurgence of unpleasant feelings from an earlier time. You may feel an unwelcome presence of some sort or feel sure you are being persecuted by something. These things are movements in you that you don't understand and cannot reason because they are unconscious. As it says, the unconscious is not conscious so you do not know it and cannot rationalise it in the common way but it is shaping experience all the time, not unlike dreams at night. It is not unusual in a dream to be chased or stalked, or for someone or something to be tracking you; it is the condition of your mind. Bowslip drew that out just as other life events may bring things to the surface from time to time. It is an act of wisdom to realise that your mind is not your own, we are accompanied by ghosts."

I didn't like the word, 'Ghosts'. He said it with such relish, elongating the 'o' sound and raising his eyebrow theatrically. It made me uncomfortable. I could tell he knew that.

"What do you mean by ghosts Ram, ghosts aren't real, I don't want to think of such things."

"A ghost may not be real but the projection is. Others may call such events delusion, hallucination, mirage or dream but that doesn't mean it is not happening as an experience and experience is real, however you name it. I am choosing the word ghosts deliberately because of its provocative power; it's the guru's tactic to shake you up. What I am calling ghosts and pointing at, you may call an oppressive feeling, a depressive attitude that comes upon you, a pervasive mood, persistent, unwelcome memories shaping how you feel and the way you view something. In those circumstances the moment is not a free state, it is a projection of the past replaying some unconscious history as a critical voice. This is the burden of the common mind. Such recycling history I choose to call 'Ghosts'."

I told him then about Duncan in a way I had never told anybody and some of it I had not even told myself. He was patient and receptive as the old story unfolded and I felt myself sinking in that guilt, doubt and sadness that was the physicality of my memory. It had such substance as if I had swallowed something and it was occupying all my corners. Abruptly, Ram put his feet on the table noisily and started to snore theatrically. It was insulting and very rude. Resentment rose in me, anger rising until he pulled a ridiculous face. Inexplicably, in an instant it was hilarious, everything seemed absurd and comical and the feelings had gone.

"What a blessing Duncan was Amelia, good for him."

"What do you mean? It was a horrible experience; it torments me still."

"It has tormented you no doubt, but only because you do not understand the nature of things. It's tedious to talk about them really because such darshan is in the realm of the tactical and we have moved away from those discussions but before we can outline the jnana more fully and more lucidly, we will be tactical for just a little bit longer. Soon, I expect you to have conquered these abilities for if we are to travel together further and deeper into Bowslip, you need to have transcended these intruders. Have you learnt anything from Duncan?"

"Well yes, I suppose, there are some things I wish I hadn't done, some things that should not have happened."

"If the situation arose again, would you act differently?"

"Yes, definitely and I'm really sorry it was the way it was. I was too trusting, I didn't know then what I know now, I was a fool."

"And that is the heart of the madness. You could not know then what you know now and in the moment you were acting in the way you needed to act. It is the gift of Duncan that is showing you the knowledge you now have. The experience may have been hard but never mind the suffering, that's another matter, the learning is the key. You may not even be able to identify exactly what the learning is but you are changed by it, developed by it, altered in some way towards an upside that you may never have allowed yourself to see and inhabit."

"But what upside could there be Ram? It was four years of mutual abuse; we were a mess. I was bad, he was bad, I don't want to think about it but I can't get over it."

"People think learning is acquiring but learning isn't always something you gain, there are many situations in life where learning is a loss, where you just have to go through an experience. No-one can ever tell you the exact reason for events but if you could only know the exquisite, perfect accuracy of your destiny in the fabric of this life, you would fall on your knees staggered by it. The dynamic process of encounter either entraps you or frees you. In this knowledge the sadhak allows and invites life, moving eagerly with intelligent acceptance, living in Vairagya, responsive to everything and attached to nothing. But you have not done that, you have clung to all the stories of guilt and shame, embarrassment, anger, jealously, regret, etc., gathering the memories as if they are a substance. It's madness Amelia. Get beyond it! The wise learn the art and skill of life through the experiences that pass through them, moving swiftly, constantly leaving things behind which is where they belong. The ignorant inhibit that possibility by the clogging accumulation of ghosts. Do you think you are a kind person?"

"Yes, I think so."

"Do you behave kind or are you kind? I know you do kind acts but do you think kind?"

"Aren't they the same?"

"Of course not. Acting is inferior kindness. That doesn't mean it's not good, it's very good, you should put all your resources into it but the superior kindness is kindness of attitude, thought and intent. Do you have a kind mind Amelia?"

"Well I hope so, yes mostly."

"Do you have judgmental thoughts, cruel thoughts, nasty thoughts about people?"

"Sometimes, it's embarrassing to admit, I suppose."

"Is it burdensome to you or do you enjoy it?"

"It's a burden, I don't like to have those thoughts and then again at times, maybe I enjoy it."

"Take it easy Amelia, don't worry, this is a common human problem, some defensiveness from the past, some survival traits, who knows, the point is, this is a ghost haunting your mind. Just one, a small example, it could be a hundred other things, different things in different people, either a memory or an unwelcome state of mind prowling about, an unholy chorus of intruders. It's not you, it is a state living in you and that is a statement you should dwell upon. Watch people and see the truth of this. For most, all is well as long as comforts are met and challenges are kept at bay. In those conditions, unseen ghosts whatever they are, sleep and snore soundly but then some little incident, you may not even notice what it is, a small irritation or obstacle, the ghosts arise, invade the moment and have their way. Incidents in your life that have been painful or you regret come back to life. Once in place this state then promotes other associated thoughts and you find yourself feeling bad about yourself, your outlook is coloured by it and so is your behaviour. Do you recognise this?"

I said nothing.

"This phenomenon is the face of the ghosts that have been stalking you in this forest but they are not in the forest, they are in you, they are not ghosts, they are thoughts. Some grace is upon you so that this is being outed here, brought forward into the light. You have told me about Duncan, well, what is Duncan now; tell me what is he now?"

I didn't answer.

"A ghost, a stalker, an intruder and nothing more. Dwelling upon him is a habit, get beyond it! This has been our preliminary conversation Amelia, you are here for a profound sadhana and we will continue it later."

He got up and left me without another word. I sat there by the range holding my hare mug looking at the dregs in the bottom thinking about what he had said. It seemed insightful and disarmingly simple both at the same time. My sadness on the walk and at the hut, my feelings of unease and unhappiness, that sense of threat and loss were familiar, an old possession that rose up and covered me like a heavy Victorian cloak, creeping out of the shadows stealthily, just as a conjurer might conceal his moves. The memory of Duncan had come to life again so vividly here but it wasn't only him. In the clarity of this place I could see that these feelings, memories and dissatisfactions were indeed of the past so why did they play in the present? These incidents were like a phantom stage I walked upon, colouring my view of the present with the content of the past.

Later that afternoon Ram returned with juniper, mustard leaves and orell root. He took a jar of mint leaves from the dresser and tipped his green ingredients into a mortar. "Pound, Amelia." he said, as he grated the orell and mixed it in. We worked together like that for twenty minutes not speaking, my senses enriched and entirely satisfied by the sounds of the pestle, the fragrance of the herbs and the presence of the two of us operating in harmony. The mixture had been simmering in a copper vessel for fifteen minutes when he put it outside.

"It isn't to cool," he said, "it is to imbibe the air." He poured it into two glass vessels. "Cheers Amelia, knock it back."

I gagged on the drink; it was bitter, harsh and revolting.

Ram looked at me with a mischievous sneer, knocked his back and let out a long "Ahhhhh..."

I felt a mild fire in my belly, then my throat and then alarmingly in my guts, building quickly into a force I couldn't resist, my heart pounded, my face became hot, I looked up at Ram and he was holding open the door with a clown's shocked look on his face.

"Fly Amelia! Fly!"

A force of nature propelled me from my chair and I rushed out into the winter bracken, pulling at my trousers with the urgency of volcanoes, all decorum abandoned.

Over the next hour things calmed down strikingly. I felt spacious and exhilarated, freer than I had for as long as I could remember. A great calm came upon me, punctuated by the occasional low frequency rumble in my guts. At first I was shocked and angry. I wanted to 'call out' my Guru for poisoning me, just as I had that time he assaulted me on the path. How could he get away with it? But either I accepted it was the guru's tactic and trusted him, or I did not. I took a bath, rested and reflected, realising that on both occasions something had profoundly, deeply shifted in me as a consequence of the experience. If something is unconscious then how could it be accessed with civility and order, wouldn't it need intervention, wouldn't it need the guru's tactic?

In the evening he made supper, saying it was best for me to continue resting. He stoked up the fire, rang the night bell and we settled down on the sofa by the hearth, the logs were smoky and the smell of pine was beautiful, rich and settling.

"You have come through the wild forest to this isolated place to exorcise ghosts, Amelia. In varying degrees everyone is in the position you find yourself in but mostly this is unseen and untackled and as a consequence, the mind is unnecessarily burdensome and confining but here is the wonder of our Brahma Vidya, we know this is not an inevitability, it is a choice. In the past, we have discussed the architecture of the mind that brings experiences and how individual minds find themselves on a roller-coaster of encounters at the mercy of sukha and dukkha. Now, because of your success in journeying here and getting to this point, I can give you the entire solution to all this. It is the solution that has been discovered by mystics throughout time and it has three pillars: Satyam, Sakshi, Sivam. It is best to approach this in three conversations; they are the reason you have come; the reason you have had the experiences you have had on the trail. I will speak to you over the next two days about Satyam and Sakshi and as for Sivam, well, we will see."

If Ram ever made anything other than porridge for breakfast I would feel cheated. There was a time when I found these same, simple routines bland, they did not titillate or satisfy. Where is the toast, the honey, the marmalade and sugar, the tasty muesli, the cornflakes? But now I loved the stable, elegant beauty. Sameness was not boring and it was enough. I took it as an example of surrender, although surrendering to porridge did seem rather frivolous. I washed up and cleaned whilst he did the goats and stacked up the wood. As always, these domestic rhythms further soothed and calmed me. Serving my teacher opened up my heart most intensely and emptied my mind. It happened so fast.

"Make tea," said Ram.

He rang the bell and fed the chickens while I brought my hare mug and his beaker to the little table between the easy chairs by the hearth. It was cold today and the wood fire was blazing. We chanted the mantras he had taught me and sat in silence listening to the wood crackling, my mind alert and amazed at the wondrous, thrilling circumstance I found myself in, here with my Guru. He opened his eyes, slurped tea and spoke.

"We are going to discuss the nature of things Amelia, Satyam, or rather Sat, is the reality, the truth of existence, how things are. The more we probe the Brahma Vidya and apply it, the more clarity you gain on how things are and the more possibilities arise. Jnana really is exceptionally beautiful in a world filled with confusion. It is the sadhak's principal refuge. How do you feel?"

"Excited Ram and reflective, deep and inspired and also anxious, as if I am on the edge of something like a precipice."

"It's not a precipice Amelia, it is space but it doesn't have an edge, you are not going to fall, you are only going to discover more of the space. Let's consider this moment here and now and declare the properties that underpin your mind and experience. What is your true nature?"

"Atman, consciousness."

"Yes but let's have it more simple, more direct. Happiness is your true nature Amelia and you intuitively know that but you have to understand what happiness is. We are not referring to a feeling of exhilaration or joy, that is the delight and play of the mood of happiness. A lovely thing, a state to cultivate and enjoy, a human pleasure but a state nonetheless. And as with all states it is bound to come and go. The source of that happiness is what I am referring to, its original light and that is the pleasure and dependability of the security of Being. This is reality and is not subject to impermanence or obscuration. The mood of happiness is the reflection of this reality, its glittering colouration if you will, and all reflections can be obscured by clouds. If you are dependent on the mood of happiness, you will experience stress but if you reside in the independence of its source, the security of Being, then any stress will be a passing cloud only, having no impact at all on the continuous sky of Being."

"I think I know this, Ram. It's inspiring; I believe it and I feel it keenly here this morning with you but even though I know it, it doesn't seem to change how I am, or what I feel, or how things move in me. It didn't change my experiences in the forest, for example, and it hasn't expelled the ghosts we are talking about."

"You cannot avoid the experiences that come, Amelia but you can conquer their impact through knowing. You are misunderstanding what knowing means, it is not just an idea about things, not a fact like a piece of information. Knowing is jnana, an actual seeing of the truth, a realising of it in the mind. When you really see the truth of something it is more than a thought, it is a dismantling of ignorance. What is the only filter with which you see the world? How are you seeing and knowing anything right now?"

"Through consciousness, chit."

"Yes but how are you knowing the coming and going of experiences themselves, your time on the track, your ghosts?"

"Through perceiving, through my senses."

"Yes but let's call it mind because then as well as senses we also include thought. It is mind which is the single filter for all the experience you have. Not only is the world appearing in your mind but the world you see is the mind. You do not have to understand this as some difficult esoteric concept; it is a statement of simple actuality. All the tone, colour, shape, density and detail of phenomena are within what we call mind. No-one is seeing absolute pure reality, what you are seeing, feeling and sensing is an interpretation of what is. This is not a mistake or wrong, it is how nature is. You are experiencing the world from a perspective shaped by your specific, individual position of seeing, by the content of your mind. All that you perceive in this kitchen and in the village and in the forest around you is not out there, it is mind. One person may look at these ancient woods and see them as dark, gloomy and full of threats; another will look at exactly the same woods and see them as inviting, light and glorious. Different structures will stand out for different observers. For one there will be a scene of dullness with details not noticed, for the other, a shimmering landscape full of life and delight. It is not because the woods are like this intrinsically, it's because you are like this. The experience of beauty or oppression is in you, not the woods."

"But everyone can appreciate a peaceful woodland glade on a sunny morning surely?"

"No they cannot, it all depends on the content and tone of mind. People can agree the details of what they are seeing but the appreciation, meaning, connection and pleasure, the range of experience itself varies immensely, as does the presence of stalkers or ghosts."

"So the forest is an illusion?"

"That is the wrong way to see it, it's not an illusion, it is an appearance relative to the observer. Some may say, 'I am frightened to spend a night alone in these woods', fine, that would not be an unusual experience; there can be hazards in the woods and dangers in the dark. It's an evolutionary thing but its impact is exaggerated by the conditions of your mind in which additional fears, threats and anxieties reside, this is obvious really. So what is it that is shaping the characteristics of this mind Amelia?"

"It's karma, Ram. Things come upon me because of the past and my actions now shape the present, my mind is my karma."

"Yes but make sure you realise what karma is. As well as your own history, personal to you, there are hundreds of thousands of years of genetic history responsible for your makeup and then billions of years prior to that, by which the primal moods and needs that move in humanity have been forged. Your mind is a product of all of that.

All sadhaks must accept that there is content within the mind that cannot be defined and which is shaping their reactions. The actual experience of this day is generated by your mind, a mind that is both a new perceiver and a repository of ghosts. The exciting knowledge is that you can spot these ghost voices, they are not hard to see, they always feel burdensome and are usually critical. And then you can easily shine the light of truth upon them and expose them for what they are, false. A ghost is a redundant echo from the past and what is an echo? Why, only a shadow, a residue of an original sound. You would never assign reality to an echo; you would not think that your hand clap was happening on the other side of the field where the echo is bouncing to and fro. But because you do not have the same clarity regarding repetitive negative states, you give these ghosts apparent weight and you hold the mood of a thing as if it has substance, whilst all the time it is nothing more than a persistent echo, a ghost that clings. It's the clinging that is not natural. It is more natural for things to decay and change like an echo. So when I say to you, free your mind, it is a provocative statement, slightly frivolous, a bit comical but it is also a most serious command. More tea?"

I got up to make the tea while he disappeared outside again for something. I was confused, I didn't like the word 'Ghosts' and I wished he would stop using it, he said it with such relish, and what about all the other influences that formed my mind, the good stuff, the positive, not everything was ghostly and to be discarded, surely? As I stood at the range waiting for the kettle to boil, I realised that the irritation I was feeling regarding the word was a force in itself. He could have said vritti, or samskara, or upadhi, or vasana but then we would be back in philosophy, a comfortable place for me because I could talk about the Brahma Vidya abstractly but here in this place, the abstract was absolutely not an option. He came back with some pussy willow stalks and put them in a vase on the table and I served him tea.

"Ram, I am affected by all my experiences aren't I? All my memories and encounters form my understanding, surely not everything that drives me is a ghost, it can't be."

"No of course not, your mind is beautiful, rich and full with wondrous things, important knowledge, insights and learning to utilise and value. It is a palace of possibilities and at the same time some of those palace corridors are stalked by a few ghosts. The moment is informed by the past, of course but the moment is not the past and ghosts are always of the past, something that has lost its vitality but still persists, out of time. Ghosts are thoughts that linger and hold you back, mental waves that confine and restrict, persistent regrets, brooding dissatisfactions or false confining beliefs about yourself. By contrast, the unsullied moment is populated by new thoughts, fresh thoughts that inspire and motivate. But you don't need to worry, you can easily know the difference, there is a flavour to this, you can sense it. The flavour of the past is heavy; the flavour of the present is light and fresh, just like happiness. Imagine you are traversing a river, life is that river, bubbling and flowing with foam and spray and current and you are happy to cross. The river is beautiful and interesting and also dangerous at the same time, so you have respect and admiration for it. But how do you cross the river of life? Through experiences, that is the nature of life's motion. Experiences are the stepping stones by which you traverse the river but remember what a stepping stone is, something that supports and transports you over obstacles, giving you the foothold to launch into the next step with vigour and stability. A wise traveller treads with skill using the balance and poise that she has learnt, you don't fall in and you don't stop. You might linger in the sunlight for a while to recover from a particular hazardous encounter and plan your next step but then you are off to the next stone continuing your course anew. Stepping stones are tools for the journey; they are not to be hung around your neck and carried with you. They are not to stay stuck on and they are not for turning around. Just like a real river, if you can take the same stepping stone approach to the experiences in life, you will thrive. It doesn't really matter what the content of your stalker is, Amelia, I am not your counsellor and am not interested in the details of those stories. I appreciate events have happened to you as they have happened to all and their impact may have been big but they are not happening now. Learning is its consequence but what bearing does it deserve to have on the fresh new moment?" He pointed his finger straight at my head. "To feel sorry for a circumstance poorly played in the moment it is playing and to do something about it, is the mark of intelligence. To then experience some sorrow or regret at the way an experience moved is the natural way learning will embed. To feel that once and grow from it is sound but to feel it over and over again for years and lifetimes, to be possessed by it like an unreleased rusty, wound spring, is a ghost. Intelligence is like light, freely shining and increasing in its intensity. Stalkers and ghosts are sunspots inhibiting the ability of that light to shine upon new situations freshly. Learn to be swift Amelia, learn to be loose, learn to skip across the stones. Free your mind."

It was mid-morning and the temperature had dropped; a bite was in the air. I dressed up in my walking gear and his old oilskin coat, borrowed some wellies, padded out with thick socks as they were too big for my feet and went out. A sharp frost crackled under my feet and stung my face; the air was arctic and beautifully clean. There were some footsteps in the garden where Ram had been busying about but as I went through the entrance courtyard and opened the outer gate, the scene outside was undisturbed except for the delicate sways and marks of the animal tracks. The village was about a hundred metres long with sixteen houses, seventeen including Ram's place. All the houses were shuttered and had obviously been shut up for a long time except for one, which was more run-down, the door hanging open. It was small, empty and dank, foxes, goats or deer had been in there and I didn't want to explore. At the end of the cobbled roadway were some stone sheds, a stone barn and fenced paddocks, all shut, ivy-covered and overgrown. Heavy clay tiles were on every building. How had this come about? It was clearly centuries old, where had the building materials come from? I strolled down the street in the silence of the frost, my breath forming plumes in the air, reflecting on ghosts and remembered the village in the olive grove twenty years ago, full of life and charm, romance and hope. In that moment, perhaps for the first time, I thought about the actual events of Duncan objectively, about what had really happened. I thought of the time and place, how young we were, how our minds were and the naïvity and desires that played in us both. It was as if I was watching a movie, like a distanced critic assessing its qualities without prejudice or preconception and without anger. Duncan was an event sealed in time, the feelings of regret, shame and resentment that had lingered so strongly and persistently, what were they other than clinging ghosts? To feel sad now about something that had not worked out then suddenly seemed to be absurd yet it had been so persistent. I realised that to bring repeated feelings of failure, guilt and regret to the present was my choice but a hard choice to break. The more I looked at it, the more absurd it became. I strolled up and down the cobbled road and in the surrounding woods for the rest of the day. Climbing the hill, I went back up to that first vantage point where I had been feeling so hopeless and so troubled by my feelings. Now, in the crisp purity of the frost and the coldness on my skin, things were different, there was a true beauty here, a cleanliness and a fresh moment. It is truly my mind which determines my experience and that is either haunted by the content of the past or is the cutting crispness of this present second. It's not out there, it's in here, it's me.

When I returned he was writing at the round table.

"Cook Amelia," he said, "I can tell you have been lost in thoughts, do something with your hands."

"What shall I make?"

"Dhal of course, goat's curd and barley."

I cooked; we ate, cleared up and sat again by the hearth.

"I am inspired by this teaching Ram, I see it but memories are strong aren't they, habits and feelings come with a force. I can't just change on a whim, just throw these feelings off. How can I activate such a change?"

"Perfect Amelia, you want to act, excellent. The Viveka itself is the principal action. You must reflect on this darshan, keep it alive in your mind, stay vigilant, stay focused, ponder upon it, test it out in your experience. The seeing of it is powerful, it gives you the option to realise these ghosts as they are happening and to step back from the willingness to engage in it. This is applied Viveka and it will free you but it is true that unravelling clinging habits takes some time and some perseverance. If you want to do something more immediate and more tangible to symbolise your intent, then take a practical action that is meaningful to you, do some puja, write something and burn it, say some prayers and mantras for the harmony of your antagonists. By all means create some processes for yourself that express your feelings like a eulogy, but don't make it too complex, remember the river bubbling beneath you, remember the stepping stones. But there is something else; the most magic and freeing action of all is forgiveness, forgiveness for the antagonists, for the circumstance, for the behaviours and principally most importantly, for yourself. Forgiveness will exorcise even the most persistent ghost. Now some experiences are harrowing, forgiveness doesn't mean you are approving of bad actions that may well deserve consequences but as you know, consequences come to all in the long game. Forgiveness means you are applying understanding, acceptance and moving on. You may not agree with what has taken place but you see that it is finished and you accept that fact. You do not always have to win. There are circumstances in this life Amelia, where it is wise to lose and to know such loss as freedom. That is what forgiveness actually means, free understanding and moving on. The stepping stone you are now on is a pivot point, a leaping point. Stand on your tiptoes, gather all your forces, feel the energy of the bubbling river of life and spring swiftly onto the next clean, fresh, unsullied and empty stone, polished by the waters of forgiveness and jnana. This change is not going to happen to you, for that is not how karma works, you are the change, you have to step out of the past and away from ghosts."

We went to bed early as Ram said we would be rising at dawn and going on a long trek. I lay peacefully swaddled in the musty bedclothes in the black of the night and the silence of the house, broken from time to time by creaks, knocks and cracks. "Not ghosts", I said to myself, "there are no ghosts except the ones I create myself." The owls hooted outside as I fell asleep.

"Where are we going Ram?"

We had finished porridge and were togged up; it was even colder today than yesterday and still dark outside, softened by the almost full moon.

"To the chapel," said Ram, "you lead the way."

A thrill jumped in my throat, going back to that beautiful and mysterious little place but this time hand in hand with the strength and security of my Guru. Nothing could be better.

"Shall I bring the torch?"

"No."

"But it's dark."

"Never mind, we can follow the road up the hill. By the time we get to the rise and the open forest there will be enough light to see."

It took four hours to complete the journey, during which time we didn't speak at all. I knew he was behind me but I barely turned around and neither did we stop except for comfort breaks amidst the bushes. A purpose was upon me, I had huge energy confidently back-tracking the route I did before, following the beeches in reverse. At the chapel we took tea from the flasks we had brought and entered together. Just as before, the place was serene, special and sacred. My thoughts went to the authors in the prayer book. It was as if I could feel their presence and that across time, they too could see me. Ram rearranged the little pews so that they were either side of the side table with the book in the middle. Still togged up in the fleeces and coats that protected us from the biting cold, we made ourselves comfy. He lit some camphor, sounded his hand bell and chanted Sri Rudram, echoing off the walls and roof as if the whole place was a living temple. The sound was extraordinary, like a whole chorus of priests, resonant and varied. I joined in with the small parts I had learned. We meditated in the deep, poignant silence that followed the sudden cessation of the Sanskrit vibrations. Ram moved to stand behind the altar as if I was his congregation. He looked magnificent, like a great seer of the Upanishads, full of power and life with a surety and confidence that was truly breathtaking, I couldn't take my eyes off him.

"I am here to speak of your glory Amelia, to tell you a most important truth that once seen can transform your life completely. I insist that you meet me here with nothing between us standing in your power. Not the power you assign to yourself because that is arrogance but the natural power of the unsullied moment, a moment without content or ghosts. I insist you do not deny this free second, nor imprint any echoes of any type upon it. This is a clear stepping stone Amelia, pure, newly quarried, fresh, stand upon it unadorned and empty, nothing else is acceptable."

We chanted Om three times together, then he rang his hand bell. I sat mesmerised, alert and open, a wordless shimmering in my heart.

"Do you know the meaning of Sakshi?" he asked, "You are Sakshi, Amelia. This is definite and without doubt. There are many other words that try to describe you; Atman, Turiyam, Self, Brahman, you know them all but they take the form of grand ideas, seemingly distant possibilities. I will conquer that problem for you this morning by showing you clearly that what you are is not different but is simpler and more immediate, a direct power perceivable and easily knowable, that will bring sunlight upon your mind. We call it 'Sakshi', it means 'the Witness' and we are going to discover what that is."

As he spoke, a sunbeam warmed the room, shining through the rose window, creating a momentary fragile-coloured aura on the table in front of me, rarefying and sweetening the air as if ethereal beings had joined us from a more delicate realm. I let out a small trembling sigh as he came down from his pulpit and sat solidly in the pew in front of me.

"Upgrades, Amelia. It's amazing to be here like this, isn't it? Completely amazing. Of course it is a delight to be in a 14th century chapel in the depths of Bowslip forest, one to one with your teacher discussing the Brahma Vidya but that is not what is amazing. I do not point to the place, or the time, or the details of this particular experience between us, I point to the power by which it is all happening and being known. Right now, clear for you and undeniable by any measure, experiencing is taking place; knowing and sensing. There is life and there is the perceiving of that life. Notice this keenly, it's incredible, isn't it? Nothing routine about it. The thrilling thing to realise is it is constant, spontaneous and never not there. Experiences change in character minute by minute of course, just as they are now but the underlying property of experiencing is always present. It is striking that this is not seen by all but understandable because noticing it is the culmination of Viveka. Commonly such Viveka is not applied, people are consumed by experiences and just don't know. The experiences are not going to stop, of course. All sadhaks must devote energy to organise the actions of life in such a way that our experience is positive and our impact in the world productive, meaningful, kind and benevolent. The doer in us is right to dedicate full resources to that goal, whilst at the same time the intelligence in us penetrates into the mysteries of the moment. When I look at you I see you doing that, I see your commitment, it is very beautiful to me but that is not all I see. I see vitality of spirit, originality and eager aspiration. I see the passions in you shaping a purer and purer vessel through which truth can be conveyed. I love you for these things Amelia; I dedicate a portion of myself to be with you in these things. You are my companion in these things beloved, we are entwined in these things."

A silence followed his words that was like snowfall. I gazed at the intensity and expression in his face and saw the delicacy of the moment softening his eyes and imperceptibly quivering the expression of emotion on his lips. Our spiritual relationship was vast and ancient and it wasn't just me, Amelia, and him, Ram, it was older, more spacious and yet so touchingly present, the timeless immensity of Guru-Shishya.

"And I see something else Amelia, which is grander and more wondrous than any of these attributes."

"What is it Ram?"

"I see God."

The crow cawed on the roof above the front door, the sunlit air vibrated between us; the notes of the wren outside serenaded the seconds as they passed and my lips quivered too in the spiritual purity of it. A force came upon me then, it was confident, sure and direct, no hesitation or doubt was possible as my words sprang out of me.

"And when I look at you also Ram, I see God."

He opened the book on the table and turned it to a blank page patting his pockets. "Where are the pens? I can never find the pens." I pulled out my own and offered it to him, careful to ensure the top was secured onto the body rather than have it thrown around and discarded as I knew he would otherwise do.

"Good, good, 'I see God', write it Amelia, write it big and write it three times."

Taking the book I dated it and copied out the words.

"Speak it Amelia, speak it three times."

I followed the instruction as he watched me intensely, holding the book like an exhibit in front of me.

"In that simple short statement Amelia, we have the whole wonder of Sakshi that I have brought you here to know, it's a device that reveals the truth. Look at the first word, 'I', so simple; we use it hundreds of times a day. But for the sadhak who is enquiring into its nature and applying Vichara, the tapas of 'Who am I?' can become a question over-analysed, a question so familiar that it becomes a convention, it loses its power like an exhausted battle. If I say to you now, 'Who knows these thoughts?' you will give me an answer, 'Atman or consciousness', all fine in itself, correct as an idea but these words are just thoughts in you. The question itself is a thought and you answer it with another thought. That is not enough. To date, you have existed in the personal; you have been working and searching through your sadhana for an improved personal 'I'. You now need to reach beyond the personal for that is how Sakshi is discovered. Tell me what the personal is, Amelia."

"I don't know, 'me', I suppose."

"The personal is your thinking, sensations and feelings."

"But that's everything Ram."

"No, it isn't everything."

"So what could there be other than thoughts, sensations and feelings that isn't personal?"

"Intimacy."

"But surely intimacy is intensely personal, my intimacy, my closest feelings?"

"Intimacy isn't personal, thinking about it is but the intimacy itself isn't. Look carefully at your words, that which says 'my' in your sentence is thought. Intimacy is intimacy; it's not *your* intimacy. It's not thought, nor is it a feeling."

"Well, what can it be then?"

"You already know the answer intuitively and securely in your heart, intimacy is 'I'."

"But you said it wasn't personal."

"Quite so Amelia, the personal is thought and is duality, the experience of two. Intimacy is not personal, it is Being, it is non-dual; not two. Don't worry about cracking the words and struggling to understand; feel it as I describe it. Thought and feeling are second things, the personal thinker is a second thing, but intimacy, 'I', is not a second thing, it is primary, it is unchanging, it is Advaita."

"Ram, I am trying to understand but it's hard, if only we could communicate this in another way, the words are so limiting, you have a great gift with them but it seems a poor medium for the subtleties of this."

"Don't use that as an excuse for non-vigilant thinking Amelia. Strive in your intelligence and don't give up. We have to use words and it's an exhilarating game. What we are trying to capture in the word 'I' is similarly approached through all the other Upanishadic words that we use in our tradition but whatever word we pick and however it is analysed, it is definitely pointing at intimacy. Maybe a language scholar would describe the meaning of the word 'intimacy' as closeness, so very good, can there be anything closer than 'I'? No. Maybe that same scholar would say it means familiarity, well, good, can there be anything more familiar than 'I'? No. Maybe that same scholar would say the meaning was togetherness, well, good, can anything be more together, in other words, present, than 'I'? No. Intimacy is first, the eternal, persistent flash of existence, the dweller within. Don't think that statement is some esoteric point; it is a literal point and don't be confused when I say it is not personal, be vigilant in your thinking. You cannot have intimacy, you are intimacy. Intimacy is universal and is beyond personal and at the same time it is 'I'. That is not a paradox, moving past the feeling that it is a paradox, is Self-realisation." He jabbed at the book with his finger. "So what is our second word Amelia? Tell me it."

"See, I see."

"Yes and what does seeing mean?"

"Looking."

"No that's wrong, looking is an action, an event, seeing is the power which looking utilises. To see is to experience something, to know something. Seeing is the perceiving of experiences, it's a global term, it's more than eyes. Seeing is knowing. Seeing is awareness. It is not the thing being seen; it is knowing itself. The ignorant see awareness as something in the head, some property of the senses, some capacity of the mind. That is not awareness, awareness is the primary perceiving power by which anything and everything is being known and experienced. Do you have any control or even influence over this power of seeing in the way I have described it?"

"Well no, it is just there."

"Exactly! It is just there, and do you have any control over the intimacy we just considered?"

"No. It is just there."

"Exactly. It is just there and that's true right now, isn't it? You see how magnificent that is without any effort on your part, it is just there and something must be responsible for its presence."

He picked up the book, took the top off the body of the pen and started to doodle, drawing characters and flying birds around the third word heavily embellishing the letter 'G'. I worried about the defacing of a five hundred year old book. I noticed my pen top had fallen to the floor.

"The third word is God. It's a big word, isn't it, well actually it's a very little word but its impact is infinite. We spoke last time you were here about what God is. I will not repeat that now. I see the understanding of it in your eyes, in your humility, in the fire of your love and your wonder for people, nature and things, I see it in your welfare and your grace and I see it in the way you most beautifully conduct yourself with your teacher. I know you realise what God is, at least as much as is possible right now but today our point is more dramatic, more incredible and more massive than we have discussed before. Our point is, God is here, not abstract, not distant, not elusive, not other or over there but actually, literally here, this. This whole, this chapel, these woods, the relationship between us, the life, the form, the motion, this is God. This God is the creation and destruction of planets and at the same time the whispering descant of a wren's lingering note at the last decaying second of dusk. This God is the deep, ancient and at the same time as fresh and new and delicate as buttercup dust. This God is potent beyond imagination and at the same time, the soft delicate kindness of your most understanding compassionate counsellor. God is here in every particle, in all the waves of movement, in every speck of space, in every unit of time. This whole wonder is his abundance and that very same abundance is also the intimacy that is Sakshi. Look at all this Amelia. This is not an abstract world, this is not insentient chemistry, this is God, existence itself! Look at it Amelia, see it."

A great hush came upon me in that moment, the air was shimmering, every element alive and vital. Dust trailed in the sunlit beam between us like an orbiting twinkling star. Everything was close and fresh, shining with existence. It was right, it was full, it was complete, the moment stretching itself with such ease and perfection, I could not see anywhere where I was not, I could not see any other.

"This is beautiful Ram."

"Moments ago Amelia, you said to me, "I see God". In that simple sentence there is contained the irrefutable intimacy of 'I am', the irrefutable presence of knowing and the irrefutable magnificence of divine expression. These three aspects are one, flowing seamlessly in one reality right now, here in this pew, a non-dual trinity that actually is this moment. The realised know this to be so; the unrealised find these simple descriptions confusing and continue to see the separation of me and things. You may not understand the truth of these words fully because this requires the deepest reflection. So I have this gift for you, an identity that will in time, draw forth the Vidya from your mind and show you the real. It is not a new identity, it is the timeless reality which illuminates the bubbling water, skipping and twirling, light-footed on the stepping stones. The you that is you can be given a glorious name, Sakshi, 'that which is witnessing'. What you are Amelia, in this moment, is the witnessing itself; the intimacy that knows all experience. When you were a child, a young woman, now, today, and on and on, Sakshi is the continuum, providing the constant unbroken sense of 'I' even though everything changes. Sakshi is the dweller within, the illuminating light, the eternal existence being experienced right now as 'I know, I am, I love'. Be vigilant and alert, do not let the inadequacy of words and translations confuse you. The witness is not austere or aloof, how could it be? The witness is rushing like a cascade, nourishing the field and refreshing all who breathe in its spray. Anything can be washed in such a cascade, the dark, the dirty, the miserable, the selfish, the selfless and the glorious. Everyone is affected by such sparkling water; everyone comes out clean. Sakshi is a perpetual fountain of consciousness, persistent in all states, flawless. You are that and as a consequence, all this is. You are Sakshi. Take some time, let it all move within you. At 11:00pm we will walk back to the house through the woods in the moonlight."

What a time. Nothing that had been said to me was dependent on being here in Bowslip or dependent on some special circumstance. It was applicable anywhere in the universe. I knew it was rare and that it came from an enlightened place. I would have to reflect upon it over and over again but that is the way with the Brahma Vidya. Just as Mary and the others pursued Self-realisation across centuries without even knowing the context, so I pursued the same goal,

moment by moment. What was my history? I could never know. What will my future be? I could never know. But what is certain is that here I am and my next step will lead me somewhere. And Mary, was she me, or was that just a romantic fancy? I could never know but it did not seem impossible. We spent the afternoon and evening in and around the chapel. I made a fire which Ram was very impressed with as it was usually him that made the fire. We brewed more tea in a vessel he got from around the back of the chapel, sang songs, kept warm, meditated and cleaned the chapel with utensils that were hidden under a tarpaulin in the roots of the beech. The dusk fell and the moon came up full and bright in a clear, cold crisp sky. Our four-hour night walk back to the village would be illuminated by moon
and stars.

We set off at 11:00pm arm in arm, I could not see far enough ahead to identify the next beech tree but the forest floor was clear enough and the way seemed to be working out. We had walked in silence for an hour before Ram broke it.
"What if I tell you our relationship is at an end Amelia."
"What do you mean?"
"What if I send you away, don't talk to you anymore."
"I would be devastated Ram, why would you say that?"
"What if I told you that I have another student now, someone who is better than you and I must devote all my time to them and cannot teach you?"
"I would hate that Ram."
At that exact moment a loud crack happened in the silence of the woods, off to the right.
"What's that?" I cried out.
He didn't reply and kept on walking in silence for ten minutes. I felt shocked, disturbed and very uneasy, not sure what to do about what he had said. My mind leapt. What did he mean, what was he trying

to say? Did our history mean nothing? Was it something I had done, had I failed, was I not good enough? And who was this other? Jealously began its creeping ascent. A second crack came loud and sharp. I looked at him for reaction, startled, yet he was expressionless. What was this? We kept walking.

"How do you feel, Amelia?"

"Frightened Ram, worried."

"Who is frightened and worried?"

"Me, I am frightened."

He turned and grabbed me. "No! This is a pivotal moment. You are not frightened; you are witnessing the fear. You are definitely the witness right now, you are definitely not the fear, do you see? And by the way, I love you and am committed to your realisation, I am going nowhere. Where could I go? I am here. Another of the guru's tactics, I'm afraid. It's always best to teach by example don't you think? And what if the opposite scenario happened, what if I told you, you were the best student ever and I wanted you to succeed me and live with me here in Bowslip?"

I was reeling, breathless at the waves of relief, its impact sang in me like a tuning fork and also I wanted to punch him.

"Well it might take some getting used to Ram, it would be daunting but truthfully, I would be honoured and thrilled."

"And who would be thrilled?"

I didn't need to respond.

"Your mind would be motivated by that pleasure, you would feel confirmed by it, you would feel special. Different feelings from the threat and the fear of rejection but the principle never changes. Sakshi is constant, states of experience are not."

Crack! For a third time and closer, the penetrating noise seemed upon us, it was shocking. Instantly Ram clapped his hands three times, sharp and loud, there was a rustling in the undergrowth then nothing. "It's a stag, Amelia, testing his authority. He won't come back now but he will be watching. If it was the rutting season and there were hinds about I would stop and make a lot of noise to ensure he had gone, but here in the winter I know it will be threat only. Who just acted then, who clapped his hands?"

"Sakshi?"

"No, again this is a critical point of understanding, not Sakshi, the body acted, the mind acted, the doer acted and quite rightly. There will and must always be action and Sakshi is always the witness. If my statements to you just now had been said with intent, then as well as the natural witnessing, something in you would have acted, thoughts and feelings would have raised a response in you, you would have investigated, negotiated, debated, enquired. That is right Amelia, it is how you tread the stepping stones, it is the natural to and fro of life. The point is, the doer in you can either do that skilfully, maturely, wisely taking action that is relevant to the moment and passes swiftly or, that same doer will take action that is not relevant to the moment but is a consequence of ghosts. And what are ghosts, Amelia? I know you haven't liked the term but it's played its part I'm sure you agree. Ghosts are redundant, false thoughts that can be discarded. Putting this into application is now your offer. It's a rare position, it's a place outside of conditioning and it's truly sacred. The Brahma Vidya is philosophy, you have to have it, but taking action is the sadhana. This is how you free your mind. Act, act, act."

Owls called to one another across the canopy, there was the odd sound in the wood but I didn't try to give it any cause or story. I was struck by the fact that my previous time in the forest had been racked with fear and imagination, it was strong, it possessed me but it was also entirely false, it was my mind alone. If I knew that and didn't forget that principle, could my future experiences be different, could they? As always, I knew that my time here with him was rarefied, the insight was strong in me now but how would it be back in the day-to-day of my life and relationships? I stopped him on the path, he didn't object and we gazed up at a startlingly clear sky. The moonlight was strong but we could still see millions of glittering stars most clearly. Two shooting stars travelled across the vista above us, one after the other, bright, thrilling and then decaying in an instant.

"Om Namah Shivaya," said Ram.

"Ram, I know I will leave here soon, so when I am alone amidst all the responsibilities and interactions with people, I understand that Sakshi is continuous but how will the doer in me know what is right action, when to change circumstance or when to change my attitude and opinions?"

"Ah-ha! No-one can answer that; it is the art of life, isn't it? The skill of the mature and the wise, it comes to you as a consequence of sadhana and as an output of Viveka. But I can give a simple formula to inspire you. Bring your mind to auspiciousness, alert to the moment and free of the past and in that auspiciousness, act."

His phrase hung in the air; it was a beautiful statement. He looked at me, his face implacable, deep compassion in his steady kind eyes amidst an unwavering, determined confidence and authority of expression that I knew would give no ground. This was the face of the teacher, something beyond convention, it was indeed guru.

"An auspicious mind is the Sivam I mentioned to you, it is the third pillar of my darshan to you and for another time, you have enough for now. When you come again, we will travel to the mountains where the snows are, where the leopards and the hares roam, where there are purer atmospheres and speak of auspiciousness there. Be patient, Amelia, I have given you much. It requires long reflection. Go away and get fit, apply what has been given to you, see that Sakshi floods each and every moment with the security of Being, and that the moment is taking care of itself as long as there is ghost-free action. Enjoy the stepping stones, clinging to nothing except the very best, the Brahma Vidya, the Guru-Shishya and if stepping

stones get destroyed because of some storm, it is those powers that will carry you across to new rivers, better rivers. Stay for a few more days; enjoy yourself here with me, living the day here with me, worshipping the moment here with me. The darshan is done and when you leave I will escort you back, I need to put that stag in his place. I know where
to find him."

"When shall I return Ram, when will I come back?"

"In a thousand years, Amelia but don't despair, that's not conventional time, it's Timecoast time, and it could come round in a second, a day or a year, meet me there. Shall I send you a note?"

"Yes please, I will wait for you, don't let it be too long. What will you do when I am away Ram?"

"Many things Amelia, I have much to do in the village and I have an outside trip to make."

"Do you mean outside Bowslip? Where will you go?"

"To my yak trader."

"Hari Om, Amelia."

"Hari Om, Ram."

Chapter Seven

Snowfield

one year later
winter in the village

Amelia had never been this side of the river before. Ram's house and the village were off to the east, there had been no reason to explore the western bank. In front of her in this isolated place a huge beech tree lay broken on its side. It had fallen right opposite the six stepping stones that had caused her to cross the river in the first place, stones that seemed to lead nowhere; there wasn't any path this side of the brook only rough undergrowth. She scrambled up through the giant root ball torn from the ripped earth below her, upended and ungainly like a chaos of spiders, stones and earth caught up in all its crevices. She sat down on the trunk in reflective mood, marvelling at the exciting fact of being here in Bowslip engaging once again in sadhana with her Guru in these most precious of surroundings. What had brought her to this point? When did her spiritual life start? What even is a beginning? She could not remember a time when this passion for seeking was not. If asked to tell her tale about the origins of the spiritual compulsion in her, she would pinpoint certain desires and experiences, various questions she had but really these were just incidents, bubbles in a flowing stream. The metaphor was pleasurable as she sat listening to the sounds of the wood and the trickle of the water splashing against the sides of the stepping stones behind her. Swinging her legs back and forth beneath her like a child, she thought more about the early days, before this place, before she found her teacher. Then, awakening was a pastime, now it was everything. There was nothing in her world that was not spiritual anymore because spiritual was simply being alive in awareness, living this life, responding to all that arose, constantly investigating herself, the world and God. All her wits had become fully absorbed in the astonishing challenges, provocations, encounters and insights that had been packed into these passionate years with her teacher. She knew that an optimum time to learn from your guru is twelve years, so maybe after eight years she was coming to some kind of transition point. She had asked Ram about this milestone as she had done

before, he had scoffed at her rudely.
"Twelve years of constant sadhana and service Amelia, constant devotion, twelve years for the dedicated. For the inconsistent and the indulgent multiply it by ten."
"That's more than a lifetime," she had responded.
"And?"
Standing on the thick trunk like a surfer on her board, balancing five feet off the ground, she walked gingerly forwards down the length of the fallen tree, positioning herself on the thinnest spur she could safely reach inside the tumble of the upended top. The forest ahead of her was a bedraggled tangle of winter, the trees drooping languidly amidst the damp silence. It was obvious nobody ever came here, you could feel it in the dirt, that unsullied silence of leaf and mould and the scattered chaos of brittle dead wood already feeding the saplings and new shoots soon to rise in spring. One magnificent single oak stood proudly like an ice queen before her, its skeletal winter canopy devoid of all its jewels, occupying the sky with the tracery of lace, just as a snowflake may grace your hand.

Amelia had arrived yesterday afternoon. She spent the day settling in, acclimatising to this powerful place not sure exactly what was ahead, only that she was here for the sadhana of Shiva. That had been the outstanding element from her last big trip when she received teaching on three pillars of wisdom. Ram had described the first two, Satyam and Sakshi in the most dramatic of ways but the third, Shiva, was deferred, postponed for another time he had said and now here she was. To describe teaching as pillars seemed structural like a geometry of the mind.
"Everyone needs a framework Amelia," he had told her, "all mansions stand on a foundation, without architecture you will not be able to attain any steadiness and steadiness is good."
The impact of that last trip influenced her life profoundly in her time away because she had given Satyam and Sakshi all her attention and

commitment. Integrating the teachings into the detail of herself and her world was the way she practised spirituality now. The theoretical had become the experiential because she looked at life that way, worked at it with her intelligence and her vision. It gave her such faith in the teachings themselves and the rightness of her direction in Vedanta. It was jnana made real. She remembered a time when things were somehow not so deep. She would be inspired and affected by her interactions with Ram while they were happening but once apart that focus would drop off as she fell back into old ways. That weakness had died in her now, thank God. She had made the discovery that all sadhaks must eventually make, that progress was a property of vigilance and application. You simply remembered, thought about it and applied. Amelia understood the way of Vedanta now, she really did, it had merged upon the preliminary sadhana she already knew and strengthened it immeasurably. She was now embedded in her path, the confidence of it consolidated in her mind by the description Ram had repeatedly transferred to her.

"I am pointing you at a principal blend of bhakti and jnana together Amelia, love and intelligence converged. The bhakti is your relationship with God in all forms, expressing your heart in the joy of nature, companionship, puja, prayer and satsang. The jnana is your exhilarating intelligence, your thrilling investigation into the nature of reality. Love with intelligence equally combined is my teaching, not love alone and not intelligence alone. This collection of forces is a complete equation of spirituality. It is not difficult. Put some arrangements in place, adopt positive habits and discriminate with how you use your time."

This focus and change in priorities had felt like a maturing for her. She watched, she considered, she read Vedanta but not too much to the point of being tied up in knots. She wrote down her own ideas, prayed to God, keeping open that marvellous personal dialogue of inner private communication. She made some modifications to her behaviour, cancelling out some old negative habits and creating some new ones that served her better and she enjoyed the continuous loving resources of her Guru. These ways had simply become her truth and while everything practical and domestic went on, she knew that this pursuit of realisation was and is the first priority of her life.

Through the tangle of branches and twigs in front of her an object right at the very apex of the fallen tree caught her eye. What was that? Balancing to the side and standing on tiptoe she could see the top of a white stone pillar. It was conical, standing alone in a thick bramble patch, the spiky undergrowth covering about two thirds of its height. It must be about eight feet high. The beech had fallen like a plumb line, landing just a metre from this thing, dragging down the thick surrounding vegetation to expose it. This was not a natural object. A pillar in the forest and stepping stones leading nowhere? Maybe they were connected. Back across the river she paced down the four-mile track heading for the village, the afternoon was progressing and she needed to return before dusk. Shiva, what a word, what a name, she pondered it as she walked. Was she to learn about the great and mighty Puranic God dancing the universe or some other mystery? What would be the purpose of this particular trip? What would be the outcome? She realised she could never know that in advance, she could only experience it as it was happening but it was hard not to try and shape it in her mind. Once she was over the rise and looking into the valley below, the abandoned village and the lights shining from the house of her Guru came into view. What is Shiva? She would ask him as soon as she got back.

Ram had been living permanently at his place in the village now for three years. Actually, he had always lived there but Amelia never knew that. The pathways around Bowslip House where she used to meet him were abandoned now, at least for her, because all things move. She had moved and the teacher must move too. The old hut had been the place for her preliminary days, teaching about the basic way of things, the person and the person's challenges. Then they had spent that time at the temple, it had been an amazing adventure and he knew those days held a tender familiarity for her which she might pine for at times. As far as he was concerned reminiscing like that risked becoming like comfort eating. The moment right here and right now was everything, fresh and immediate, blazing with the eternal thrill of the bright and the new. This was the place to engage. Any thoughts of wanting it another way must die as soon as they tried to rise, and he would see to it that they did. Since he had given Amelia the darshan of Sakshi two years ago, she had visited him briefly on two occasions, using the new route in that he had given her. Her previous journey from Bowslip House took her three days; the new way was for the accomplished shishyas and could be done in four hours. He had played it down but actually it was a sign of attainment that she had been trusted with that information. It was curious that access was private and exclusive like that as Bowslip was not guarded or purposefully hidden at all, it just required a certain determination to explore the landscape and a persistence that few people had. You couldn't just be given the directions, you had to earn them. Off the B3151, down an unclassified road onto what looked like an abandoned forest drove; gated but not locked, walking for two miles to the intersecting brooks and then pushing through the reeds for five hundred metres until the land cleared out. Then you could walk through the peaty ground alongside the brook following it east. It was a four-mile trek but you could do it in ninety minutes. The turning point had to be specifically explained and you had to find the right hillock to crest amongst several but once over it and into the woods on the other side, the pillar was just two hundred metres in. It was eroded white stone and blended into the landscape but five feet high and

discernible if you looked. The village was another three miles through the thick forest.
"It's not a marker post," said Ram when she had asked him, "it's a tethering post but it serves the function of pointing out where to go, maybe I should remove it in case of unwanted visitors but it's been there a long time."
Her two trips had been for weekend short stays, once in the spring when the whole place was alive with magic and energy, it was very beautiful but she couldn't sleep. She had helped Ram fix up his hay store and animal shed in readiness for his new working animal that he said was on its way. Another donkey she thought, dear Donkey, he was often on her mind. The second time in midsummer when all was shimmering in an abundance of colour, life, noise and heat. She had taken it easy, just resting and sitting in the garden. Ram had been gentle, social and friendly with her, chatting about the forest, cooking, reading her stories of early adventurers in Tibet and India. Amelia hadn't been read to for thirty years, it was lovely. She curled up on his big sofa, light and easy in her summer clothes and lived like a child in the warmth of it all. He gave her a present on her last day, perfectly wrapped in leaves with a bow made of creeper and left her to unwrap it. It was a small Tamil book with a message that said:
Read chapter two of this before twelve years are up
எல்லாம் ஒன்றே
"But it's in Tamil," she said to him.
"Then get it translated," he replied.
Amelia had no doubt that she would.
"Have you enjoyed yourself Amelia?" He asked as she had been about to go.
"Yes Ram, it has been lovely. Thank you."
"And you are feeling refreshed, settled?"
"Yes, I am feeling really good."
"Come again in the winter and come for a month; autumn and

winter are the best times for sadhana when the decay is on the ground. Come then, when the snow may fall, come for Shiva."

It had taken her several months to organise, negotiating a sabbatical from work, explaining to family and friends that she was going on a private trip to study Vedanta for a month, trying to avoid the probing questions and not least sorting out the cats and her routine affairs. She had travelled in yesterday on the 668-country bus with a rucksack and holdall, alighting one mile from the entrance to the drove. The walk in was tough with the bags, she had to stop frequently to adjust straps and weight but after two and a half hours of tramp, it was pleasing to finally be closing in on the very last corner, around which she knew the stone pillar would come into view.

She had smelt him before she saw him, standing there around the bend just twelve feet in front of her, wild and massive, dominating the pathway like some shaman's effigy, a great pungent beast, shaggy head, prominent horns looking down into her face. Her heart was in her mouth, tension squeezed her guts. Beast snorted and swayed against the tethering post as his great pylon legs shifted on the stones and crushed the pebbles. Shaking out his hairy forelock he pawed the ground once and fixed her with a stare. Amelia was poised to run immediately, to defend herself from Beast, shoo it away, scare it off but it was tethered to the post blocking her path. Perhaps she could climb up the scree and trek across above him she thought, make a detour but it was difficult, there was no clear way. Beast let out a sigh at that point, opened and closed his soft-lipped mouth and continued to look straight at her. Tied on the post was a note; it could only be from Ram. She took off her rucksack watching Beast like a hawk. He didn't move, solid and implacable like the great bull of the Vedas. Picking up a stick she tried to hook the note but it was hopeless. She took a single step to the right and then another, nothing happened, Beast didn't rear up or stick her with his awful horns. His eyelids blinked and his cheek twitched as she planned her next move, continuing to stand and stare at her, breathing with a sound like the rush in a sea cave when the waves recede. Keeping her eyes on him, alert and ready to leap for cover, she edged to the post, grabbed the note and sidled back slowly not wanting to rouse or spook Beast. Ripping open the envelope she unfolded the paper:

This is Milo he is from Mongolia you can load him with all your gear ride him if you want once you untether him he will make his own way he wants to come back to me talk to him kindly he is insulted by your fear and an insulted yak is a dangerous thing xR

Ram was in the yard when she arrived.

"You didn't ride him then? An opportunity missed."

He had gone straight to Beast, nuzzled him and whispered in his ear, pulled a handful of corn from his pocket and given it to the yak who crunched as if he was crushing rocks, a great, guttural grinding noise. Amelia and Ram had embraced like the spiritual siblings they were, greeted each other and talked about her journey as they unloaded yak, organised her kit and settled Beast in his new byre; a good space, with a stash of hay, a water tank, a chicken pen and two goats. They spent the evening sitting in the kitchen on the big yellow sofa exchanging stories and ephemeral things. Now a day later, returning from the broken beech tree Amelia is approaching that same kitchen with her mind full of the intrigue of Shiva. As she approaches the door in the early evening light of that second day, feeling sweaty from the pace of the walk, with the Shiva question on her lips and ready to burst, she can tell her own story.

"Make tea," said Ram.

He signals to the range as I come in the front door ducking under the low lintel. The kitchen table is scattered with papers, maps, notes and coloured pencils. He is standing, hunched over this display with the corner light trained on the space before him. The room is buzzing with speed and energy. It hits me in the belly the moment I enter as if I've been poked. I stand still at the range staring inquisitively at the intensity before me as the kettle starts to whistle.

"Astronomical charts, Amelia."

"Are we going to the stars then?" I reply and regret my joke immediately.

"We are going to the snowfield, there are only star points to navigate by, if the timing is awry, we will never hit the mark."

"What is the mark?" I ask.

"The mountain hermitage, in the snowfield."

I think to myself, what snowfield? We are in Somerset, there are no mountains, but I choose to keep quiet.

"We have to be very exact in our discipline if we are to not be fatally lost. The snowfield is a serious place Amelia, the only way to find the hermitage is by an exact polar line measured from the alignment of this star and that constellation at a specific predicted point in orbit; it's a tricky calculation, it takes time."

I carry the teapot and cups to the table and wait while he makes room amidst the sprawl of work and sits back in his chair. The chart is astonishing, intricate and complex, actually I had never seen anything like it, I wondered how it could even have been produced, there must have been several thousand individually named objects, each displayed with their Latin names, all with intersecting sight lines, geometric information, scale lines and symbols like way-marks.

"This is incredible Ram, where did you get it?"

"It belongs here. This is one very small region of the Milky Way; it is as much information as we can realistically take in and work with. Look at the immensity of it Amelia. It is not surprising that our ancestors looked around them and saw not stellar objects but Gods. The idea of insentient matter is quite new you know and that's not

what they saw, they saw living entities, a sky and an earth full of consciousness. We now look on that as primitive because we have decided on viewing things a different way but what is better, to relate to the sun as a product of insentient material physics or as a living entity? You like the summer, don't you?"
"Yes of course, it is a beautiful season."
"You are lucky to know it like that. The sweet warmth of summer is the diluted rays of that sun, a single star that would incinerate you in a nanosecond if it were not for the atmosphere. What you feel as pleasing rays upon your face is the edge of a stellar ferocity, continuously transforming matter in a great nuclear furnace ablaze for five billion years. Stars, Amelia, my God, one day we should really consider their nature for I promise you it would shock your tiny mind into absence. And it is the alignment of these very same stars that will guide us to the hermitage."
We drink the tea in silence. A great stillness descends upon me sitting there in the kitchen next to my Guru. I stay quiet, not really thinking as he carries on his work around me, pushing the papers, calculating with a metre long ruler and a protractor, referring to his notes and scrawling on his pad. I move to the sofa and stretch out comfortably, watching him leaning over the table amidst the teacups and papers, my eyes close to the thoughts of ancient Gods.

The sound of the runners clattering on the curtain poles stirs me as he pulls the heavy drapes closed and opens the door indicating for me to come outside and onto the step. It is early evening and dark. With the door closed behind us it is pitch black.
"Look up Amelia."
Above us the sky is peppered with an infinite spray of points of light, misty long bands of trailing illumination spread upon the dense darkness of the sharp winter evening like rivulets of glowing dust.
"This is your galaxy Amelia, the Milky Way. It is here, there and everywhere you can see, in a vast spread-out disc. You live in the

Milky Way; this garden is in this very same galaxy. Contemplate the vastness, it's big, have you noticed that? If you could somehow travel at the speed of light which is 186,000 miles per second and you took a journey to cross this single galaxy from edge to edge, it would take you 100,000 years at that tremendous speed. Consider it, the energy, the forces and the unbelievable distances, both in space and time. It's hard to understand why the interests and preoccupations of people are so superficial and small-minded when you recognise the grandeur of all this life within which we live moment by moment. Look at all these points of light scattered in every direction you can see, mostly these are stars, just like the sun. How many stars do you think there are in this, your own galaxy?"

"I don't know Ram, a lot I'm sure, a million maybe?"

"That would be a lot but no, multiply it and multiply it again. There are two hundred billion stars in this one single galaxy. Consider it, two hundred billion. I want you to get excited about the cosmos Amelia. The enlightened are almost dancing with joy with the reality of it, whilst the ignorant sleep and dream of tiny things, caught up in mundaneness. It's a terrible disease and it's unacceptable for the sadhaks. Look up Amelia, feel it. Ignorance is dense and does not know how to experience beauty like this, people just look and see a thing but that's not how the mystics behave. The only way to know beauty is to stop thinking and feel it in your heart, the experience, not the object but the experience. I tell you once you engage like this with living life, there can be only one outcome, joy. My God, I am a part of all this, this is happening, I feel it, I know it, I am it. Can you conceive of the size, can you conceive of the wonder of existence? Is it shimmering in your senses, is ananda bubbling in your heart or are you bored by the stillness and consumed by mundane transient things?"

His words provoke me, bringing to the surface an inadequacy that I have avoided facing because it just made me miserable. The truth is I can never connect completely with beauty. I can see it, appreciate it, enjoy it of course, just like everybody does, there is nothing wrong with me in that sense but to me it is always something other, something over there to watch or feel as a passing experience and that is never completely satisfying. It seems to satisfy others but it doesn't satisfy me. I know I am missing something that the saints had, something I have read about, something that Ram has; the openness, the freedom, the gaiety, the pleasure of it and I do not know how to get it. In fact, many of the spiritual practices I have done in my life were unknowingly for this purpose; to try and find that natural subtle ecstasy. But right now, on this step next to him, this moment is different. I am not looking at something; I am with it, really with it. I feel my emotions trembling as the weight of this dawns. I am not thinking about anything else or wanting anything else or more importantly, comparing or contrasting this with the next thing. None of that. I am experiencing, just experiencing. Oneness is this experiencing itself, without secondary thought, my God. In other memorable moments of significance in my life, moments of deep love, flowing grace, the common feature was joy. I had always thought it was the thing that was joyful, the event but it is quite clear, right in this moment that it isn't. It is the merging into it, the experiencing that expresses joy. This seems to be a secret being revealed to me as I gaze into the night. My skin tingles with the significance. This is what oneness is, not some other dimensional dissolution, it is experiencing itself.

"I can't conceive it Ram, the galaxy is beautiful, beautiful."

"Do you know how many other galaxies there are like this in the known universe Amelia?"

My eyes fix on the milky band above me; I think of the two hundred billion other stars within it and shake my head.

"Two trillion and all this is a tiny fraction of that we sometimes call Shiva."

The tremoring inside me accelerates and I burst into tears.

I wake at 2:30am following a fractious dream. My mind had been unsettled since coming to my room and turning out the light in the silent house. It made no sense from the sublime moments on the step earlier in the evening. All I can say is that the high of that perfect moment has crashed into a kind of unease. I feel all at sea, confused by the vastness of things, uncertain of my way and troubled, just as you feel when you have something and then it's lost or turns out not to be what you thought. I am only a whisker away from starting to feel hopeless. I read but can't concentrate and stare at the ceiling listening to the creaks and groans of the house, feeling oppressed as if I'm being watched, like I am unsafe. Old threats and inadequacies move tensely in my head. I can't sleep and at 6:00am, feeling jet-lagged and bleak, I come downstairs to find Ram already at the table working on his chart.

"Sit down Amelia and do this calculation for me."

It was simple maths adding up three sets of figures.

"Do they balance out?" he said.

"No."

"That's a problem, check them again."

I sigh, get the same answer and look at him resentfully. He holds my gaze for a moment.

"Some turbulence is upon you Amelia, you don't need to understand it and you definitely shouldn't judge yourself by it, if you do your thoughts and conclusions won't be reliable. Everyone experiences it in different ways as their senses become exposed to higher energies. It's not permanent but it is common. This is a powerful place and these are powerful times. Right now why don't you make porridge and tea, give me the sums."

While the kettle is boiling and the pan heating up, I open the door and stand outside for a moment. The dawn hasn't broken and the sky is still full of stars but now I feel dense and detached. What is this sensitive instability of my mind? I must ask him once again. His teaching to me on Satyam had addressed it directly last year. I had thought about it, I understood it but it hadn't brought me the freedom I expected. The reality is, my mind is still not in my control, it's affecting my life and it's not an easy thing.

"Have I got two minds Ram?" I say as I put the porridge on the table.

"Absurd, what are you talking about?"

"Or more than two. My thoughts and feelings, they change on a whim, just last night all was peaceful and inspired and then this morning it's all up in the air. There is no stability. It's like there are two of me, or three or four."

He looks at me with an expression of intense kindness. His eyes saying, "It's all right Amelia, never mind, you are doing your best and I love you, don't worry about it". I sit opposite him and think to myself; this is really lovely, should I just stay in these rays of acceptance and nurture? Is this what I want from him, the pleasing atmosphere of love and grace to settle this particular moment, to hold me close or do I want conquering sadhana? I can't decide. The truth is I want both, I want many things. My eyes close to the sound of the clock ticking on the wall and the aroma of porridge.

"Which one of you is this?" says Ram playfully, "Number one or number two?"

"The happy one is me, the positive one; I want her, the one who was here last night. I don't want this dissatisfied troubled one."

"It's the wants that are the problem, why don't you just give them up and be patient, none of this is substantial. You are talking about the experience of mood activity and you give it too much attention as if it's solid, when it isn't. Moods are the common condition of every mind so why are you surprised and what are you complaining about? If you are waiting for all of that to completely stop you will waste your days. It's a bit like nature, the turning of the seasons, only a fool tries to deny the seasons, the wise one just adapts in the flow of things. There is no-one that has a constantly clear mind, that is not how minds behave, it's a myth to think otherwise."

"Do you mean then that the mind can't be fixed?"

"The desire to fix is a great burden. You need to stop obsessing about these vrittis; they come, they go and they pass swiftly unless we cling to them and give them more value than they deserve, then they stick. Unwanted and undesirable thoughts move in all minds like a stream. The more you give it attention and meaning the more it seems important, the more it bites and the stronger the current of that stream is. Let it all flash and move with great speed, get with the speed and learn to keep your perspective, the one that constantly sees beyond it, then the stream becomes a trickle and nobody cares about trickles."

"But why does it happen?"

"We have discussed it before and that is enough. You don't need to understand everything perfectly; often things don't have a meaning. Why does the weather happen? Multiple forces interacting, movement and change. The desire to understand it all assigns energy and false purpose to things which can simply be transcended. This life is dynamic, it doesn't all need to be defined and understood. Growth is often painful because you have to recognise you can't have things in the way you want and you have to let those parts of you die. The dying off is less painful than the clinging on Amelia. The wise have become heroic; they have learnt to dissolve their wants, to enjoy these little deaths."

"Am I at the mercy of my mind then, my moods, feelings and thoughts?"

"No, you are not and we have discussed this extensively. Mind can be improved immeasurably, desires left behind, habits overcome. The puja, the tapas, the yoga, all improves the tone of the mind. You know that and you experience it frequently. Keep your perspective, work hard to do that. But really these methods of making it better are just psychological tactics, effective in the moment but not conquering. Soon we will travel into the mountains where the air is clearer and the darshan can become conquering. Then we will speak more of transcendence but as for now you are in no fit state for anything. Get out, do something practical, go and clean out Milo, make yourself useful about the place. Pull up the old rope from the well and disengage it, we need to replace it when I get back."

He returns to his work and ignores me. I take my tea outside and sit on the step wondering why I am here and even if I want to be. Once again his conversation has shaken me up. I knew my relationship with my teacher to have the greatest affection and also to be the most challenging exposure at times. There was a spiritual force to it, sometimes it upset me, usually it enthralled me but mostly it exhilarated me. There would be moments of heart melting tenderness, fulfilling beyond any common relationship and then this incision of intelligence that hit the mark without diplomacy or softening. It was the experience of direct honesty and it was amazingly rare, I valued it more than any other experience I had ever had but right now it just felt unyielding and tough. Just give up wanting, how could I possibly do that? Psychological tactics, that seemed dismissive and this trip to the mountains, it didn't make any sense, there are no mountains, why can't we just stay around the house in these comforts, and I didn't want to deal with Beast, why should I? The yak disturbed me; there was nothing sweet about him, nothing gentle or human like Donkey, only wild nature. The chickens started to move about and the goats poked their noses outside, bleating. One came over, stood close to me and I stroked her neck. It's alright for you, I thought, simple, easy, why is my mind so all over the place? As I entered the byre Beast made his rattling, grunting yak noise. I cranked the wind-up lantern hanging on the beam, releasing its weak glow out of which he peered at me like a Minotaur, his shaggy locks scraping the ground and falling across his face. I did my best to clean out his dung, filled up the water trough and tied up a new sheaf of oats but I couldn't get right in amongst him in his stall; that was asking too much. I tried to avoid touching him, left him to his oats and took the wheelbarrow to the muck heap.

The meditation bell rang at 9:00am and I went to the temple room. It was a beautiful space at the back of the house, clean and empty except for the comforts of practice; cushions, chairs, blankets, a wonderful old Indian rug, various puja objects and always flowers. The French windows looked out across the garden where the sun rose and the room was full of light. I loved being in there, it was like a nest of perfection, so soft, a place where the mantras were chanted every day and had been for longer than I knew. Ram was very affectionate to me and kind, offering me blankets and water, singing a sweet little bhajan and speaking encouraging, soothing words, checking on me and settling me down, making sure I was comfortable. We chanted Om, he rang his hand bell, silence washed upon the room but it didn't wash within me. I was too distracted and disheartened, I knew it would be hopeless, meditation wouldn't work. I would just end up sitting with my eyes shut thinking other things. My meditation had not been going well for some time and wasn't improving. I had raised it with him in a casual way when I was here in the spring, complaining that distraction and intrusive thoughts were preventing me from meditating. He gave me an immediate challenge there and then, to stand up in the kitchen and not move a centimetre, keep my eyes open, not shift my gaze and not think for thirty seconds. I responded eagerly; it was a fun challenge. To not move was easy, to keep my eyes still was reasonably easy but to not think, that was hard. Patterns of thought popped up within seconds. I worked at this and was able to eventually resist the normal movement of thought but there was still something else there waiting in the wings, it was like an expectant watcher held in abeyance, me trying not to think. I was frustrated by this and sought his advice.

"That's the intruder you have found and she is the whole problem, it is she who is responsible for your stagnation. Now that you have identified her you will be better prepared. That intruder has to be released. Double the exercise, do it for a minute."

So I tried to practise it and struggled. Having a silent mind empty of common thought was one thing, which was getting easier but being free of this intruder who waited behind thought like an overseer, that was something else. I needed some help, some more detailed guidance on where I was going with my meditation. I will have to ask him but right now I will just listen to the birds and the sound of my breath, maybe I will fall asleep. During the rest of the morning I didn't see Ram once and he didn't turn up for lunch. I spent my time sitting on the sofa thinking to myself and working on the heavy old rope at the well-head. It was long and jammed in the pulley and I was getting filthy trying to free it but eventually it was out and coiled on the ground. I was at the outside tap rinsing the caked blood from my scraped knuckles when he came back down the path with his foraging bag, went straight to the byre and let out Beast who proceeded to roam the garden, grunting and taking an interest in me as I waited at the well-head. I kept my eye on his horns and his slather and kept repositioning myself around the well-shaft to stay out of rubbing distance. Ram came out of the shed with a skein of fresh rope and a bag of tools. I helped him replace and strengthen the wooden pulley which had become weakened and cracked by age. It took an hour of fiddly work, muscles and sweat. We sat there on the grass when the job was done enjoying the cool fresh water that I had just pulled up while he observed and tested the wheel mechanism. Beast had moved into the border and was lying, chewing in the long grass.

"Good work Amelia, are you feeling better? Good to be effective isn't it? To do things, to initiate actions. Creativity and activity are natural consequences of an awakened life, it reflects happiness and banishes dullness. It's impossible to be dull when you are awakened to God, so it's best to act rather than mope about, don't you agree?"

We looked at each other in great intensity for several minutes in the silence of the garden, only grunts from Beast and the trilling of birds. I appreciated him trying to lighten the tone. His manner when we had been together this morning had been very tender and I knew from experience that he was inviting me. I must grab the moment and open up about what was on my mind. A robin fluttered down and sat right on the well-head wall just a metre away and started pecking at the moss.

"How can my meditation improve and advance Ram, what should I do, what is the nature of progress?"

"It depends what you want, what you are capable of; it is not the same for all. Why do you want to meditate?"

"For enlightenment."

"Aha! Good answer Amelia, I love you for it, it's why you are here in my place. Meditation improves through evolution just like all things. It's a combination of skill, discovery and attainment; you get better at it because you are experienced in the skill. It advances in character because you have developed some spiritual and mental muscles. The majority of people don't acquire those muscles, they meditate because they have a wish for simple happiness and peace of mind, that's all and that is a totally worthwhile aim. They know those qualities are good for them because they are experienced daily. If you wake up from a great sleep you benefit because you have been in the void of unconsciousness which is naturally pure. Meditation is the same as the purity of deep sleep but with awareness. People intuitively know the pleasure of peace of mind and that's what they want. So they should; creativity, intelligence and well-being are the result of an inspired mind, refreshed by meditation; everybody should meditate like this. But for the likes of you, the benefits of such an approach are a foundation only. Your meditation has plateaued at this point. You should shape up, renew your focus and get beyond it. What are you waiting for?"

I knew he was goading me again as if somehow I hadn't got it and I should try harder. My sadhana had suffered from that before; always striving for something else. When I did try harder it just made my practice tense. He had even told me many times not to do that. But he was being mercurial with me now, behaving differently. Potency arose between us, ready to engage, not the soft appeasement of Donkey but the uncompromising reality of Beast. I realised it was this that was rattling my nerves but despite my sensibilities it was intensely stimulating. I let myself relax profoundly.

"We won't speak of the preliminary meditations," said Ram, "suffice to say all meditators require the ability to establish a foundation of stillness, first for the body and then for the mind, to be steady and at ease with silence. And then, in those conditions, to work at achieving a concentrated mind, able to overcome fidgeting, boredom, distraction and all those agitating forces which are the enemy of stillness. This is the essential capability for all. If you ever think that such control is weak in you, then don't just accept it but continue with all speed to do your sadhanas, watch the breath, control the mind and unravel the agitations in you through puja and service. This is basic, Amelia. From that foundation, meditation then develops through Vichara and becomes something different. Vichara is distinctly two-fold in character; firstly an active, thinking enquiry in the normal waking state, using your normal faculties to consider the reality around you, in the world and in your mind. You are thinking, throwing questions and doubts upon your teacher, pondering, watching, wondering, reading the Vedanta, using your intelligence. This is active Vichara and is essential to overcome the ignorance in you. Secondly you are meditating in silence. Vichara is then not active thinking at all but a subtle perceiving, using an ability of mind that we call inner enquiry, to look into what is. You know all this but I am reminding you of the qualities of that enquiry because that is what you have been in danger of forgetting. What do I mean by subtle perceiving? It is not the normal probing of an object, not something to look at and examine with the ordinary senses, neither is it a line of thought. You should experience it as acknowledging, appreciating and allowing. These are not doing actions nor are they passive, it is something in between where intelligence realises what is present within the appearance and comes to recognise it. To stimulate this, Vichara begins with the thrilling inner curiosity, 'Who am I?'. Looking into the condition of yourself. You discover the everyday experience of me is a combination of senses, sensations and thoughts, a kind of subtle stuff. Now that is a good discovery but hold on, that stuff, including thought itself, is being watched by something else, a someone who is doing the Vichara and that we can call the thinker. Common meditation is just like this where this someone is in place watching the peace. Even when all thought is absent she remains in full measure behind the eyes, waiting for something to happen and thinking about the peace. That is the intruder I described to you last time we spoke and she is your problem. The reason you feel stuck is that you are allowing her to exist because you believe she is you and you continually endorse that identity during your meditation because you are invested in that belief. The fact you do not know this is the essence of ignorance. To realise this is an achievement and a stepping stone to greater progress. If by using that intuitive ability of perceiving you look into the nature of this thinker, then you make the bigger discovery. The thinker is itself only a thought, not a thought that moves and thinks but a thought nonetheless, an underpinning assumption best described as a concept. Now you have to meditate with persistence, faith and patience to determine that and you have to think about it outside of meditation to support your efforts and gain clarity. Realising it defies many but it is a true attainment and poises you to make an even greater discovery; the thinker is itself being experienced. By what? Well, that's the big prize. The answer is by the fullest, greatest power within you which is nothing objective at all, it is the experiencing itself. The thinker has seemed to be the innermost one but it never has been because that status is held by experiencing itself. You cannot look at that, you can only be that. Now we are at a high point, now we can realise that experiencing itself isn't a something at all, not a me in the way I have imagined me to be, it is unlike anything else, a no-thing yet at the same time, the full, affectionate, intimate abundance of existence; present, alive, intelligent, conscious. I am not going to give it a name today although there are many. The risk if I do, is that you will again turn it into a thing and try to find it, or see it, or watch it and whenever you do, that it is the thinker thinking. The point to understand is that thinking and the thinker itself is an activity happening within experiencing. Reflect on that statement, your answer lies within it. The foundation of Vichara has been supported by the inner enquiry but once this experience becomes near at hand, there is no need to enquire anymore as you have been doing because there is no need to think, only to appreciate, recognise and allow. Now the philosophy of the Upanishads is apparent in your own experience; there are not two; a thinker and intimacy, now there is only intimacy. The word intimacy is, as you know, my own word for sat/chit and describes my direct experience. Abiding in this without reverting to the thinker is the meditation you seek. For this to evolve in you, freedom of mind is an asset and for that we must travel to the hermitage in the snowfield and encounter Shiva. Before that you must meditate here with me for seven days and then we will leave."

The early evening sun shone through the latticed window on the kitchen work surface where I had come to cook. I had spent a lovely half hour in the veg patch and greenhouse and had harvested some beetroot and a squash to go with our lentils and rice. The greenhouse smelt fragrant from the cut branches of Tulsi that were drying on the rack. Our conversation on meditation was fantastic; I was uplifted by it and had gone straight to my room afterwards to make urgent notes, spending an hour on my bed just reflecting on what had been said. His points had been technical, they demanded careful attention but when I thought about them I realised that in that detailed guidance were the instructions I needed to overcome my obstacles and that without those instructions I probably never would. Sometimes sadhana is so nebulous, indistinct, contradictory even, conveyed in a kind of dreamy vague language of obscurity. Clarity and direction are what the meditator needs, specific guidance and points of knowledge. I was so lucky to now be with my Guru enjoying those abilities. My mind was clear, I knew what to do. What a change from this morning, I hummed to myself as I cooked, enjoying the moment, astonished by the ups and downs of my tumbling mind. And seven days meditation, wow! What a cosy and relaxing thought. The idea of meditating with my Guru in concentrated practice seemed like heaven. I could try everything out in the intimacy of soft cushions, gentle silence, bells, the warmth and charm of his room and the powerful compassionate current of those peaceful rays guiding me and bringing me securities. Perfect. I went to bed that evening in a warm wash of contentment and excitement looking forward to the morning and the days ahead, wondering if I would dream about Shiva and the snow mountain. What would I meet there? Shiva, my goodness! Is that even possible, did I have any idea what that actually was? Truthfully it was making me tremble.

It is 5:30am. I am shocked into an awkward wakefulness by the intense clanging of the morning bell, tolling again and again, the resonance building like a storm with each new clang. I scramble out of bed and look out to see Ram in the gloom standing at the oak frame of the big old ship's bell yanking on the rope. I dress and hurry downstairs, the kitchen is cold, there is no tea on the range and the front door is wide open. A pile of woollen blankets and sheepskin coats are on the table smelling musty as if they had been just discarded by nomads. Ram appears to the resonating sounds of the fading bell and stands in the doorway. His face is incredible, an ocean of tender kindness expressing the most beautiful soft assurance, while his stance emanates power and presence and his eyes flame with brightness. I can't take my eyes off him, I can't speak, I can't even shape my thoughts. He passes me a small wooden cup tipping his head toward it. Putting it to my lips with my eyes fixed upon him I swallow it in one. A warm mustiness like stale cinnamon and the residue of cathedral incense percolates my throat, resting in my belly. With my Guru standing like Shiva himself filling the open-door frame before me, I realise the winter air is freezing. He nods to the pile; I pick up a hide coat and sink my arms onto its heaviness adjusting it around my shoulders. Grabbing a blanket, I give it a shake, releasing the scent of attics and medieval chests. With the coat around me and the strange heat growing within, I follow him to the well in the garden. Working the chain he pulls up a newly filled bucket of water from the aquifer deep down in the chalk, pulls me toward him, plunges his hand into the glacial liquid then places his iced wet palm right onto my forehead holding it there as my brain freezes. It is as if my senses have become twenty years younger. The drips fall down my nose and cheeks and drop onto my lips like rain. I am standing in the morning gloom with my Guru, silent but for the dripping of the water deep down in the well and the ethereal cry of a lone buzzard patrolling the early morning sky. The space in my head, the flame in my guts and the envelopment of my animal hide cloak drive all sense of norms from me. I walk with him across the garden as if we were parading through a cloister, imagining that once back in the house I can have tea then sit in the corner seat in the back room propped up by the pillows. He will ring his bell; the log burner will glow comfortingly as the birdsong trills in the garden and we will sit in that spiritual silence close together and meditate before porridge and breakfast.

We head instead for the byre through the low entrance into the wood-slatted shed. Beast is dominating the space, his shaggy black massiveness swaying in the dim light. Ram breaks open a hay bale and works to spread it out bunching it up into two piles. Beast munches on his tethered oat sheaves, his breath cascading clouds of mist in the air, his black eyes examining me from across the shed floor. I don't know what to do, are we here to muck out Beast first? Ram eases himself down on one of the piles and assumes his meditative seat, an aura of the wild about him, or the priest, or both. It was compelling and unsettling. The chickens scratch around in their inquisitiveness stretching out their feet and weaving around my legs, pecking at the frills on my long hide coat. I hiss at them and shake my boot in their direction to scatter them as goat bleats noisily banging his hoof against the stall wall. Taking in the feral fug of hay, chicken debris and Beast dung, I sit on the second loose pile of hay, bunching it up under my buttocks and try to overcome thoughts of mice and spiders. Ram says his prayer and chants Om twelve times. I listen to his reverberating baritone and fear the silence that is about to come after it, a recognition painfully dawning. Seven days? Surely we were not to be in the byre for seven days? I shift my position, anxious that in doing so I will reveal some weakness. I think of the conversations we had since I arrived, were they alright, did I say the right things? I shuffle again, trying to get my foot into a better position, then sit still, my face tight, my eyes closed, but I am right behind them, fully present, alert to every sound and listening for rats. I had not seen any rats; we had never spoken of them but what if they are here? My lips are tense, scrutinising the soundscape for any rustle or squeak and all the time, Beast looming massive, eight feet away from me like a torment. I try moving my foot silently, tiny bit by tiny bit. What is the time? It can only have been ten minutes. Seven days, my God, it's impossible! How long will each session be? I hadn't asked him, why hadn't I asked him? I begin to feel useless, resentful, angry at him. Time passes in a kind of sombre tension. I think about the comforts of home, all the ways I could feel better, why was I even here? I begin to plan how I will leave, to escape Beast and him and this place. I think of my past, resentments from ten years ago replay in my mind; moments when I had been embarrassed resurface and grab at my emotions, anxiety builds and builds, my head aches.

The pain in my foot wakes me, it is sharp and cramped. I grit my teeth and screw up my face as I try to ease it out from under me. Beast has his eyes closed but they open like great moons as I brace myself in the hay and stretch out my poor legs. The goats and chickens are outside and Ram isn't here. I can hear the well-chain rattling; he must be pulling up water. I've been asleep! I stretch out and come to all fours working my back and legs into a better kind of order, then puff up the hay and lay down on my back, rocking my foot as sensation returns in pins and needles. Beast breathes out, the sound rumbling in the throat of him and begins to grind and chew the oats. I settle back and listen to the noise and the intermittent rattle of the chain. I don't know what time it is or how long I have slept but I feel alright, something had changed. After a while Ram returns followed by two of the chickens and settles in his seat. The vast peace of him sitting there is comforting, before it was threatening but something has happened. I don't change my position only settle back into my prone state, comfy at last lying flat supported by the hay. The chickens leave, Beast stops chewing. I lie, gazing up at the slats in the roof and watch the sun play upon the rafters. I know I will sleep again and that is alright. On the 4th day I experienced something new. I was settled in the hay, alert after an excellent night's sleep, tea and porridge had happened, the morning bell, water from the well, water on my face, chickens, Ram, the smell of Beast and now stillness but it was just as if I hadn't done any of those things and neither was I doing anything now. Everything was happening as normal; all details were fully present but there was a difference. I hadn't been thinking about any of these things abstractly, I had just been doing them. The insight thrilled me. I had been alert, awake, responsive, doing things, interacting but without commentary, not thinking and in this immediate moment, right now, I didn't want to comment either because I didn't need to be that commentator. I realised that my normal meditation was sitting in an expectant state, senses alert and actively avoiding thought but this was a kind of forced suspension. I was still fully present; waiting, watching and often commentating. This state of waiting was the intruder he had discussed and I could see how I could simply let that end. Beast urinated like a great fire-hose. The loud noise reverberated in the byre and through me and it met no resistance. I had no reaction; no thought about it, no opinion, no response, there was just the noise. I was fully aware and that was enough. I opened my eyes to his steaming flow noticing the physicality of Ram sitting so close to me in his statuesque poise. I knew instantly that he had no opinions too, somehow this was intensely beautiful, a unity of presence without anything needing to change. How common it is for engagement to be impaired by intruders, how magnificent that these had vanished.

"Pull it straight," said Ram, "it needs to be tight."

We were assembling the gear for the big trip and had been at it all morning. My arms were around Beast, trying to join the harness buckle underneath his shaggy matted flank.

"Get under him," said Ram, "so you can see."

I was a strong woman, brave I thought, but crawling around beneath the belly of Beast and inside his hooves seemed too much.

"Well?" said Ram, "Go on, I will hold him."

Forcing myself I knelt in the soiled hay and crawled underneath his girth, shaggy yak hair brushing against my face, the sound of him grinding oats rumbling in his belly as I stretched my arms around.

"He's purring Amelia, Milo likes you touching him, it's soothing him."

I had been here ten days now, much of that time up close with Beast in the byre but he still unnerved me, his size, his power, his ways but

I knew it was more than that, it was the untamed wild which Ram would just say was the real. "You can't have it on your terms Amelia" would be his comment, so I just kept quiet about my feelings for Beast and tried my best to get on with it.

"Poor Milo," said Ram, "so misunderstood, so out of place with puny little humans - maybe you should eat her Milo, what about it?"

Crawling out from my precarious spot I dusted myself off and left the byre. I still needed to clean out the water containers and package up the dried fruit and nuts. We were to leave tomorrow morning and the trip would take four days. I was still completely puzzled as to how we would get to a mountain range, particularly a snowy mountain range when I knew for certain that there were no such places between where I thought was here and Wales, two hundred miles away but Bowslip had behaved in surprising ways before. Once Ram said to me, "you may think Bowslip starts in Somerset but that's not where it ends." So, I put logistics out of my mind, stopped thinking about it and just completed the tasks. That evening I cooked dhal and we sat in the kitchen silently eating. Ram spread out his modified star chart and placed on top of it a one page, hand-drawn map, jabbing at it with his finger.

"This is the village Amelia, we are here. This is the hermitage in the high snowfield where we are going." He had marked it with two long elongated triangles like ordnance survey pillars. "I will meet you at the convergence of these two streams, right here at the base of the ascent and here is the forest point where you will start."

"But I am coming with you?"

"No, we travel separately."

"What do you mean? I don't want to travel by myself; I don't know where to go!"

"I am showing you now, that is why I have drawn you this map, it's all marked. Milo and I will track across the moor and beyond, you go through the forest."

"But I want to come with you, why can't we go together?"

"That is the way of it for this trip, it's necessary. Anyway, I want to be alone with Milo, he knows you don't like him and it would disturb him but he will get over it if he is with me."

I felt distraught and angry, dismissed and not listened to, picked up the little map and looked at the various symbols and pointers in confusion and disbelief.

"Why can't I come with you?"

"Because this is your sadhana, to be alone, not dependent on me and to practice emptiness."

"But where will I walk, in which direction?"

"Cross the stepping stones, use that pillar you found as your marker and walk in line with the fallen beech straight ahead, it's all on your chart, follow it, it's perfectly adequate."

"But what if I get lost?"

"Have faith in your guidance, stay alert and press on."

"But what if I do?"

"Press on."

"But I might not be able to decide which way to press on."

"Don't get lost Amelia, walk and practice emptiness."

"But Ram seriously, what if I do get completely, hopelessly lost?"

"Then you will die."

Snowfield

It was early afternoon as I leant on the beech tree, the river was trickling behind me and a gentle breeze was playing the forest leaves. I had thought it best to get going earlier but one thing and another meant that the sun was almost about to dim and dip. After crossing the stepping stones I was having a sip of water holding the map in my hand. I looked at the little drawing of a mountain with the elongated triangles. It seemed impossible, daunting but I had done some pretty difficult things with Ram and been through situations that exposed every last corner of my sensibilities, so a four-day trek through another forest was nothing really new. All my adventures in Bowslip had been progressive, building on themselves; they only made sense to me in retrospect. "You can't have it on your terms Amelia". This was more than just an annoying comment, I was coming into acceptance of it. I knew it wasn't unsupported.

I once came across Ram chanting the Vedas in his hut, lingering and lilting Sanskrit intonations with a compelling rhythm of poetic power; it was enthralling and wonderful in a way that seemed to silence the mind. It was the only time I had seen him do that particular mantra. Later he said it had been for me and for him, for us together to banish pride and that all the practices to bring about receptivity and subtlety were for one principal goal.
"What's that?" I had asked.
"Emptiness, you need to be empty of your self-obsession before fulfilment is possible and so do I."
I had found it so touching, the thought that he was dedicating something of himself for me and was doing that in unseen ways. Emptiness was exactly what he had asked me to practice in this forest but where were the detailed instructions, the guidance, the ordered sequence of technique to achieve emptiness? He had given me nothing. Maybe it's some guru's trick, a test, perhaps he would pop out from behind a tree at some point and say, "Hey Amelia, let's go back to the house for tea."

The thing about woods is that I had become used to them, maybe that's how you conquer fears, by becoming used to the circumstance of a thing, sort of tired of feeling bothered by it and you realise that the thing you are afraid of isn't really anything substantial or permanent, it's just a habit. I had already been exposed to my fears in radical ways like last time when he sent me all alone into a wilderness at night and again previously to that when I had been so terribly affected in the darkness of the dhuni. Those experiences and coming through them had somehow made this forest ahead of me alright. Maybe that is what he had been doing to me with all these various encounters, exposing me to aspects of myself that first reared up as fears or stubbornness, then once exposed just became inconsequential and diluted rather than important things to defend. I didn't need to work it out anymore. What a wonder it all was. But why didn't he tell me about emptiness? What was I supposed to do? I picked up the pack, hoisted it over my shoulders, stood at the very edge of the bramble patch with the tip of the white stone pillar behind me, aligned myself with the angle of the fallen trunk and stepped out towards a mountain which was not even in sight and, I suspected, may not even exist.

It was a pleasure for Ram to walk alone across the moors, he didn't really need company and was often better without it. Companionship he appreciated, especially with the best of sadhaks, there was a true joy in that spiritual togetherness which only a fool would not welcome but it was clear to him that the finest companionship was roaming about in the oneness of God. Milo felt the same, but for him Ram was God and Milo never wanted to not be at his side. Milo's plodding thump on the ground as his hooves crushed the winter reed stalks set a rhythm for their trek like the drummers on the galleons of old, beating out a pace for the rowers. He was also Ram's sadhak and a most blessed one. He had been entirely alone with Ram for many years. They were together constantly, often Ram had slept in the byre with him and occasionally Milo came into the kitchen but not often as it had caused some damage to the floor but it was worth it. Having tea by the range with Milo slurping his from a washing up bowl was a total joy for Ram, hilarious. He wasn't sure anyone had previously witnessed a yak laughing but Ram was certain he had. In the far distance where the horizon blended into the sky he could just make out the mountain but only just, like a mirage, half there and half not. In this clear landscape of flatness and space to see the mountain at all required the sharpest vision. It wasn't a matter of optics; it was a matter of realisation where the mind was a clear mirror, not projecting or rejecting, nor calculating or desiring. He knew it would have disturbed Amelia, she would never have got it and that itself would have inhibited the possibilities. So, he had sent her through the forest where all sadhaks must travel, where the distractions are both interesting, appealing and provoking. To have something to think about and something to do, a purpose and an action would bring her mind to a more receptive state than the austerity of nothingness. To teach someone of Amelia's capabilities was of great interest to Ram because he was the guru and that's what the guru did but he also knew his active role in teaching her all the detail of life was over. He kept it alive out of a sense of love for her but now, after so long, the persistent nature of the petty concerns of the person grated with him more than it had before. Sadhaks were needy, demanding on one hand and defensive on the other, puffed up with pride in one moment and timid in the next; lost in their own delusions. It was not Amelia's fault of course; it was the nature of ignorance and desire. Every mind, everywhere, in this realm of existence carried the long and ancient legacy of fears, projections, self-importance and doubts but that was not true everywhere and it was not true of all. He knew that when this work was done there would be another realm where there was more grace and purity but for now he was where he was and she was his shishya and that was alright. He was doing his best for her because he loved her profoundly and it was thrilling for them both. And despite all and any obstacles the thirst for moksha shone through all the issues of the ego's defence. That fact was for him, the most beautiful aspect of all. He saw it in her and he recognised it. It was a beacon for his heart and beacons always need to be responded to. Bringing Amelia to an intellectual acceptance of realisation had been his most recent task. It had itself been a challenge as it always was because it was a subject of great subtlety. "What is your reality Amelia?" That was the topic they had addressed again and again from multiple viewpoints, first in elaborate detail then latterly in simplicity. He recalled their last conversation on the subject of reality…

"There are two statements you can make about yourself Amelia, I am and I know. Stop there and really give that all of your probing attention. Your goal is to see that the only reason you are able to say either of those things is because those powers are real, right now, constant, present at the very heart of you. Come what may they are the powers that define your existence as they do for all. That is a complete truth and a window to what realisation is. The only reason you can claim I am at all is because you know it. Now what is dependent on what? Is the I am dependent on I know, or is I know dependent on I am? Which is it, Amelia? Everything is dependent on something, what do you think?"

She had replied that knowing is dependent because you have to be here before you can know. It was a reasonable answer, a thoughtful one but it wasn't true. In Ram's clear vision it was evident that you cannot separate either power. The two words were names for two sides of the same thing. As he strode by Milo enjoying the rhythm of his gait and the expanse of the moor, sat/chit was his entire totality. He had used the words 'Am' and 'Know' with Amelia rather than the Sanskrit because simplicity was his goal but he also knew that however simple he made it, she was still searching from a conventional perspective of subject/object thinking and was stuck in that duality. "Realisation is a different way of knowing yourself Amelia, intuiting the intrinsic, rather than looking for an objective experience through the mind and the senses." That was the message that had been his refrain and he knew it eluded her. It was subtle, that was her problem as it was for all; assertions of mind do not easily give way to perceiving differently. Amelia was not a mind looking, she was awareness knowing a mind looking and that was also a fact that eluded her. Awareness was her entire existence, itself dependent on nothing else. But you need a very clear mind to know that, a mind free from old convictions; you need emptiness. His way with her to bring this about was not just to convey Vedanta and Vichara through theory and abstract description but to illuminate nuances of reality by example, encounter and his own immediate vision, for that is what the guru does. He would take her to the hermitage and then they would see. The hermitage wasn't the last step because that was ahead of her and for another time but it was advancing towards that pinnacle. If it went well then he knew where he would take her because he knew the goal and could feel its closeness. That journey would only be possible if the encounter with Shiva succeeded. Amelia did not know the importance of this trip but Ram did and he would keep it like that. He was used to containing discretions because he was used by now to the loneliness of the guru. Ah, the guru had to be wise; it was a burden at times but a pleasurable one. Ram climbed upon Milo's back and lay forward a moment burying his face in his yak's thick lanolin neck hair, taking in his musk then adjusted his position to ride with the rhythm of Milo's gait. Ahead, the moor spread on and on in its flat expanse, it was tremendously beautiful to an empty mind and threatening, bleak and boring to a full one. The mountain shimmered like a phantom whisper in the long horizon ahead. Ram wondered if Milo could see it but it didn't matter, he would see it for them both.

The great thing about sleeping in the woods is how fast you get attuned to the natural rhythm of the light. The worst thing is roots sticking into your back no matter how carefully you think you have prepared your spot; that and the damp. I opened my eyes to see the high canopy of the elegant slender conifers swaying above me in the morning breeze, filling the air with whoosh and swish, intermingled with the birds darting about. It was a great morning; I had slept well in the comfort of the enveloping forest, silent in the black of night.

There were some odd sounds creaking and rustling at times but it was fine, it was what forests did. My map was actually clearer and more useful than I had thought, specifying the main contours of the land, and when to turn. It was enjoyable to trust it and just be at ease with my task. Once I noticed I was doing this, it released a great happiness in me, I was going somewhere, I was exploring alone, I was in charge of myself and I was feeling fine about it, what a change, what an excellent change. My breakfast was fruit and nut mix, honey and milk. Feeling like a woodland creature I stretched out, did some asanas, organised my gear, checked the map and headed off across the forest floor to my next waymark labelled, 'meteor crater' and depicted by a three-pointed compass. Ram's words earlier about psychological tactics were on my mind. At first I had found that title a bit dismissive, even insulting because I put so much effort into it but now in the sparkle of the new morning with my mind brightened after sleep, I realised he meant that those things were mental activities. That didn't mean they were not necessary and important but the teaching he was now pointing me towards was of a different order, beyond mental management and into something else. I was pleased I had worked this out and inspired by it. Was emptiness part of it and what might emptiness mean? The instruction I had been given was so short with no explanation 'Practice emptiness'. Did he mean meditate? Should I walk with concentration and silence like the Buddhists, did it mean nothingness and could you even have nothingness? Maybe emptiness means consciousness but how do you practice that? I knew I had misunderstood consciousness for most of my life without really knowing it. Previously I had assumed consciousness to be the things I knew, being awake and thinking. Then last year after the profound Sakshi teaching it became clearer to me this was only a part of what was being described. We had been sitting at the fireside on the last day summarising, talking about me going home and back to work and getting back into all that and I remember saying to him,

"I suppose things are only a problem when you are conscious of them".

"Well, they don't exist unless you are," said Ram, "but be careful, consciousness is not only the experience of things, that is a state, an application if you will, whether there is the activity of things or whether there isn't, consciousness is the constant ground and you are never not that."

We had debated it for a bit in that lovely fireside way when you are with your teacher filling the air with exhilarating conversation about reality, curling your toes in the thrill and warmth of it all. He had explained to me what the Upanishads meant by consciousness; we had talked about it many times before but it was only really then on that evening that I started to grasp the truth of it. It's like that isn't it, where aspects of teaching seep into you sometimes over years, you just have to keep interested, keep thinking about it, keep investigating and exploring in yourself and checking doubts with your teacher.

"Awareness and consciousness are the same, Amelia. There is only one power, do be clear about that; it is existence itself. There are not lots of separate consciousnesses even though it may have appeared so. There are lots of individual minds but it's an obstacle to view consciousness as limited to your individual self. It will help you to distinguish consciousness more clearly if I give it two names. Simple consciousness is sensing and thinking, the awareness in your body illuminating your mind, feeling and knowing what's going on. It's everyday ordinary awareness, the common field of wakefulness. But this simple consciousness is a mode of experience rising and falling like everything else and it disappears every night. That into which it disappears and from which it arises we call pure consciousness or any of the other twenty words that describe it, Sakshi being a very beautiful one. Usually when people use the word consciousness, they are unknowingly talking about their active mind, simple consciousness. We know however that mind is a function being illuminated by pure consciousness which is its entire support and is not limited to you. Sometimes this pure consciousness is called God. The best way of you realising this is to understand it with astronomy. Your mind is the moon illuminating the waking and the dream state through the power of its reflected light. That light we call simple consciousness or individual consciousness. It is real light with its own properties but it is entirely dependent on the sun, which is its source. By contrast, the magnificent sun is neither reflected nor dependent, shining upon the moon and upon everything else everywhere through its own potency. That light we call pure consciousness. This is a good analogy but it falls down because sunlight is finite, an event in time. Pure consciousness is not finite but eternal and constant, radiating everywhere independently as existence. Understand that despite appearances moonlight and sunlight are not two lights, it is only ever one light merely manifesting differently because of the properties of nature. Pure consciousness is the eternal power; simple consciousness is what is being temporarily experienced in this life as a reflection through this body. Interestingly, all human beings can look lovingly upon the sensuous moon but no-one on earth can look into the sun with their senses. We can however, enjoy the sun immeasurably and thrive in its illustrious rays. The moon brings us pleasure, the sun brings us joy and light and life. Perceiving this is subtle isn't it, delicate, it would be best if we didn't meet here for talks such as this. In this common waking state your mind is full and solid in the foreground with all its assumptions and characteristics intact, it's like trying to see through a piece of old glass that has been tumbled in the sea. It takes a lot of work and is often pretty ineffective. We should meet when you are asleep and dreaming of love. Or better still in the night space between sleep and waking where all veils are thin and shimmering, then there would be an easier receptivity, then we might get somewhere beautiful."

"Is that possible Ram?"

"No, at least not yet but never mind, we can simulate that receptive condition through emptiness."

I had forgotten he said emptiness but right then it flashed thrillingly in my mind. I stopped dead with a start. My feet had come to rest one metre from a steep drop. I was standing right on the descending edge of a big depression in the ground. I would have to be more alert, I had hardly been aware of my movements, lost in my thoughts. Before me the ground dropped steeply in a great circumference like the empty bowl of a deep lake. It must have been a hundred metres long and fifty across, a big elliptical gash in the forest floor. There were exposed boulders on the sides and uprooted trees laying rotting and scattered on the slope. The undergrowth was thick in some places whilst others were barren patches of mudslide that had dried and cracked decades ago. What was this thing? There was something spooky about it. It seemed grim and alone. Instantly I thought of Goblin Wood, the story book that had scared me as a child and troubled my mind for years, the memory of those childish terrors creeping in my belly. I knew it was ridiculous but there it was, triggered, released. The air was almost still, I couldn't hear any birds; the faintest rustle of grasses like a tiny sigh was the only thing occupying silence. I clapped my hands to see if there was an echo, it was instinctive and straight away I wished I hadn't, it was too revealing to goblins and forest things. I was a day in, maybe twenty miles from the fallen beech tree. There was absolutely no-one else here. The weight of that recognition rose quickly to bite me. Then I saw the object, a single white rough stone pillar down in the very base of the crater. Someone has erected that there. Beneath the undergrowth I could see that the eroded sides of the basin had been layered, stepped. This was an earthwork and a mighty one, a very big structure. Looking across to the apex of the ellipse I was even more disturbed to see a second pillar right on the lip of the crater. It was big, twice my height at least and then a third, much smaller at the other side just below the lip. What was this? The place was threatening, I didn't like it, what was I to do? I felt I should do something. Ram had said nothing about it. I looked at my map again and realised that the small drawing of what I thought was a compass with three needles on it was in fact these three pillars and this was 'meteor crater'. I was to use it for alignment to get my next bearing. That would mean circling this ghastly gash and getting the three pillars to line up to show me where to go. I suddenly felt awful. Moments ago my mind was bright and full of stimulating thoughts, travelling happily along thinking about consciousness and now, because of this gash in the ground I am full of anxiety. The instability of my mind was unsettling, I felt angry about it. Only two days ago I had understood Ram's teaching on moods that I should be less concerned about it but here again right now my pleasure and ease was shattered by upset and a childhood story about goblins. Toughen up Amelia, be strong, I could, I would, I am strong but I would have to be vigilant, forceful about it. With that determinism in my mind I circled the gash, aligned myself with the posts and strode off, not looking back and thinking of other things.

What Amelia didn't know was that the pillars in the ground that disturbed her so much were ancient ritual objects, markers of the time when clear and brilliant minds saw the world differently and instinct ruled more than thought. Even Ram was not sure of the whole story of the place. He knew that Bowslip and the village itself were the legacy of those who placed the pillars in the landscape marking the way for seekers. This was the heritage of Vedanta, a wisdom and truth that he was now a living teacher of. The crater was the remnant of a great Yajna temple for fire ritual, mantra and puja. It was a place of immense beauty and the greatest stability. The fact that Amelia found it spooky was understandable. The purest possible spirituality is bound to unsettle impurities in the mind and that was indeed its purpose. In earlier times vagaries of the mind would not be addressed by psychology, therapists or self-ambition but would have been subject to ritual. The sadhaks of old would chant and do puja, sacrifice to the fire, serve their guru and the people unstintingly, undertake prayers and sublimation, surrender and submit. Purification was understood to be the eradication of pride, defences, desires and ego and thereby coming to emptiness. Now people are different, few have the humility and selflessness to devote in this way, instead people are interested in their determinism and self-worth, in getting their needs met and asserting their independence. Equality rather than surrender is seen as the mark of achievement and points of view are asserted rather than appeased through fire sacrifice. Ram knew this and he knew it was folly to rely upon methods of the past. The trajectory upon which he was now directing Amelia was neither old ritual nor psychological tactics alone because in that she would not be well served. She was destined for realisation and he was guiding her to that. She required a secret to be unravelled, a mystical one that he would reveal at the hermitage in the snowfield, assuming she made it through the obstacles still in her path. For now, the pillars marked the route to the mountain and using them was Ram's great pleasure. Giving away your self-importance through the shedding of dependencies was sacrifice. Amelia was in the woods undertaking that yajna even though she may never know it. Sending her that way was puja to the Lord. The ways of the guru are mysterious indeed, they are either invited or resisted and Amelia was in-between the two; which direction she would go in would be revealed in the snowfield.

On a Tuesday in March, the morning of Shivaratri when the air was chilled and the sun filtered through the thinning trees, I stepped out of the forest. I had been walking through light snow for a couple of hours and had reached the boundary line and climbed the little rise that was the last object on Ram's map. As I crested over the top I stopped dead in stunned disbelief. Two hundred metres ahead of me a vast snow-covered mountain dominated the whole sky. Impossible! I stared open-mouthed at the dramatic immensity of this frozen mass, my amazement obscuring the fact that it was immediately, ferociously, dangerously cold, stinging aggressively, biting into my fingers, probing my bones. At the base of this wall of ice two small rivers converged, snaking through the snow on the lower slopes. Smoke curled up from a little camp on the bank of the flowing waters distinguished by the shaggy black form of Beast standing distinct against the world of white. There was a canopy under which Ram was attending to a cooking pot. He was enveloped in animal skin, boots, fur mittens and fur hat. I wanted to drop to my knees in disbelief but couldn't, fearing the biting iciness of the snow. My lips trembled as the pain of freezing bit deep. The sound of a conch broke my spell. Ram was blowing it and beckoning me with his hand.

"Come down Amelia, come down!"

I heard him shout but I felt confused, uncertain, frightened, look at the severity of the place, the awesome power and danger of it! To go on or go back; I didn't know what to do. I could see no track, nothing, just a trail of prints along the river where they would have walked in, everywhere else in every direction was virgin pure and unbroken whiteness. My body was shaking strongly, my concentration slipping. I saw Beast thundering up towards me with Ram on his back scything through the snow, great snorts of breath bellowing from him, his ice-tangled mane flopping and rattling from side to side. I stood stock still, feeling dreamy and distant as Beast slid to a halt and Ram jumped off, coming towards me with a bundle of skin and fur and draped a heavy Mongolian coat over my trembling shoulders.

"Get this on quickly Amelia or you will die!"

Roughly he pushed the hat down over my ears, forced my hands into mittens, started beating my back through the skins and placed

my left gloved hand under Milo's tack.
"Hold on Amelia and walk, come on, one two, one two."
Half pulled and half trudging I followed Beast back through the broken snow to the camp. Behind the canopy was a small yurt, he pushed me into the interior and we sat either side of a little brazier, warming and drying my reddened feet.
"You can't get cold Amelia, once cold gets into you here, you are lost. You have to stay in this gear all the time now, don't get exposed again. This is a place for heroes, stay alert."
He made tea and hot porridge and told me we were to spend the day and a night here acclimatising and preparing for our trip to leave in the morning.

Warmer in my skins and fur-lined boots I was able to get a more measured sense of the place. It was like I was on another planet or back in primaeval time, another dimension even. There was nothing other than snow, as if the world was made of one thing. There were shapes, peaks and ridges, overhangs and protrusions in the surface features of the landscape but it was all entirely covered in untrammelled snow, no patches of exposed rock, or scree, or flora anywhere. I didn't know how to process it and couldn't decide whether it was beautiful or disturbing but it was certainly majestic. A vast spaciousness of unmarked emptiness glowing with a wild intensity. I didn't really see the presence of snow so much as I saw the absence of everything else, a stunning total purity. I am not in charge here; I cannot direct or control. I am simply here or I am not and it is powerfully clear to me that this is a choice. I can either accept this snowfield on its terms and open myself to experience its nature, or I can stand distant from it and keep it at bay while I try to find some personal vantage points, some way out. I stand there speechless and feel very alone. Ram stopped his preparations and stood next to me with great tenderness.
"The snowfield is an unsullied place Amelia, just like the spiritual

heart, it's a metaphor isn't it but a real one, an actual one in which you are standing with me and Milo. When you go into wilderness there are two reactions; one is threat and the other is relief, both are affecting in their own way depending on your disposition. There is tame wilderness, a kind of partial purity you can come in and out of on your own terms, then there is deep wilderness untainted by any imprint, the place where the heroes go and become absorbed in its ways. Its nature is inviting and magnificent but not accessible to the demands of your assumptions or the needs of your feelings."

Ram knew that a common question for the sadhak is, can I let go and if I do what might happen, will I lose myself? That which they are afraid to lose is identity and control but they do not know that. The teacher says, 'Yes, let go and have faith because those things you are clinging to are not the way' but it often has little impact because a person can't let go unless they sense some security in the heart of themselves.

"Do you feel safe Amelia?"

I didn't reply and continued to look out at the white vastness feeling small and vulnerable.

"When your security and belonging is wholly dependent on the activities of the world, the continuation of your habits and your current ways, then you will want to defend it and wilderness will be a threat. If by contrast, you sense security radiating from your own nature even to a small degree then you sense that the wilderness is the source of that and exploring it is a compelling joy. It must be apparent to you now that spiritual security in the way I am speaking of it is not found in people, activities and things going your way. It is only found in God for which the deep wilderness is another name. Human companionship is wonderful; life, activity and experience in all its lustre and beauty but depending upon it for your security is severely limiting because it will continuously change and be ultimately unfulfilling. The wise enjoy a deep companionship from a much deeper truth; the aloneness of Being and that is found in the intimacy of the wilderness."

His words, 'aloneness of Being' moved me deeply and seemed to reflect the nature of this place but it was disturbing, I wasn't experiencing it as beautiful at this moment but devoid of comfort, a place that gave no quarter to the needs of my mind.

"Do I need to be a hermit Ram?" I burst out.

"Definitely not and nor should you wish for it, such rejection and isolation would be an indulgence and a torment but solitude, that is something different, that is a delight because in it there is a peace in which you are never actually alone. This snowfield is solitude of place but the higher solitude is of the mind or more eloquently, of the heart. You are not here to be a hermit but to become hermetic, in other words impervious to the temporary risings in your mind that bring you trouble and cloud the landscape. There are two principal strands of teaching in response to those rising waves. The first is tactical, taking the mind and the seeker at face value, accepting its ways as real and meaningful, giving specific guidance to the intelligence of that mind so that it can see how it is behaving and can choose to alter those habits. The second strand denies that you are the mind or that there is a seeker at all, points out that you are other than the objects of the mind and brings you release from conditioning. You have been exposed to both teachings and you are where you are because of it but now there is somewhere else for you to go, a new subtlety between the two and we are here for that, a superior mode of mind, a wilderness of mind, where the snow falls and is unsullied."

"Are we going to meet someone?" I asked.

"We are going to meet Shiva." he replied, "Let's go."

Ram had packed everything away in quick time including the small yurt, its stove and fuel, telling me there was no room for personal belongings only the food, shelter and heat we needed for basic living. Beast made off, swishing through the deep snow, parting it like a plough, his great bulk expanded by the rolled-up yurt, its poles sticking out before him like a jouster's lance. I plodded off with Beast in front and my Guru behind. Since Beast had run up to the forest to collect me in the snow, I felt something new for him. His doleful face framed by ice-encrusted locks had expression, I was beginning to see it as kind and true rather than wild, not tame, but kind and true nonetheless. The snow was soft and the crunchy surface collapsed when you walked. It was manageable to follow Beast's track but without him it would have been impossible to make hardly any headway at all. We were not walking on any trail, this was virgin snow, unmarked and untravelled. I wondered how on earth Beast knew where to go across unmarked ground, he wasn't being led by us, we were following him. After two hours we stopped for rest, Ram told me tea was an indulgence and we had no room for it, instead, pulling out a water flask that he had kept inside his coat, we sipped at it before it froze. Inside the coats, mittens and hats and as a consequence of all the exertion, I was warm enough.

"Another two hours then we can pitch the yurt on the moraine ahead," he said, after again consulting his map.

I trusted Ram, he was resourceful and capable in all practical ways but this was a very perilous place, what if his calculations were wrong, what if we get lost? I turned around and looked back from where we had come. For some time it had been possible to turn around and still make out Bowslip forest behind us, a comforting link to normality, a way out, but not now, there was only snow in every direction. Beast's trail was a marker but if it snowed again as it already had a couple of times that would soon be gone. Should I stop now, speak out now, should I say I wanted to turn back, to go home? Shiva, what did it mean? I wanted to know, I wanted some certainty, some context, some evidence of the meaning and purpose of what we were doing and our destination. What were these mountains, where were we? I wanted to negotiate terms, to have some say, to decide if this was for me.

"Whoa Milo!" he called.

Beast came to a halt instantly, turning his hairy horned head towards his master, his face implacable, calm and settled. Ram came forward and started working the tack loose.

"We can pitch camp here," he said, "it's flat enough."

And so we worked, erecting the yurt and piling snow up against its skirt, sealing the inside from any wind. Right now the air was calm but he had told me that if wind did come and came hard we would not be able to move, perhaps for days. I really wanted to cry at that point, the feeling of homesickness built and built. Ram went off to take a bearing, taking Beast with him to push through the snow.

It was the first time I had been completely alone, not moving and silent. The stillness was incredible, a solid wall of un-movement. I wanted something, anything to break it, to give me something familiar but this was emptiness and I felt out of place, an intruder in some other dimension. I wasn't sure I was welcome, just like in the forest it reminded me of when I was little and afraid of the dark but this wasn't dark, it was whiteness and solitude of a totally different order, it was listening to me and I didn't want to be heard. It was watching me and I didn't want to be seen. He came back, unpacked a pouch of dried yak dung and built up the brazier. As the warmth built up we made porridge with nuts, seeds and dates and drank melted snow. I yearned for tea.

"Where are we and why are we here?" I asked directly, "I really must know."

"Steady yourself Amelia, it's alright, you are bound to feel unsettled just because it is unfamiliar to you, find your courage, I know you have it. We are still in Bowslip just as before, albeit a realm of that world that you will call strange, but it would be better to call it advanced. There are no common sensibilities here, no markers to confirm your assumptions about yourself and that will rattle your bones but no-one can approach what we are about to approach with their personalities intact. Be patient and try to actually experience faith, perhaps you never truly have. Faith is not an idea; it is a whole experience. All those prayers you have made over all those years pleading for purification, help, guidance and enlightenment well, here we are, this is what you have prayed for. The day after tomorrow we will arrive and your questions will be answered."

Next morning we started early and walked along a long ridge for about three hours. It was a beautiful day. Beast had forged ahead or perhaps I had become slower, not so much from tiredness but I think I was more settled somehow since our talk, more accepting of the place and its features. My mind had slowed down into a kind of trust that this was okay; I was doing the right thing. Ram had fallen back and I turned around just to see if all was well, he was about a hundred metres away. I looked ahead to Beast to see he too had now stopped, his head turned to look at me and then for the first and only time in the whole trip he bellowed a single note that reverberated on the snowy crags around me echoing in the still air. He had spoken to me; I was sure of it but why had he stopped? I could see he was stood on the edge of a feature in the landscape like a rounded corner. I closed the gap between us and coming close to him stepped next to his flank and stopped dead. If I could have bellowed like Beast I would, instead I gasped in shock. "Wow Milo! Wow!"
Instinctively I reached up and embraced his shaggy matted flank; he leaned into me in response and grunted low and deep. Ahead of us the landscape flowed in all directions like silk upon the mounds of the moon, soft undulating curves lying like the bellies of sleeping buffaloes, a huge arena of inviting lilting hillocks blended into a poem of form and grace. It was the best, the absolute best view I had ever seen. Up above in a clear faultless sky, a bird swooped, circled above us then glided effortlessly across the terrain with the faintest of calls that seemed to whimper at the beauty. Milo purred and I held the side of his great thick neck and wept for the faultless beauty.

My tears came rolling and trembling in relief, absorbing into his tangled fur, the greatest most welcome and freeing release, right there on the edge point of heaven.

"What is it my Milo, what is it?"

Ram came up quietly beside me. I looked at him excited; wanting to share, ready to burst but neither was possible. His face was an unmoving mirror of wordless perfection, an open neutrality, not showing any common emotion, no flicker of the mouth or widening of the eyes and yet, conveying the full majesty of love. It was as if his face and the wonder before me, the very air itself, was one thing. I couldn't speak; I did not want to speak, as my face by some means unknown to me matched his. I realised that I had stopped thinking and this experience itself was emptiness. My tears rolled gently like jewels in a waterfall. Milo's flank reverberated with his rumbling purr. Over to the left, a patch of broken snow caught my attention. It moved in little rivulets as if someone had bowled something through it, like a mole trail accelerating over the ground and then another, moving to intersect with it. They converged and stopped in a little explosive puff of snow. Up popped two sets of ears, disappeared and flicked up again. Two creatures leapt into view, bounding in a flurry of action then still as stone facing us.

"Snow hares!" said Ram, "Watch them." He clapped once. Instantly they were off, bounding through the snow, leaving the imprint of their feet like breadcrumbs through the forest. "Away Milo," said Ram, and he trundled off following the footprints.

We walked with him into the wonderland before us in the high plateau of the world. It was impossible, mesmerising, we were following two snow hares into this spellbinding landscape. Was it even real? I grabbed his sleeve.

"Ram what is this? I have a hundred questions." He put his finger to his lips. "Wait until we have made some ground, experiencing it is better than analysing it."

"But where are we going?"

"We are going to the hermitage in the snowfield to meet Shiva. There is nothing unreal about the hares, they live at the hermitage. Now there are intruders in the field they will instinctively return. Following them is the only credible way to safely reach our goal."
"Do you mean we are really going to visit Shiva?"
"Yes, exactly, nothing less than that and the hares are your guide. We need one more pitch for tonight, tomorrow we will arrive."

Once the yurt was up I lay still and silent, resting my bones and enjoying the peace that had come upon me. It was much milder outside, the bite and ferocity of the previous serious freeze seemed to have gone, maybe this area was more protected by the mountains, it was just cold like it might be in the worst ordinary winter at home. We didn't need all the skins and sat in lighter layers smelling like nomads in the glow of the brazier. Meditation came upon me, it wasn't an effort or even a practice, it was just there naturally. In the isolation and the total silence, my mind was empty of its content and it wasn't austere but abundant and fresh, happiness without any details. The whole evening was like this, we ate, organised the gear and then I was lying down on my coat to sleep with the hat as a pillow and feeling just the same, it was like meditation started and then didn't stop. I fell asleep in a state of delight.

"Good morning," said Ram, "breakfast?"
It was a question not an offer. I washed in the snow and busied around organising the oats, fruit, nuts and milk. Outside the yurt Ram had been working on a bundle of dehydrated silage. It had compressed into a small pack but now was expanding in the snow melt into a hay bale sized mass of seaweed-like matter. Milo looked on with eagerness in his eyes. After breakfast, we left Milo at the yurt feasting on his bale. The snow had been getting firmer as we climbed,
not sinking as before, it was easier to walk and make progress. It

was just the two of us with a single small pack that I carried. Standing at the threshold to our journey, Ram pulled out his conch and blew it three times. All the fears and doubts that had plagued me for days shattered, all associations with anything in the past shattered, I had no needs. I was here in the snowfield with my Guru, we were alone and that was all, there was nothing else, nothing. Ahead of us the undulating curves and hillocks of the snowfield glowed with a sheen like fresh velvet, empty of all sound and any movement. Without Milo the solitude was even greater, this was the purest place I had ever known, purer than I could have imagined, this was complete emptiness. There could be no-one else alive and still this place would outshine all of us, existing aloof, not dependent on us or desiring us. I felt the ancient, I felt the majestic, I felt the beauty. As the landscape ahead began to level out, it seemed there was a top. I could see we were approaching a plateau of sorts and on the high point there was an uneven raised area like a crag and something next to it, white against the snow and hard to see. Earlier, I had been imagining what the hermitage would look like, maybe a stone building like a temple hanging in the mountainside, small and old with thick stone walls and a shaped tiled roof, a place of dignity and majesty with prayer flags and bells but there was nothing like this in sight. We stopped right on the edge of the plateau. Before us was a smooth table top of silken snow gently curving at its edges and broad in its middle. Behind us was the snowfield and in the distance the great peak we had circumnavigated to get here. On this high point I could now see the true grandeur of our setting. In every direction undulating contours traced the ground as if an artist's hand had moulded gentleness in form, it was stunning. What I had seen as a crag from lower down on the path was actually the frontal feature of a long spur bulging up from the plateau, standing out like a snow-covered blister in the smooth curve of the hill. It was a rounded hummock like the long barrows of England, symmetrical and striking. At its central point stood a tall white stone pillar. A snow hare darted across the track in front of us, scampered up to the structure and stood on its haunches, alert and twitching, its black eyes and little black tips of ears the only things that gave its location away. We were being watched and probably had been all morning. We stood ready but I hesitated, I didn't want to step in virgin snow there on that top because I didn't want to break its pristine state, not just the snow, I didn't want to move at all, the air itself contained that same virgin quality, I didn't want to break it.

"Go on," said Ram, nudging me forward.

The moment ticked by in complete isolated silence.

"You go first," I said, "please."

He blew his conch three times. I waited with my heart in my mouth. Would there be a response, would someone come out? But he was up instantly and striding forward. I gathered myself and followed. As we closed the distance, a single black feature on the side of the structure became clear against the surrounding snow. Now I could see that the pillar was actually one of a pair, each about twelve feet tall. They were either side of the black feature and it was obvious they were framing an entrance. I fell back a little while Ram strode ahead, reached the entrance and disappeared inside without a pause. I wasn't sure about this, how are you supposed to be when you are expecting to meet a God? Was I good enough, was this alright, how should I behave, what should I do? But I really didn't have a choice. I walked through the black arch doorway. Like a bat I could sense the dimensions of the dark chamber from the echoes of my steps rather than my sight. It felt to be about the size of the small village temples I had visited in India but rather than camphor, it smelt pungently of hares. The floor was solid, the walls were rough rock, it was bone dry and quite warm compared to the outside. As my eyes slowly adjusted to the gloom I saw we were in a completely empty space. There were no carvings or markings that I could see, no structures on the floor or furnishings of any type.

"It's a cave, Ram, just a cave."

He was sitting on his haunches watching me as I explored. The whole area was about thirty feet long and fifteen wide. There was a fire hearth but it was only a scrape in the ground, no stone surround, just a place where you could tell fires had been. The floor had some debris on it which seemed to be just ash and some random sticks, old remnants of firewood I supposed.

"It's an ordinary cave Ram."

"It is a cave Amelia but I don't think you can call it ordinary. Here we are in the high snowfield, sitting within the earth marked by the very ancient potent and most powerful pillars of the Vedas."

"But Ram," I whispered, "where is Shiva?"

"Make some fire. I have a special gift for you and we need fire."

The floor of the hermitage was scattered with lots of hare droppings. Using my hands and two flat stones I scooped up a large pile and set to work on arranging the fire, using the droppings and the sticks that were scattered about. I wondered what rituals may have been performed and over what time period in this place. The fire was thick and smoky from the hare dung. With our feet we pushed it closer to the door to resettle it so that the smoke naturally drew outside. It would have been visible right across the snowfield and I wondered what eyes might be out there that would see us. Out of the pack Ram unfolded his collapsible pan and melted snow, then gave me two cups. I waited expectantly for other ritual objects.

"Hold out your hands Amelia and close your eyes."

Two soft objects fell into my palms.

"Om sri guru bhyo namah hari om." said Ram.

I opened my eyes in immediate delight. Tea bags! We used the pan to cook up oats and had a feast of nuts, fruit porridge and hot tea. As the afternoon gathered in, we sat in the doorway of that extraordinary place between the two tall pillars looking out into the grace of the snowfield.

"Ask me your question," said Ram.

"Where is Shiva?"

He threw open his arms to the world before us.

"Here, there, up, down, far, near, in, out. This entire, all-inclusive magnificence, everything, everywhere, can be given the name Shiva but let's not pretend we understand what that is. The universe and its source is something beyond the attempts of humanity to categorise or fully know. We may think we understand how the physics of the universe might work but physics is a tiny aspect of what is. This whole grandeur of existence is itself Shiva. Some people say there is no God; what a foolish and limited assumption. It is an act of severe folly to make such definitive statements or to deny realities we have no experience of. Our problem is people have learnt to conceive of God as something limited, personified, contained in a form. I have not brought you here to this exalted place to see a form of Shiva. I have brought you here to meet the energy of what Shiva is. You are not here to engage with Shiva as a noun; you are here to engage with Shiva as an adjective; a power, not a thing. The Sanskrit word Śivā is entirely descriptive and it is this I want you to know. Śivā means the auspicious one, the Lord of auspiciousness, the conqueror of negativity, the transcender of illusion, the destroyer of darkness, doubt and selfish desire. Śivā is auspiciousness itself, that is what the word means and that is what you are here to meet. If we were gathering in some common satsang environment in the Orangery at Bowslip House, the word auspicious may flow over you like so many other religious and spiritual concepts. We would define it further with other words such as benevolent, benign, altruistic and all the properties that go with that of graciousness, kindliness, generosity, positivity and so on but I tell you, my dear Amelia, you are not in the Orangery but here in the hermitage of the Vedas and this is not ordinary. Auspiciousness is not to flow over you, it is to become you. Śivā has never been explained to you in the way I am about to here in this place, for we are speaking not about a concept but about the very structure of your mind. We have come to this place through the intensity of your sadhana so that you can be poised to meet Śivā right here, no more than a hair's breadth from the intimacy moving in you right now; a hair's breadth, that is all. Tomorrow morning when the sun rises I will give you the whole darshan of auspiciousness, the knowledge and sensation of Śivā."

He went outside and sat in his meditation pose in the snow. I watched him in silence, the tiny sound of my gentle breath the only sound there was. I felt peril in his words; something was tremoring in me, quivering in expectant awe. I couldn't place my feelings nor did I want to, there was a kind of intriguing chaos. I neither felt certain nor uncertain, nor did I want to shape in any way what he had said. Normally I would have evaluated, calculated, put the ideas into order but I couldn't, didn't want to, the sensible me was disintegrating in peril and it was delicious. I kept the fire going for another couple of hours just sitting, breathing and watching. As the evening passed the grandeur of the night sky came into view. I thought about that conversation back in the house nearly two weeks ago; two hundred billion stars in our own galaxy, two hundred billion. The sight before me was simply perfect, if I could have died into it right there and then I would be content but not tonight. All this way, all this preparation and a build-up I now realised had been taking place for years. With the fire finally dying and huddled in the coats with the single blanket shared between us, sleep came, perfect sleep as though I had never been born.

The Darshan of Auspiciousness

I awoke to the sound of the conch and lifted my head to see the disappearing tails of the snow hares scampering down the hill.
"You have spent the night in a burrow Amelia. Good morning, let's get the fire on and have porridge and tea."

I washed in the snow and busied about, arranging myself and organising breakfast. Once again we took our positions between the two pillars with the cave behind us and the snowfield beyond, the hare trails the only sign that anything had moved. I looked into the horizon with all my senses alert as my Guru started to speak.

"Are you in a snowfield Amelia? Do you think Bowslip is a physical environment out there, separate from you in an objective world? A rational person would say, 'yes of course' but rational people do not usually follow a yak into the wilderness and lose their wits in the process. So, what is your view, is it wisdom to base your life on that understanding which implies a separate me looking out at a separate world, what do you think?"

"Well, I am not sure, it seems like that, I see the world like that and live in it. Is it not real then?"

"It is real because real only means that which is happening. Reality on the other hand is something different, pointing to the underlying form beneath the apparent appearance of things, the truth of it and that is what we are interested in. We are here in this very privileged place to face a most advanced yet simple realisation. Appearance is dependent on its underlying form. Your experience of yourself and all this is dependent on your mind and how your mind moves is dependent on its underlying form. This is important to know. By what mechanism are you discerning this situation right now, this experience you are having of snowfield and conversation?"

"With my mind."

"And what is mind?"

"My thoughts."

"Yes, but not only that. Mind is the instrument which is responsible for all your experiences. You already know there isn't a single thing called mind, no inner organ that can be identified. The word itself is a compound word encompassing differing types of perceptions, all the rising waves within consciousness; your senses, your memories and mental impressions, your sensations, your thinking, your emotional reactions and moods, all these reacting together perceiving and responding is what we call mind. All your experiencing is contained in that and nowhere else. Where is the snowfield, Amelia?"

"There," I replied, pointing out into the distance.

"And your sense of sight?"

"Here, in my eyes."

"And your thoughts about the snowfield?"

"Here in my head."

"This is how it appears, an outside and an inside but where would you say the actual felt experience of seeing itself is, the richness of it?"

"In my mind."

"Exactly, not in your eyes, nor in the space but in your mind and the same applies to all your senses. Seeing or sensing is entirely in the mind. The experience of snowfield, Bowslip, me, Milo, hermitage and everything else is within your mind, whether it is a mountain fifteen miles away, a memory of last week, the Milky Way, or this conversation. When you have any experience at all it is happening within mind and how that experience appears is dependent on the mind's underlying condition. You may not have realised how immense mind is, look how vast it is in scope and possibilities, look at what it can contain. And that's not all, mind is not only receiving, by no means, it is also aspiring, initiating, generating. It wants to assert, it wants to project, it wants to make you think and feel, it wants you to act. Where does your action come from?"

"My ideas."

"Yes, and your reactions. Those movements themselves which seem to just appear for you are the fruits of desires. You hold opinions, you assert attitudes and respond to things in a certain way based on what you would call your feelings. All of that rises from the desires in your mind. That simple fact is very wise knowledge. These are not dry things, certainly not, we are not talking abstract here, we are talking about the very stuff of you. Perceptions, feelings, reactions, thoughts have impact, you feel them most acutely. The motivations that shape, those things and give them character are a result of the underlying state of your mind and the pathways that have taken root there. This is a place you cannot think or understand because it is unconscious, you cannot reach it but you sense its nature and are affected by it. Your moment by moment experience is a consequence of it. It is important that it serves you well. Are you working to improve your mind?"

"Yes, definitely."

"Why?"

"Because I want to be a good person and to be free from limitation and negative thoughts."

"And how have you been doing that?"

"Through sadhana, meditation, discrimination, all the things you have been teaching me."

"Beautiful, admirable, all excellent necessary things of great value, such has been your spiritual training as it is for all, but these are psychological tactics adjusting the surface of your mind only. The higher knowledge addresses the default disposition of your mind, that which is dictating your experience, not only your inner experience but how you express yourself and how the world actually appears to you. That's everything, think about it. I often give you the metaphor of the weather to describe changing moods but in what does weather appear? It appears in the sky. Now that sky has flavour of shade and light, it isn't nothing. Similarly, the unconscious sky of your mind, its underlying form, isn't nothing. The status of that realm dictates what rises, how your mind moves and how the detail of the world plays for you. Your experience in response to events is not the fault of the world; it is a consequence of your mind. This is big stuff and my proposal to you, here in this place, is to transform the underlying unconscious form of your mind to reflect auspiciousness then the world as seen by you will itself become auspicious; your ideas will be auspicious, your actions and the direction in which you apply intelligence will be auspicious. You don't then have to work to, sustain this as you do on the surface because it has become you and is your natural way. This is the experience of the realised, this is my experience, this is the experience on offer to you in this place. That is enough for today. You are in an expanded state Amelia, this is big sadhana. Let's cook and eat, sing some bhajans and see if we can coax those hares back. Tomorrow morning at dawn we will speak to the big question on your mind. What is it?"

"How do I bring this about?"

"Exactly."

Ram went back inside and an easy meditation fell upon me. Do you know that experience when you don't have an edge? There is only silence and a contented harmony where everything is stimulating without the need to do anything, thrilling in a way which you know is divine. I opened my eyes to see the snow hares, both of them standing alert and quivering in the snow twenty metres away. Their cuteness was irresistible. "Come on," I whispered but they darted away in a tussle of snow. The rest of the day was spent easily in rest and reflection. I thought about his phrase the higher knowledge and where it might now lead. When I thought back to the early days and compared how I was then with how I was right now, it struck me how far I had come. I still felt the same person but my experience was different and my needs were different. And now the offer of achieving what he was describing was, well, simply amazing and seemed to address the sense of stuck-ness and repetition I had been experiencing. If I just looked straight into my motivations, spiritual happiness was the goal that drove me on, or rather, absence of unhappiness. Sometimes I gave that other names, wisdom, grace, love, peace, but happiness summed it up. It wasn't a common happiness that had called me, although that was lovely but a deeper truth and it wasn't an indulgent desire, I knew that. It was something big, important to do, as if there was a justice to happiness, a rightness to aspire to this deeper spiritual state, not so much to enjoy happiness but to be happiness itself, in which moods didn't really matter. Perhaps this was happiness's underlying form; I had tasted it in glimpses and knew it to be real. Earlier in my life without understanding anything about spirituality, I had unknowingly sought this same fulfilment in people, states and things and had discovered, as all sadhaks do, that permanent happiness or even meaning, is not in these changing forces. This was not a comment on enjoyment or caring, far from it, I continued to engage in the play and creativity of life, relishing companionship, experiencing pleasure, contributing and sharing affection but I no longer expected to be made happy by people, states or things. And it was because of Ram. I watched him and saw his steadiness; he had his own source of happiness. He did things in the world, he expressed and engaged constantly but he did not seek fulfilment in dependencies. His fulfilment was in himself; his happiness was in himself, untouched by any transient display of feelings. It was an affection he shared in abundance and now he seemed to be describing a window into how this could be. We went to bed at dusk in the silence of the snowfield and I slept for ten hours, waking fresh, bright and inspired by the new day, excited in anticipation of what was going to come. Sitting in the hermitage doorway next to my Guru, I waited for him to answer the question I had put the night before, "How do you do it?"

"Auspiciousness is a real recognisable power," he began, "an actual fabric of existence. You can understand it as a sheen upon consciousness, a brightness that overwrites dullness and uplifts negativity. It is tangible as a lightness waking up around you and in you, just as spring wakes up inside the forest. You sense it as love and purity and you want to share it and express it. You recognise that the positive rays that are its projection, such as decency, kindness, goodness, fairness, truth are shining through existence, influencing behaviour and you marvel at its operation. To me, these realities alive in my mind and in the minds of the wise are the actual form of Shiva manifest, that to which I give worship. It is to that reality you align by holding this vision in the forefront of your mind and acknowledging its truth. You have to get to that place of recognition so you are convinced. You cannot have commitment for something you do not endorse. You have to see it and believe it."

"But..."

"Stop. I know what you are going to say but the speed with which you say it just shows how isolated you have become. It's not your fault, it's the way of the Earth. Don't worry, say it Amelia, say your question."

"What about the selfishness, hardship, pain and suffering? I see it all over the world and in myself."

"What about it? Never mind about the darkness, it is a feature of this realm of life. Inauspiciousness is as real as auspiciousness and nobody but a fool would deny it but you give it too much attention and lose your perspective. There is darkness in the human condition but as we have discussed many times, there is not only darkness. That simple point must become your everyday vision and you must fight to attain it. It isn't difficult, you just need to look and see clearly. Auspiciousness is ascendant and that is demonstrable in the world and obvious when you have thoughtful eyes. Out of incidents of darkness come initiatives for justice, charity and positive change. The fact there are incidents of darkness is not evidence against auspiciousness but evidence for its triumph. Your life is motivated by the initiative you feel to improve and amend areas of discord within you. You don't want to go with the discord; you want to reach out for harmony. You do not feel you want to make things worse. Why is that? It's because auspiciousness is already running within you as altruism, goodness, compassion, forgiveness and all the other ways benevolence manifests. In your best moments you simply want to be productive, loving and kind. That is auspiciousness and it is already a living reality in the world. The fact it is only present in degrees and other inauspicious elements also rise, is not a proof against it but only indicates that auspiciousness is not primary. You want to make it primary in you and for inauspiciousness to recede into the dust. The probability is you have become too passive in relation to your own mind. It needs to be led. I want you to recognise the power you have to initiate, assert and persist. I want you to stand up and take the attitude of a wise commander scanning her mind and surveying all her forces. You discover that mind is by no means solely your domain. Intruders have crept in by subterfuge and gained influence. Some of them are very ancient. At its worst the mind is a prison of torment. At its best, a beautiful arena of possibilities and expression, a force to be reckoned with, capable of wonderful things. The commander knows that and knows what she wants to achieve but she does not stand alone and isolate herself in her campaign for freedom, she seeks to identify allies and align with others. Your immediate allies are like-minded people, your teacher, the guru in all its forms and the teachings themselves. These will assist and support you but your principal ally is the might and rulership of Shiva himself and it is to that you appeal because you realise that Shiva is very close at hand and you choose to reach out and be with that. See your reality as a great living and interconnected wheel of possibilities, the influencing force is that which is at the hub, the spokes are the individual minds in which those possibilities are expressed, the rim is the world. Shiva in other words, auspiciousness, is the hub. Your initiative is to actively attune to that reality with your attention. The fact that there are evidently other forces that also prowl the landscape need not concern us or distract us. The cosmic air is full of radio waves, if you take care to tune your receiver perfectly you will receive a clear pure signal and hear a ballad that lifts your heart. If you tune it imperfectly you will receive distortion and if you mistune it, you will receive any amount of chaos."

I was mesmerised by what he was saying, that experience when you are enthralled, just receiving the thrill of the dharma. I neither felt convinced or unconvinced; I was just alert and receptive. My questioning mind, my doubts, my assertions and cautious habits had disappeared into absence, which I realised was what he had meant by emptiness all along. I felt alert innocence, absorbed in something. I opened my mouth responsively but I didn't want to speak. He nodded that single short nod that was a trademark of the relationship between us, carrying within it an infinity of language and meaning.

"The greatest power you have at your disposal is attention. I want to give you a remarkable equation. The quality of your life depends on what you choose to notice and concentrate on. It's remarkable because it's powerful and even though it's obvious it is not commonly known. If you concentrate on your assets you will feel cheerful, if you concentrate on your deficits you will feel miserable. If you become used to focusing your attention on difficulties and resistances rather than opportunities for grace, that will intensify into a kind of negative persona and there will be no end to it. The wise have broken this conditioning and seen it for the false intruder that it is. Previously you have said to me if you are caught up in some strong feeling of threat or negativity you can't just overcome it, you can't just ignore it but even if the capacity to do that is as yet undeveloped, you are wrong to imply it can't be done. You cannot choose what arises but where you apply attention in response to what arises is something you can wield and direct. This is the higher knowledge. It really is a choice whether you indulge in an uncomfortable mental wave or whether you transcend it. Such directing of attention is exactly the potential of your mind, its possibility. Obviously it takes some vitality, undoubtedly it is out of the range of the beginner or those struggling in ignorance but you are not that anymore, you are strolling around the hermitage of the advanced and you need to step up and open your mind to be occupied by Shiva. Enough of the explanation, now you must act to bring this about. I am going to give you the direct tapas of the darshan of auspiciousness and it is in two parts. First, I want you to pray right now on this day in the passion surging in your heart. I want you to pray there and I want you to invoke that divinity, that in this place we call Shiva and to whom you can relate. It is not a timid prayer. You are making an appeal to the gigantic might and purity of Shiva himself, declaring allegiance with that power of auspiciousness, the consciousness of goodness. You are inviting that protection and influence into the very intimacy of you, making an offering of your own mind, declaring that space and aspiring for that very space to become auspicious. You are appealing to a real force, a power beyond your ordinary senses, close at hand, immense but subtle. You are making a vow, committing yourself to actively collaborate with this influence because you find the idea beautiful and appealing. These feelings of attraction and motive are important because then no longer is it a stray thought, it has transformed into an intent. This is volition, what you affirm. Do not expect God to do it to you. The doing is an equation between the influence itself and the degree to which you exercise your own internal powers in response. I will not give you the form of words for your prayer; you must draw it forth from your heart. You need to want it and it is your choice. If you do, you will create and exercise this prayer yourself. I am going to see Milo and will return before dusk."

Ram picked up the little pack and made off down the slope soon disappearing below the rise. I was alone in the intensity of solitude, the purity of this sacred place, full of clarity and determination. All his words washed through my intellect with no resistance it was palpable that I was sitting amidst truth. All the previous naïve ideas I may have had of Shiva in form had been exploded. I was literally to commune with purity itself, the lord of auspiciousness. Sitting in my meditative seat amidst the snowfield, in my own emptiness, between the pillars of Vedanta I made my prayer and sat in long communion, feeling the impact of the words I had spoken and their intent, feeling the receptivity of the Lord. I will not speak of its detail for that is too sacred and is for me alone, just as it would be for you alone, should you feel similarly moved. Should you also want it. Should you also choose to act.

Ram came back at dusk and cooked for me, saying that he had to serve me. We spent the evening entwined in affectionate silence, revelling in the delicate perfection of what he had given me and what I had done. I loved my Guru with a spiritual depth that just continued to expand and he loved me because that power is the natural energy of this relationship of freedom. He told me that he would complete his initiation of the tapas to me the next day and then we would immediately leave for the forest.

I was sound asleep when he tapped me at 6:00am and called me outside to watch the dawn rise. Bundled in our coats in the freezing crispness of the air I felt that all my previous life had melted away. I was ancient and at the same time brand new, a fresh perfect space. To see the golden-red disc rising in a clear sky, spreading her rays everywhere was as if Shiva himself embraced me. Ram made me breakfast insisting again that I must be served by him. We cleared everything away so that we left no mark other than some blackening on the floor where the fire had been. I even smoothed out the snow around the entrance with my boot so that when it fell again the surface shape would be as flat and perfect as when we came. We packed up and all prepared to leave, sat in the entrance between the pillars gazing out across the high snowfield for the very last time. There was nowhere on earth I would rather be, sitting here in this grace, poised and receptive to hear his final part of the teaching, voiced with the illuminating authority of divine intelligence.

Namah Shivaya.
May my whole mind be auspicious in thought and action.
Harih Om.

This is your mantra. Think about it; understand it based on all we have said. Become familiar with it so it lives with you right in the forefront of your awareness.

When you wake up in the morning make this invocation in the privacy of your own mind, either verbally or silently.

Before you fall asleep at night make this invocation in the privacy of your own mind, either verbally or silently.

During the day, give this spiritual activity you are engaged in frequent attention so you remember your intent and it is a living companion in your mind.

During the day, bring your attention to Śivā often so you feel familiarity and accessibility with that power.

Develop deep respect for what you are doing and hold it close with sincerity and cheerfulness.

Do this without break for a hundred and eight days. At that point, make your own decision to continue it for a time period you specify so it is then your own vow.

Discuss any details with your teacher. This is your tapas.

"As you live with this sadhana, think of auspiciousness, enjoy its reality. Take frequent solace in the knowledge and presence of benevolent protection. Remember the power of attention, that your well-being is a consequence of what you give your attention to and make some adjustments in your life as needed. Turn away from pointless superficiality. Turn away from anger, cynicism, aggression and the harmful in all its forms as far as that is possible in your worldly affairs. If it is not possible be patient. Whatever happens to you during the day respond as needed, it doesn't matter what difficulties or pleasures you face; the ups and downs of the moment are superficial and are not the measure of this sadhana. Look to your own council, keep the company of the wise when possible and turn towards the benevolent within the attitudes of your own mind. This is not a question of tense morality, do what you like to do freely but it is obvious where goodness lies, keep that in mind and let that shape your choices and your thoughts. Where inauspicious waves move in your mind learn to give them less attention as if they are someone else's voice, a dwindling voice. In any moment of acute hardship where you need support or encouragement say silently to yourself "Om Namah Shivaya" and bring your thought to that strength. Remember you are the commander of your mind in alliance with the Lord of auspiciousness. Let's go."

It took us five days to get back to the village down through the snowfield and through the forest. Ram talked to me about everyday things and I knew he was trying to ground me and re-orientate me to everyday affairs. We had a great time; he was funny and irreverent and we played like you can in the woods when there are no goblins. When we got to the Yajna temple we lit a little fire there, blew the conch and sang bhajans, all light, friendly and easy. It was immediately obvious that auspiciousness was in this play and lightness, as much as it was in the sacred aloneness of Being. That recognition was marvellous and freeing to me. While we were there

I asked him about the darshan of auspiciousness and how it had come about, whether he had invented it. He told me it was from the Rudrashtadhyayi and would have been known to the people who created the Yajna temple before us.

"They would have enjoyed it in its original form, Amelia, for you, I have adapted it to be more suitable to your sensibilities, more accessible."

"Did you practice it yourself Ram?"

"Of course, and it is still active in my heart, a part of me. The teacher must always have experienced that by which they instruct others, remember that when you come to teach yourself. It is a rule of spiritual ethics, only a fool or charlatan would break."

I felt very happy and complete, so secure in the integrity of my Guru, who in a very plain way modelled the teachings he conveyed to me and demonstrated them in his actions. I felt so lucky.

For the last day I rode Milo, he was so great and also seemed to be happy, even skittish which at first unnerved me until I understood that was how he played, so I played with him rubbing his neck, giving him bowls of tea and making him a necklace out of wild garlic leaves which he seemed bemused by until he ate it. Back at the house I spent two days working with Ram on practical projects about the place. Then we washed Milo with hose-pipes and a potion of woodland herbs sloshed on from a bucket with a bar of soap chipped into it. A yak with wet dreadlocks is a hilarious thing and as he showed from his purring grunts and little jigging movements, a happy one. It was a perfect, satisfying, joyous connection between us all, like a loving family, we had been through so much. On the very last morning I had everything packed and was sitting astride Milo at the well-head ready to ride him back to the tethering post. He was slurping from the bucket while I just enjoyed the moment reflecting on the amazing circumstances I had been through in these four weeks. The darshan of auspiciousness and its tapas was just incredible, the more it had sunk in, the more I realised how special it was. I could think of no temple or location anywhere in the world that was as rich to me as Bowslip. Now it was time to go. I was reconciled to going home but as always felt sad to leave this astonishing place. How could you not? Ram came to my side, stood on the well shaft wall, took my hands, looked me right in the eyes and said:

"All things are the Beloved; you, me, people, Milo, everything. Seeing that as so is unconditional love and that is the full vision of auspiciousness. Go back to your duties, they are where you belong. Do not be afraid of the dream, never reject the dream, it is where you can put into place all that has been given to you. It is where you act and you are not alone because your mind is no longer your own, it is a shared space; it is the abode of Shiva himself. Not everyone can visit a mystical snowfield, but never mind, we know it's a metaphor. The real snowfield is the human heart, cleared of chaos and ignorance where anyone can walk side by side with the guru… Go Milo!"

Beautiful, strong, wild and sweet-smelling Milo lumbered down the track with me astride him.

"I will see you in a year Ram."

"Yes, come in a year. *Harih Om.*"

Epilogue

four months later
with Amelia

On a spring morning at the end of May, Amelia was sat in a meeting at work discussing a project plan with her five colleagues. Since returning from the forest nearly four months ago all her professional and domestic routines had reassembled themselves piece by piece. It had all been quite natural, a little jarring at first but that passed quickly once she consciously applied the simple yet powerful tool of acceptance. She simply didn't resist, such a transforming power, it felt like a new virtue living in her mind, dispensing gestures of magic. Looking around the room at the faces of her colleagues confirmed the wave of private affection she now had for them. A warmth of appreciation vibrating tangibly through her heart, even toward her colleague Paul who had previously raised her hackles more often than not, focussing as he did on his ever so slightly superior status. It was all a wondrous drama. She had to keep her wits about her and stay alert to what was expected of her but that was alright, that was part of it too.

Implementing the magnificent insights she had gained on the mountain was proving transformative, a rich and fascinating encounter facing down the previous assumptions and defences that were the cause of unnecessary limitation and tightness in her life. This way of being in the world was not exclusive to special circumstances but applicable in the flow of every moment, including Monday morning team meetings. Applying sadhana in this way was thrilling; at the beginning she may have said difficult or even daunting but now she chose to say thrilling because it was true. *'May my whole mind be auspicious in thought and action'* - no longer an approach preserved for private conducive moments but a generalised vision here and now as life itself. What a discovery.

Such spaciousness and freedom of thought within her was of course not just a spontaneous arising. It was a consequence of the jnana, of all the sadhana she had been through during these magnificent years. But not only that, she was also fortified and constantly inspired by the pleasure of knowing that this unfolding destiny that had been awakened in her, was not done. The adventure was by no means finished and there was more to come. A two-hour distance away, the Bowslip estate existed in all its potency and beauty. Ram was there with Milo, living and thriving within it. The Vedanta teachings, his own particular take upon them and the revelations they contained shone brightly in the security of his stewardship and it was not over, by no means.

Last night she had dreamed she was in a huge lecture hall at a debate on the nature of spirituality, with an opposition of atheists and a sceptical audience. It wasn't Ram addressing the floor it was her. And that's where she had met him seven years ago, in a debating chamber, that mysterious figure, first aloof, then inclusive, first accommodating, then provocative, first bewildering, then incisive, first remote, then as affectionate and accessible as her own heart. And all the time throughout all these adventures there was one overriding quality, rigorous honesty with a clarity and consistency that took her breath away, sometimes literally. Where else could you experience such a gift, free of all the usual layers of attitude, projection, hesitancy and defence. It was the rarest most precious thing. Amelia knew she was in love with that unique potency. It was an easy, magnificent love, smooth, dependable and true, a hidden dimension of nature to which she had been given a secret key. This was the territory of the real, beyond the play and transience of the world, this was the scaffolding of existence and it was glorious. She would not see Ram for many more months, maybe a year and that was alright, at least mostly, the connectivity between them was secure and as intimate as skin. Now was the time for application, the time to explore her own resources, the time to assimilate all that she knew and implement it in the real world of people, events and things. This was the opportunity of a lifetime. Every encounter that came upon her, lived from this perspective, was as precious as jewels. When the time came around, they would engage directly again. What would come next was hard to imagine but she knew there was a next, the fact that was mysterious to her was alright. 'One step at a time Amelia, stand on the step you are on, make it steady and stable'. That was the instruction that enthused her mind and she was doing it here and now in this place. If Ram had been approached, he would have held his council on the question of what next but you never know, if he had been cajoled in some way, he may have shone some light upon it. To set the context he would probably have said something like this. 'There are three principal goals Amelia, awakening, realisation and moksha. That is the direction, this is its momentum and that is all.'

Amelia was awake, this was clear to her now and to those who knew her. Spiritual awakening had occurred and was embedding in her as her very own vision and truth. She had seen beyond the physical, the conditioned and the assumed, into the subtle aspects of her nature. She had an expanded understanding of life, world, mind and God. This was becoming so vivid now and established that it could no longer decline or be compromised by old habits or concerns, even if they did arise. It was an attainment. Amelia was awakened. The next step on her ladder of evolution was realisation. Self-realisation. Goodness!

Bowslip held all the mysteries, just as they had been held in various ways throughout human history. To one such as Amelia, Ram was ready to reveal them all through the student and teacher equation; a timeless, passionate equation and a spectacularly beautiful one. Let her live in the world for now, let her rely on her own resources, let karma take its course. Time and distance were irrelevant to Ram and were becoming increasingly irrelevant to her. Amelia would return in a year, or something like that and then they would continue. As for now he had left her with a single instruction, his most vital instruction of all.... Proceed Amelia. Proceed.

The sequel of Amelia's story to Self-realisation continues in the second companion book:
Illumination in the Forest of Vedanta

Enquire through vedantarama.com

ACKNOWLEDGEMENTS

Something very profound is moving in this life. Poets may refer to it as a calling, psychologists a passion, religious leaders a devotion. This wonderful vitality of spiritual exploration and creativity has been a constant impulse. My deepest gratitude for its precious and compelling voice.

My fondest respect to all the thousands of encounters that have taken place with all the students that have come to me over these many years. Little of any value would have been truly accomplished without the power of these engagements. It would be wrong to isolate names, there are those at a distance, those nearer to hand and those up close, in whom something extraordinary has passed in the shared intimacy between us. I honour you all as a magnificence of students.

Special thanks to the small team of individuals who have worked practically with patience and skill to enable and organise all the output over the years including the efforts needed to bring this book into existence. It has taken much to achieve and would have been impossible without you.

All praise and worship to reality itself. The fact that human perception is capable of seeing beyond its own limitations and evolving into ever higher vision of its own potential, is stunning and divine. To that divinity I offer my eternal salutations.

ABOUT THE AUTHOR

Derek Thorne is an accomplished Vedanta teacher living in Somerset, UK. Since childhood he has followed a strong and committed destiny of spiritual investigation alongside full participation in society, work and family responsibilities. Having deeply fulfilled his own sadhana through the insights of Vedanta and now retired from professional life, he dedicates his time to writing, teaching, guiding seekers and leading the Vedantarama spiritual community.

vedantarama.com

Printed in Great Britain
by Amazon

62764590R00173